COMPUTING USING BASIC:
An Interactive Approach

THE ELLIS HORWOOD SERIES IN
COMPUTERS AND THEIR APPLICATIONS

Series Editor: BRIAN MEEK
Director of the Computer Unit, Queen Elizabeth College, University of London

The series aims to provide up-to-date and readable texts on the theory and practice of computing, with particular though not exclusive emphasis on computer applications. Preference is given in planning the series to new or developing areas, or to new approaches in established areas.

The books will usually be at the level of introductory or advanced undergraduate courses. In most cases they will be suitable as course texts, with their use in industrial and commercial fields always kept in mind. Together they will provide a valuable nucleus for a computing science library.

INTERACTIVE COMPUTER GRAPHICS IN SCIENCE TEACHING
Edited by J. McKENZIE, University College, London, L. ELTON, University of Surrey, R. LEWIS, Chelsea College, London.

INTRODUCTORY ALGOL 68 PROGRAMMING
D. F. BRAILSFORD and A. N. WALKER, University of Nottingham.

GUIDE TO GOOD PROGRAMMING PRACTICE
Edited by B. L. MEEK, Queen Elizabeth College, London and P. HEATH, Plymouth Polytechnic.

CLUSTER ANALYSIS ALGORITHMS: For Data Reduction and Classification of Objects
H. SPÄTH, Professor of Mathematics, Oldenburg University.

DYNAMIC REGRESSION: Theory and Algorithms
L. J. SLATER, Department of Applied Engineering, Cambridge University and H. M. PESARAN, Trinity College, Cambridge

FOUNDATIONS OF PROGRAMMING WITH PASCAL
LAWRIE MOORE, Birkbeck College, London.

PROGRAMMING LANGUAGE STANDARDISATION
Edited by B. L. MEEK, Queen Elizabeth College, London and I. D. HILL, Clinical Research Centre, Harrow.

THE DARTMOUTH TIME SHARING SYSTEM
G. M. BULL, The Hatfield Polytechnic

RECURSIVE FUNCTIONS IN COMPUTER SCIENCE
R. PETER, formerly Eötvos Lorand University of Budapest.

FUNDAMENTALS OF COMPUTER LOGIC
D. HUTCHISON, University of Strathclyde.

THE MICROCHIP AS AN APPROPRIATE TECHNOLOGY
Dr. A. BURNS, The Computing Laboratory, Bradford University

SYSTEMS ANALYSIS AND DESIGN FOR COMPUTER APPLICATION
D. MILLINGTON, University of Strathclyde.

COMPUTING USING BASIC: An Interactive Approach
TONIA COPE, Oxford University Computing Teaching Centre.

RECURSIVE DESCENT COMPILING
A. J. T. DAVIE and R. MORRISON, University of St. Andrews, Scotland.

PASCAL IMPLEMENTATION
M. DANIELS and S. PEMBERTON, Brighton Polytechnic.

SOFTWARE ENGINEERING
K. GEWALD, G. HAAKE, and W. PFADLER, Siemens AG, Munich

PROGRAMMING LANGUAGE TRANSLATION
R. E. BERRY, University of Lancaster

ADA: A PROGRAMMER'S CONVERSION COURSE
M. J. STRATFORD-COLLINS, U.S.A.

COMPUTING
USING BASIC:
An Interactive Approach

TONIA COPE, B.Sc.
Computing Teaching Centre
University of Oxford

ELLIS HORWOOD LIMITED
Publishers · Chichester

Halsted Press: a division of
JOHN WILEY & SONS
New York · Brisbane · Chichester · Toronto

First published in 1981 by
ELLIS HORWOOD LIMITED
Market Cross House, Cooper Street, Chichester, West Sussex, PO19 1EB, England

Reprinted 1982 twice

The publisher's colophon is reproduced from James Gillison's drawing of the ancient Market Cross, Chichester.

Distributors:

Australia, New Zealand, South-east Asia:
Jacaranda-Wiley Ltd., Jacaranda Press,
JOHN WILEY & SONS INC.,
G.P.O. Box 859, Brisbane, Queensland 40001, Australia

Canada:
JOHN WILEY & SONS CANADA LIMITED
22 Worcester Road, Rexdale, Ontario, Canada.

Europe, Africa:
JOHN WILEY & SONS LIMITED
Baffins Lane, Chichester, West Sussex, England.

North and South America and the rest of the world:
Halsted Press: a division of
JOHN WILEY & SONS
605 Third Avenue, New York, N.Y. 10016, U.S.A.

© T. Cope/Ellis Horwood Limited, Publishers 1981

British Library Cataloguing in Publication Data
Cope, Tonia
Computing using BASIC. –
(Ellis Horwood series in computers and their applications, ISSN 0271–6135)
1. BASIC (Computer program language)
I. Title
001.64'24   QA76.73.B3

Library of Congress Card No. 81–6882 AACR2

ISBN 0–85312–289–X (Ellis Horwood Limited, Publishers – Library Edn.)
ISBN 0–85312–385–3 (Ellis Horwood Limited, Publishers – Student Edn.)
ISBN 0–470–27279–1 (Halsted Press – Library Edn.)
ISBN 0–470–27280–5 (Halsted Press – Student Edn.)

Typeset in Press Roman by Ellis Horwood Limited, Publishers
Printed in the United States of America by Vail-Ballou Press

Table of Contents

Acknowledgements

This book has necessarily been the result of a team effort and I would like to express my gratitude to all who have contributed towards it. In particular:

Frank Pettit, who first fired me with enthusiasm for computers and computing, and who continues to give generously of his time and inspiration;

Charles Beesley, (CHASx) the co-designer of the artistic features in this and earlier versions;

Martin Hall, for his varied programming help which includes the Solutions section in the Appendix and the Index;

Helen Tweed, whose hours spent on a wordprocessor made the original drafts intelligible;

Paul Taylor, of the Age and Isotope Laboratory of the Department of Geology, Oxford University, for his collaboration in preparing the application in rock dating in the final chapter;

Steve Thomas, who has been proof-reading draft versions of this book longer than both he or the author cares to remember! He is the co-author of the version of BASIC used (Research Machines BASICSG Version 5.0).

The following have contributed in various ways, particularly by reading or working through various draft chapters: Richard Jackson and students of Burford School, Jonathan Darby, Roger Treweek, Nick Rushby, David Small, Ian Every, not forgetting several students of Oxford University. The background support of my mother and optimistic friends is also much appreciated.

Lastly I would like to than Brian Meek, the Series Editor, who has waded through the manuscript in its various stages and made encouraging noises.

Preface

In recent years the use of computers has not only become commonplace in commerce and industry but also in the home. Within the next few years every secondary school in Britain will be equipped with at least one microcomputer as educationalists seek to keep pace with the world today. It is increasingly necessary to have some grounding in computing, whether or not it is a required tool in the pursuit of a career.

For many, the mystique surrounding computers has created a seemingly insurmountable barrier to understanding and participating in this new technology. In these pages an attempt is made to dispel that mystique, partly by keeping jargon to a minimum. That which is necessary is explained as it occurs.

This book is about how to communicate with a computer, in a dialogue-style, using the programming language BASIC. It will be valuable for anyone who is new to computing and is designed as a 'teach yourself' manual for all who have access to a computer, as well as being suitable for class teaching. It originated at Oxford University Computing Teaching Centre where earlier versions have been successfully used by over 1000 people of widely differing backgrounds ranging from school children and students to businessmen and university professors.

The book is divided into two sections. In Section I the elements of the language are presented including the more recent extensions to BASICs such as High Resolution Graphics. No previous knowledge is assumed. The beginner is quickly motivated to write small programs and good programming habits are encouraged from the outset. It is also designed to provide a useful reference source for the more experienced person.

Section II introduces the reader to more advanced applications of BASIC such as sorting techniques; simulation, including the use of random numbers; and design, as used in the manufacture of fabrics.

The underlying theme of structured programming is stressed throughout, in concepts such as modular design, and the need for an orderly approach to problem solving.

All the programs were developed and tested on a Research Machines 380Z, using BASICSG Version 5.0, and are readily adaptable to run on most other computers. The exception to this claim is the chapter on matrices in the appendix. Although not currently included in RML 380Z BASICs, matrices are a valuable tool in many areas of programming, for example in statistics, and are a part of several existing BASICs. The appendix also includes convenient features such as a summary of the language and the solutions to the problems.*

The profusion of different dialects of BASIC is often a source of confusion. It can prove difficult, particularly for those new to programming, to use a book which is not specifically written for ones 'own' computer. In an attempt to ease this difficulty attention is drawn throughout this book to the most common differences. These are elaborated in 'Variation on a Theme' (ϕ) in the appendix.

*Note   The BASIC on the 1981 RML 480Z does not differ significantly from that used here and programs should run without alteration.

The programs which appear in this book
are available on floppy disc (CUBdisc)

5¼″ double sided single density
8″ double sided single density

Please write for full details to the publishers
ELLIS HORWOOD LIMITED
Market Cross House, Cooper Street, Chichester, West Sussex, PO19 1EB, England

Chapter 0

WHY have a
chapter 0 ?

Chapter 0 gives
useful background
information which,
although not a part
of the BASIC language,
is necessary when using it.

0.1 INTRODUCTION

As the title suggests, this book is about Interactive Computing. It uses BASIC as the language to communicate with the computer.

BASIC, one of hundreds of computer languages, is growing in popularity particularly with the advent of the microcomputer.

Prior to 1963, the influence of the business and research world dominated computer language development. At this time Professors John G. Kemmeny and Thomas E. Kurtz, of Dartmouth College, USA, devised BASIC (Beginners All-purpose Symbolic Instruction Code), an easy-to learn and easy-to-use computer language. It combines in an elementary way the most useful features of other languages such as FORTRAN and Algol 60.

A question sometimes asked is: 'Isn't BASIC *just* a beginner's language?'. A look at the second half of this book should give a clue to answering that question. BASIC with its modern interactive capabilities, including filing, editing, matrix operations, its provision of a good basis for simulation, is used not only in teaching those new to computing, but also by business firms, scientific researchers and engineers.

But what is a computer? Fundamentally it is a machine that processes information. Information may be recorded, manipulated and retrieved. It is a machine capable of carrying out a sequence of logical operations called a *program.* The program and data it may use are stored magnetically or electrically within the computer or on an associated storage device.

There are many different computers and many different dialects of most programming languages. It is well nigh impossible to write a book on BASIC to suit every variation of every dialect. In an attempt to simplify this problem this book has been written using throughout the version

RESEARCH MACHINES 380Z BASICSG Version 5.0

A large proportion of this version of BASIC is common to many other dialects. Where differences exist the symbol

$\oint$ representing **VARIATIONS ON A THEME**

will appear in the text. The reader seeking an alternative version should refer to this section in the Appendix and also in the literature for their own machine.

RESEARCH MACHINES LIMITED may be referred to as RML from this point on.

0.2 THE KEYBOARD

A quick survey of computer keyboards reveals some surprises. Not only are there obvious differences from one to another, but some include keys of no relevance to the associated computer. It is therefore especially important to read the keyboard description for the computer you will be using. The details in this chapter apply to a RESEARCH MACHINES 380Z microcomputer. Most features are relevant to many other makes of keyboard as well.

Should you be in the position of having a computer at your disposal but do not have the relevant literature nor a 'local-expert' to consult, try experimenting using this text as a spring board.

Schematic diagram of a RESEARCH MACHINES 380Z MICROCOMPUTER KEYBOARD

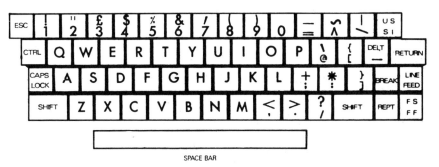

The keyboard differs from that of a normal typewriter in that three sets of characters can be generated.

1. Normal lower-case characters.

2. Capital letters | SHIFT | are generated by holding down the key while typing the required letter.

| CAPS LOCK | pressed once, gives capital letters only. (To unlock press again.) in CAPS LOCK position capital letters are generated but all other keys remain in lower case, and need SHIFT to access characters on the upper section of a key.

3. Control Characters | CTRL | are generated by holding down the key while typing another key. These are used to control the computer; control keys frequently used are:

| CTRL | Z | Interrupts a program LIST or RUN.

| CTRL | P | Echoes console output to printer.

For a complete list of control characters see the summary in the appendix.

0.3 KEYBOARD SUMMARY

NORMAL KEYS	SHIFT KEYS	CONTROL KEYS
Used for programs and data.		Used to control the computer.

Example

Z	gives z
SHIFT	Z	gives Z
CTRL	Z	interrupts a program LIST or RUN.

Other keys:

ESC	is used within the EDIT command to end an insert (some keyboards have ESC labelled ALT MODE!)
RETURN	signals the end of a line to the computer.
DELT —	with SHIFT this key will delete one character.
REPT	repeats the last character typed for as long as REPT is held down.
# 3	with SHIFT a hash (#) symbol is generated. It is used in association with file handling.

Depending on the model of your keyboard some or all of the following keys will not be connected: FF, SI, BREAK, whilst the following are ignored:
US, LINEFEED, FS.

A keyboard symbol you may not recognise;

    ^   ↑   an upward arrow.

0.4 CORRECTING MISTAKES

1. *While still on a line* characters may be deleted by touching SHIFT DELT. To cancel more than one character touch REPT after SHIFT DELT
2. *Replace a line* by typing in the required version at any stage during program development.
3. *Cancel a line* by typing the line number and RETURN.
The EDIT command provides a more sophisticated way of editing. This is described in chapter 12.

Some common errors to avoid
Although sometimes indistinguishable in appearance:

1 (one)	and	I (the letter)	are two distinct characters
0 (zero)	and	O (the letter)	are two distinct characters

MORAL   Choose your characters carefully!!!

0.5 NOTE ON THE VIDEO DISPLAY SCREEN (VDU)

> NOTE: IF THE VDU SCREEN
> IS ONLY 40 CHARACTERS WIDE
>
> ◄─────────────────────►
>
> you will find when typing in information
> it will automatically overflow onto the n
> ext line if longer than 40 charac
> ters.
> NOTE: At the end of every line type:
> RETURN
> This causes the computer to act on what y
> ou have typed.
> Got the message?

NOTE: Consult the literature on your own computer on the following, (and on any other machine-specific operations):

to load BASIC,
to load or save a program,
to connect a printer device,
to determine specific error messages,
to close down your computer,
etc.

The Basic Language

Just as when learning a natural language
such as Norwegian, some new symbols
and much strange vocabulary and
grammer, must be learnt, so It is with
BASIC (or with any other programming
language). Of necessity the early stages
involve a certain amount of drill. Works
of art are written later (by the end of
section II)! This does not, of course,
exclude the probability that the equivalent of many good articles and short
stories will be written all along the way
of learning.

CHAPTER 1
Lets get started

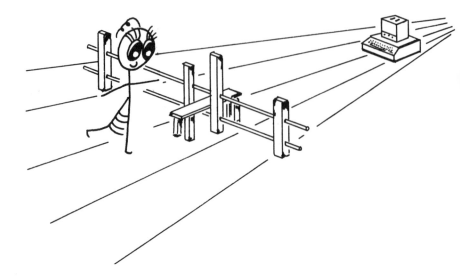

1.1 GETTING STARTED

The only way to learn a computing language is through hands-on experience. And so, if possible, before you read further, login to BASIC on your own computer and type in the program in Example 1.1. Don't worry if you don't understand what you're doing, you'll see what the computer does after you type RUN! Each feature of the program will be explained in this chapter.

> ### Note on LOGIN procedure
> There is no one standard procedure for getting into BASIC on a computer. At this stage it may be necessary to consult the introduction, literature specific to your machine, or ask someone with experience.

At the end of every line you type, touch the RETURN key.   ♭

This tells the computer to act on the line you have just typed. Before RETURN is touched, mistakes on a line may be corrected. See the INTRODUCTION for details on simple line editing.

If due to mistakes the screen begins to look a muddle, and your program is unrecognisable, type LIST. The LIST command will cause all that the computer has accepted to appear on the screen.

Example 1.1 Program Counter

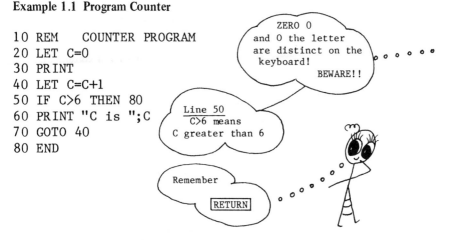

```
10 REM    COUNTER PROGRAM
20 LET C=0
30 PRINT
40 LET C=C+1
50 IF C>6 THEN 80
60 PRINT "C is ";C
70 GOTO 40
80 END
```

Now type:

RUN

and observe the result for yourself. It should be similar to that in the Solutions pages in the Appendix.

♭   RETURN : See Variations on a Theme in the Appendix.

'HELP!' my program is running on forever!' ... is a cry sometimes heard at this point. It usually implies something went wrong in line 50, the condition to end the RUN. If this is your problem, stop the RUN by holding the CTRL key and typing Z. Correct your error and RUN again. †

This simple counter program is frequently used as part of large programs. It is an easy way of telling the computer to do some counting for you!

In this program you have already met several features of the BASIC programming language. These are described in the following pages.

1.2 Note on WORKSPACE and the NEW command   ‡

The program you have typed in is held in an area of the computer memory called the WORKSPACE. It will remain there until you move out of BASIC or type the word NEW.

1.3 KEYWORDS IN BASIC

You will probably have noticed that every line in Example 1.1 begins with a number followed by a word. This word provides the KEY to the type of instruction which is to be carried out, hence its name, keyword.

1.3.1

The REM statement

REMarks are included in BASIC programs by using REM statements. REMarks describe to people what the program is doing and are not acted on by the computer.

1.3.2

The LET statement

The LET statement places the given value into a named memory location. (This is often referred to as an assignment statement.) ♭

♭ Consult Variations on a Theme in the Appendix.
† CTRL Z: The keys typed to interrupt a program LISTing or RUN differ from system to system.
‡ NEW: Some BASICs use a different word for this command.
WORKSPACE: Area of temporary storage of program and data.

Example 1.2 Typical Assignment Statements

	Memory Locations	
	name	contents

111   LET R = 2   R   ┌─────────┐ 2 ┌─────────┐

190   LET P = 3.14 * R * R (* means multiply)   P   │ 12.56 │

250   LET Q = P   Q   │ 12.56 │

20   LET A$ = "Y"   A$ │ Y   │

The equal sign

In each example above the value of the expression on the right of the 'equal sign' is assigned to the variable name on the left. *The equal sign* does not mean equals as in a mathematical sense. *It is an assignment symbol.*

Thus:

10 LET X = 99   implies 'into the place called X put the value 99'   X

│ 99 │

15 LET X = X + 1   means 'add 1 to the number already in X
                      and store the result in X.'   │ 100 │

30 LET X = X * 2   │ 200 │

20 LET C = 0   in example 1.1 gives C an initial value.   │ 0 │

Many BASICs *allow assignment* without using the word LET. Where this is true example 1.2 can be written as: ♭

111   R = 2
190   P = 3.14 * R * R

Multiple assignment is a feature of some BASICs for example:

150 LET A = B = C = 0

Here ZERO (0) is assigned to A, B and C. This is not true for 380Z BASICs.

♭   See Variations on a Theme in the Appendix.

1.4 NAMES FOR NUMBERS

Memory locations for storing numbers, are usually referred to as numeric variables. All names begin with an alphabetic letter and are:

a single letter	A,	B, ...	Z
a letter and a digit (0-9)	A0,	B0, ...	Z0
	...	...	
	A9,	B9, ...	Z9
a letter followed by a letter	PI,	SD	

To make a program more readable more meaningful variable names may be used, for example: TOTAL, AVERAGE.

However, *only the first two characters* are used to identify the variable concerned.

The names:

SAMPLE 1

SAMPLE 2

are identical as far as the computer is concerned!

Warning!

Any name which has a BASIC instruction embedded within it is unacceptable. For example the following statements would give rise to syntax errors because they contain the BASIC words indicated.

        100 LET DIFF = N - A

        120 LET GOAT = GOAT + 1

1.5 NAMES FOR CHARACTERS

Names for characters differ from those for numbers by having a dollar sign ($) appended and are, for example:

        B$, F5$, MESSAGE$

Example 1.2 line 20 is a method for storing a character in the computer.

A character or group of characters is sometimes referred to as a STRING. †

A LITERAL STRING is a character or group of characters normally enclosed by quotation marks. Consequently no string bounded by quotation marks may contain quotation marks.   ♭

♭   See Variations on a Theme in the Appendix.

†   NAMES for CHARACTERS: If your computer does not accept a $ sign check in your manufacturer's manual for an alternative symbol.
     STRINGS: See Chapter 5.

1.5.1

★ ★
★   ★
★ **The PRINT statement**   ★
★ The PRINT statement cause the computer to output information,   ★
★ usually to a screen or printer.   ★
★ Numeric and character (string) items are listed following the word ★
★ PRINT. A COMMA or a SEMI-COLON is used to separate items. Quote   ★
★ marks 'surround' strings.   ★
★   ★
★ ★

A few typical PRINT statements follow in Example 1.3. *Observe* each statement and its effect as seen in the program RUN.   †

Note: It is not necessary to type this program into your computer. However, if you do, REMEMBER to type the command NEW to clear the workspace before you start.

Example 1.3 Program WRITE

```
10 REM                  WRITE
20 PRINT "PRINT is a versatile statement"
30 PRINT "But        BE WARNED"
40 PRINT "        There are significant differences "
50 PRINT "        between BASICs in interpreting this statement"
60 PRINT
70 PRINT "CHECK YOUR VERSION FOR DETAILS"
80 PRINT
90 PRINT "Observe the different spacing effects below when using"
100 PRINT "a  COMMA  or  SEMI-COLON"
110 PRINT
120 LET Y=2
130 PRINT "Y","Y*Y","Y↑5","SQR(Y)","Y-Y"
140 PRINT Y, Y*Y, Y↑5, SQR(Y), Y-Y
150 PRINT
160 PRINT "Y";"Y*Y";"Y↑5";"SQR(Y)";"Y-Y"
170 PRINT Y;Y*Y;Y↑5;SQR(Y);Y-Y
180 END
```

Remember NEW !

↑ is the symbol for raise-to-the-power

†   PRINT: A fuller explanation is given in chapter 6.

```
RUN
PRINT is a versatile statement
But        BE WARNED
           There are significant differences
           between BASICs in interpreting this statement

CHECK YOUR VERSION FOR DETAILS

Observe the different spacing effects below when using
a  COMMA  or  SEMI-COLON
```

Y	Y*Y	Y↑5	SQR(Y)	Y-Y
2	4	32	1.41421	0

```
YY*YY↑5SQR(Y)Y-Y
2  4  32  1.41421  0

Ready:
```

If you did type in Example 1.3, and your RUN differs from that given here, check carefully for typing errors. For example, you may have the letter instead of a zero (0) or the letter I instead of 1. Other common mistakes include omitting or confusing separators , or ; in PRINT statements.

The questions below are based on Example 1.3

? ?

1. What is the result of PRINT in lines 60, 80, etc?
2. What is the outcome of a PRINT 'Anything in quotes' statement? This is illustrated by lines 20 to 40 and others.
3. The PRINT statements in lines 130 and 160 arrange for characters to be printed. What are the differences between these statements? What corresponding differences do you observe in the resulting RUN?
4. Lines 140 and 170 result in numbers being printed in the RUN. What differences do you observe?
5. What are the differences between printing numbers and printing characters?

(S) Check your accuracy in answering these questions by referring to the Solutions section in the appendix.

? ?

1.6 CONTROL STATEMENTS

Normally BASIC executes program statements in ascending order of statement number. There are several commands which can be used to alter this order as required. Two such are used in the first program in this chapter, Example 1.1 and are described below.   †

1.6.1

★★

★ **The GO TO statement** − Unconditional transfer of control provides a method of transferring the control of the program to virtually any other program statement. The format is illustrated by the two equivalent statements:

        30 GOTO 99
    and 30 GO TO 99

If the line number specified does not exist, the error message:

    Undefined statement at line number nn

is displayed and the program run comes to a halt.

★★

1.6.2

★★

The IF . . . THEN statement − Conditional transfer of control. IF a given condition is met THEN control is transferred to the specified statement number, otherwise the next statement is obeyed as normal. The format is illustrated by the examples:

    55 IF condition   THEN   123

    500 IF   C < 5   THEN   150

A slight variation on this format is seen below.

    40 IF   JO = GO   THEN   PRINT "Hurry"

    90 IF SUM > 132 THEN   PRINT   SUM

The condition, SUM > 132, for example, is called a boolean expression (after George Boole, the logician), and is either true or false. If the boolean expression is true then the statement following THEN is obeyed, otherwise the program moves on to the next line.   ‡

★★

† CONTROL: See chapter 7

Example 1.4 Program BROKE

```
10 REM Program BROKE
110 PRINT "If your balance is negative
120 PRINT "You have reached the  END of your resources.
130 REM    Line 140 is one way BASIC may say the same thing !
140 IF B < 0  THEN 200
...
...
...
200 END
```

1.7

★★★★★★★★★★★★★★★★★★★★★★★★★★★★★★★★★★★★★★★

The END statement

In good programming practice END is the last statement of a program and halts program execution. However, RML 380Z BASIC and some others, permit the inclusion of several END statements, or none at all, in a program. A good convention is:

A program should have ONE and only one END and this at the very end.   ♭

★★★★★★★★★★★★★★★★★★★★★★★★★★★★★★★★★★★★★★★

1.8 LINE NUMBERS IN BASIC   ♭

It is normal in BASIC to have a *number at the start* of each new statement. In RML 380Z BASIC the line number is between 1 and 65529. BASIC statements may be typed in in any order as they are rearranged internally into ascending order of line number. When the program is RUN statements are obeyed in this order unless the flow is altered from within the program. *A line may be erased* by typing its line number followed by RETURN.

A multitude of possible variations exist in the language. The guidelines which follow are suggested to help you develop the habit of writing programs which are easy to understand and will RUN on other computers, i.e. portable programs.

♭   See Variations on a Theme in the Appendix.

1.9 GUIDELINES FOR PROGRAM WRITING

1. Each statement must start with a line number.
2. A line number must be followed by a BASIC keyword.
3. Use a new line for each statement.
4. A statement should not be longer than a line.
5. Blank spaces should be inserted wherever these improve the readability of the program.
6. REM and PRINT statements should be included to clarify the intent of the program and the layout of the results.
7. Make the first statement of the program a PRINT followed by the program name. This ensures that both the listing and the run carry the program name.

1.10

Q Q Q Q Q Q Q Q Q Q Q Q Q Q Q Q Q Q Q Q Q Q Q Q Q Q Q Q Q Q Q Q Q

PROBLEMS

REMEMBER type NEW and ⟨RETURN⟩ before starting each new program

1a. Modify Example 1.1 to count up to 10.
  b. Print the numbers only (i.e. without 'C is'). Print these numbers tightly spaced across a line. Print five numbers on a line.
2. Write a program to print your name and address as it would appear on an envelope.
3. By adding a few statements to your program cause the address (only) to be printed out 5 more times. There should be 2 blank lines between each address.
4. Given PI = 3.14159 and R = 5 calculate the area and the circumference of a circle.   (A = PI × R × R
                                                                                                C = 2 × PI × R)
5. Extend the program for question 3 to calculate the areas and circumferences of many circles. Your results should appear under the headings:
RADIUS   AREA   CIRCUMFERENCE

SOLUTIONS in the Appendix.

Q Q Q Q Q Q Q Q Q Q Q Q Q Q Q Q Q Q Q Q Q Q Q Q Q Q Q Q Q Q Q Q Q Q

CHAPTER 2
Interactive
programming

2.1 WHAT IS AN INTERACTIVE PROGRAM?

To program interactively is to communicate in an 'alive' way with a computer, to have a dialogue in a sense! It has been put this way: 'An interactive program is one that talks back to you (!), a program over which you have some control while it is running'. Perhaps, in its most advanced form, interactive programming means that a user works with the computer towards a goal that becomes clearer as the interaction proceeds. The user may not necessarily know at the outset what all his responses will be.

This type of interaction is made possible in a BASIC program by the inclusion of the word INPUT. It enables numbers or characters to be assigned to variables by entering them at the keyboard whilst the program is RUNning. Using INPUT there is a more satisfactory solution to problem 4 of Chapter 1, as demonstrated below:

Example 2.1(a) Program CIRCAREA

```
10  REM          CIRCAREA
40  LET  P  =  3.14159
50  INPUT  R
60  LET  A  =  P * R ↑ 2                                    †
70  LET  C  =  2 * P * R
80  PRINT
90  PRINT  "R", "A", "C"
100 PRINT  R, A, C
200 END
```

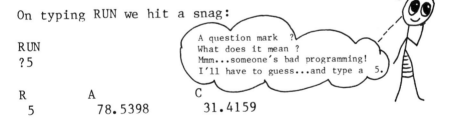

```
On typing RUN we hit a snag:

RUN
?5
```

A question mark ?
What does it mean ?
Mmm...someone's bad programming!
I'll have to guess...and type a 5.

```
R              A                C
5          78.5398          31.4159

Ready:
```

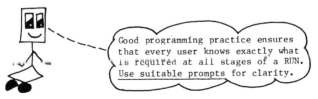

Good programming practice ensures that every user knows exactly what is required at all stages of a RUN. Use suitable prompts for clarity.

†   ↑EXPONENTIATION – Raising to the power of, see Chapter 3.

It is easy to add new statements to an existing program. Line 45 gives a clear prompt to the program user. The other statements below extend program 2.1(a) to cater for another 5 values for R.

```
45 PRINT "Give new radius each time  a  ? appears"
20 LET K = 0
105 LET K = K + 1
110 IF K > 5 THEN 200
120 GO TO 50
```

So far so good! However an important point has been overlooked. The PRINT instruction on line 90 will cause the heading R A C to be printed each time the values for R, A and C are printed, an unusual requirement! A more usual heading results when the PRINT "R", "A", "C" statement is moved outside the repetitive section of the program. For example:

```
90
47 PRINT "R","A","C"
80
48 PRINT
```

Note:

★ ★
★   ★
★   A line is deleted by typing the line number only   ★
★   ★
★ ★

The scattered lines of program in this chapter are confusing me! The trick to get out of all the confusion lies in typing the word LIST.

REMEMBER ?

Lets try it and see the result in example 2.1(b)

Example 2.1(b) Program CIRCEXT

```
LIST
10 REM           CIRCEXT
20 LET K = 0
40 LET P = 3.14159
45 PRINT "Give new radius each time a '?' appears"
47 PRINT "R","A","C"
48 PRINT
50 INPUT R
60 LET A = P * R ↑ 2
70 LET C = 2 * P * R
100 PRINT R, A, C
105 LET K = K+ 1
110 IF K > 5 THEN 200
120 GOTO 50
200 END
RUN
Give new radius each time a '?' appears
R              A              C
```

	R	A	C
? 5			
	5	78.5398	31.4159
? 10			
	10	314.159	62.8318
? 15			
	15	706.858	94.2477
? 20			
	20	1256.64	125.664
? 30			
	30	2827.43	188.495
? 40			
	40	5026.55	251.327

Ready:

In example 2.1(b) all the numbers on the same line as a ? were typed in while the program was running. The computer did the rest.

Sometimes it is good to have your program and results on paper to refer to at leisure. Most, if not all, computers can be linked to a printing device. An instruction such as LIST in BASIC will cause a LISTing to be printed provided that the link between the computer and the printer has been established. The command PRINTER will establish this link on a 380Z computer. You will need to consult your own manufacturer's manual to discover the specific instructions for your combination of computer and printer.

To summarise:

2.1.2

★ ★
★   ★

The INPUT Statement

The INPUT statement enables a program to 'ask' for information while it is RUNning. When BASIC executes an INPUT command it displays a ? on the screen and waits for a response from the keyboard. The numeric or string variables specified by the INPUT command receive the data typed in provided it is of the correct kind. Commas are used to separate items.

★ ★

Examples of INPUT statements and correct responses during a program RUN follow:

Example 2.2 Correct responses to INPUT

INPUT statement	A Correct Response	
	Computer	User (RETURN after each line)
10 INPUT A	?	5
25 INPUT X, Y, Z	?	3, 4, 5
40 INPUT A$, A, B$, B	?	"LONDON", 1, "LEEDS", 9 †
55 INPUT T$, X	?	"JIM", 1

†   STRINGS such as A$ and T$ see chapter 4.

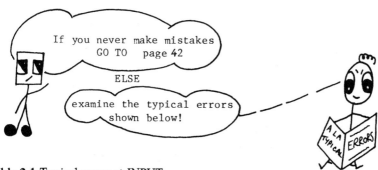

If you never make mistakes
GO TO   page 42

ELSE

examine the typical errors
shown below!

Table 2.1 Typical errors at INPUT

Valid Input Statement	Response while RUNning BASIC's Yours	Comment ⚭
20 INPUT K, J$	? RETURN ?? RETURN	*When only* RETURN *is typed* K is given the value 0 (zero) J$ becomes a null string (C) You may INPUT words or numbers
50 INPUT X, Y, Z	? 55 RETURN ?? 72, 85 RETURN	*Too few items* Three numbers were expected but after giving one RETURN was typed and BASIC responded with ?? prompting the user for more information.
99 INPUT P	? 5, 8, 9 RETURN *Extra lost	*Too many items* *Extra lost is a warning. The extra items are lost and the program continues.
a) 132 INPUT R	? no RETURN *Invalid input ? 79 RETURN	*The wrong kind of data* When a number is expected and characters are typed which cannot form part of that number the error message. *Invalid Input is given. All data for that INPUT must be retyped.
b) 155 INPUT S	? 1/2 RETURN *Invalid input ? .5 RETURN	
c) 7 INPUT P$, P	? 9, "Tigger" RETURN *Invalid input ? "Tigger", 9 RETURN	*Mismatched data* Quote (" ") marks are optional. They are only essential when string contains commas (,) or leading spaces.

⚭   See Variations on a Theme in the Appendix.

You can of course build in your own responses and error checks as in:

Example 2.3 Program CHECK

```
10 REM    program    errorCHECK
20 PRINT  "Select a number less than 10";
30 INPUT N
40 IF N < 10 THEN 70
50 PRINT "WRONG ! Read the question. Try again"
60 GOTO 20
70 PRINT "You have chosen ";N;" I wonder why ?"
80 PRINT "Goodbye"
90 END
RUN
Select a number less than 10? 15
WRONG ! Read the question. Try again
Select a number less than 10? 9
You have chosen  9  I wonder why ?
Goodbye

Ready:
```

As an alternative to using the PRINT statement to prompt the user, some BASICs allow an explanatory string, e.g. an instruction, after the INPUT. This is enclosed by quotation marks and followed by a semi-colon. Lines 20 and 30 in Example 2.3 could be combined:

```
20 INPUT "Select a number less than 10";N
```

The effect of the RUN remains unchanged.

2.1.3 A simple interactive program for typing practice:
The keyboard sometimes present difficulty to those who are not typing experts, so here is a program for converting dollars to pounds for you to type in to give you practice:

Example 2.4 Program EXCHANGE

```
1 REM        program    EXCHANGE
10 PRINT "Today's Dollar rate please ";
20 INPUT R
30 PRINT "How much Sterling ";
40 INPUT S
50 PRINT S;"Pounds is";S*R;"Dollars"
55 PRINT
60 GOTO 10
70 END
```

Now type RUN and your result on the screen should be similar to:

```
RUN
Today's Dollar rate please ? 2.4
How much Sterling ? 100
  100 Pounds is 240 Dollars

Today's Dollar rate please ? 3.0
How much Sterling ? 33
  33 Pounds is 99 Dollars

Today's Dollar rate please ? ↑Z

Interrupted at line 20
Ready:
```

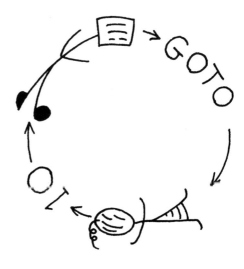

Have you noticed that this program could run on forever? Why?
Simply because there is no way
out of the GOTO 10 loop. This
program RUN was stopped by
touching the CTRL and Z
keys together.

2.2 To interrupt a program RUN

★ ★
★   ★
★   To interrupt a program RUN or program LISTing, press the CTRL and   ★
★   Z keys together or the equivalent for your computer.   ♪   ★
★   ★
★ ★

Have you noticed the effect of the ; at the end of line 30?

Well done!
Right first time!

It results in the next print item being printed on the present line.

In other words a ; or a , at the end of a PRINT statement inhibits a new line. †

---

†   See PRINT statements, Chapter 6.

Finally here is a summary of the very useful LIST command. This command instructs the computer to LIST all or part of a program currently in WORKSPACE.

2.2.1

★ ★
★   ★
★   **The LIST command**   ★
★   LIST   Lists the complete program.   ★
★   LIST L   Lists the line numbered L.   ★
★   LIST-L   Lists all lines up to and including L.   ★
★   LIST L-   Lists all lines from L to the end.   ★
★   LIST L-M   Lists all lines from L to M.   ★
★   ★
★ ★

If for example, you are working on the program 'EXCHANGE', (example 2.4) and you typed the following LIST commands you would get the results as recorded below.

COMMAND	RESULT
LIST 10	10 PRINT "Today's dollar rate please ";
LIST 55-	55 PRINT 60 GOTO 10 70 END
LIST 20-30	20 INPUT R 30 PRINT "How much Sterling ";

2.3

QQQQQQQQQQQQQQQQQQQQQQQQQQQQQQQQQQQ

PROBLEMS

1. Modify example 2.4 so that:

   (a) The program ends naturally without using CTRL and Z.

   (b) The dollar rate is entered once only, but a specified number of conversions is made.

2. Gas Mark $= \dfrac{F - 275}{25} + 1$ †

   This formula can be used to give an approximate conversion from degrees Fahrenheit (275 and above), to the British Gas Mark on a cooker.

   Write an interactive program with clear prompts which will:

   (a) Allow a user to enter a temperature in Fahrenheit and return the Gas Mark.

   (b) Inform the user when a temperature below 275°F is entered, the user is given another chance.

   (c) Terminate the program RUN when a temperature above a 1000°F is entered.

3. Produce a conversion table for dollars, lire, francs, and marks in relation to pounds sterling.

   The Bank buying rates on day x.y.zz. which are quoted as:

   2.368   1994   9.78   4.22

   should be built into the program. The sterling to be converted should be INPUT. All relevant information must be shown on your printout or VDU display.

4. The formulae $V = 4/3\pi R^3$ $A = 4\pi R^2$

   give the volume and surface of a sphere respectively, where R is the radius of the sphere. Design a program to calculate the volume and surface area of a sphere of given radius. The program should be capable of processing several sets of data sequentially. All output should be clearly labelled. Use pi=3.14159.

QQQQQQQQQQQQQQQQQQQQQQQQQQQQQQQQQQQ

---

†   Priority of operators. (Chapter 3)

Some basic tools

3.1 THE BASIC CHARACTER SET

BASIC uses a precisely defined character set. This may differ in detail from one interpreter to another. The RML380Z version described below is used throughout this book.

```
**************************************************
*                                                *
*           THE BASIC CHARACTER SET              *
* Letters            A B C ... Z                 *
* Digits             0 1 2 ... 9                 *
* Arithmetic operators  +  as in A + B           *
*                    −  as in  A − B  or  −(X + 7)  or  −123 *
*                    *  multiply as in  X * Y    *
*                    /  divide as in  (A + B)/(C * D) *
*                    ↑  raise-to-power as in 10↑3    ♭ *
* Brackets           () indicate 'do this first' as in   A/B*(A − B) or *
*                    A(N),  Z(8)                 *
* Space              as in GO TO (for GOTO)      *
* Point              .  decimal point as in 3.14159  *
* Comma              ,  used in lists such as PRINT A, B, C$ *
* Semi-colon         ;  used in statements to indicate 'PRINT next *
*                    item in next position'      *
* Assignment operator  =  eg.  X = Y↑2 + 1  means:  put the value of *
*                    Y↑2 + 1 into X. ('=' does not mean equals *
*                    in this context)            *
* Relational operators  < Less than as in  IF A < B ... *
*                    > Greater than as in  IF A > B ... *
*                    for more details see (Chapter 8) *
* Quote marks        "  used to surround anything to be printed or *
*                    read literally             *
* Character indicator  $  as in A$ defines a string of characters *
* Separator          :  as in 10 PRINT "number please"; INPUT N *
* Other characters   %  !  ?  '  #  @  &        ♭ *
* recognised by some versions                   *
*                                                *
**************************************************
```

♭   Variations on a Theme in the Appendix.

3.2 OPERATORS AND EXPRESSIONS

BASIC allows you to write both simple and very complex expressions. But first we must examine the use of operators. BASIC follows the normal algebraic conventions for operators. Examine the table below:

Table 3.1

Operator	Symbol	Example	Algebraic Rep.	Order
Exponentiation	↑	10 LET P=T↑5	$P = T^5$	1
Multiplication	*	20 LET L=4*G	$L = 4G$	2
Division	/	30 LET A=15/N	$A = \dfrac{15}{N}$	2
Addition	+	40 LET N=A+B+C	$N = A + B + C$	3
Subtraction	−	50 LET E=R−99	$E = R - 99$	3

The order in which operations are carried out is indicated at the right of the table. If two operators of the same order follow one another in an expression the operations are carried out from left to right, as in:

    99 LET S = T + R - A * W / B * E ↑ 2

Use brackets to indicate a different order of operation, or simply to make the formula more readable, as in:

    99 LET S = T + R - (A * W / B * E ↑ 2)

You may have brackets within brackets, (nested brackets), to any reasonable depth. The computer first calculates the value of the innermost bracketed sub-expression, and works its way outwards. This is illustrated as follows:

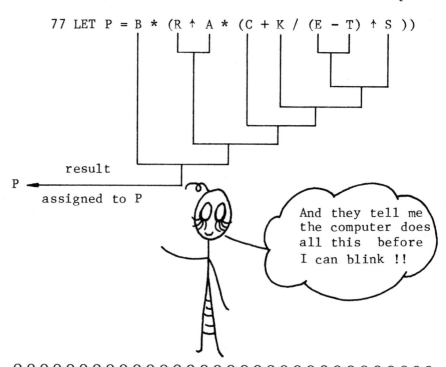

77 LET P = B * (R ↑ A * (C + K / (E − T) ↑ S))

result

P ←

assigned to P

And they tell me the computer does all this before I can blink !!

Q Q Q Q Q Q Q Q Q Q Q Q Q Q Q Q Q Q Q Q Q Q Q Q Q Q Q Q Q Q Q Q
Q
Q   *Can you spot the errors* (or conditions creating errors) in these BASIC
Q   statements?
Q
Q   100 LET A = 2D
Q
Q   200 LET R = A(T*T + Y)
Q
Q   300 LET J = K↑−3
Q
Q   400 LET N = 2.5P + I
Q
Q   500 LET A = B/C/D
Q
Q   600 LET Y = 1/SIN(X)
Q
Q   700 LET E = X↑Y↑Z
Q
Q   If you doubt your decisons, read on . . . †
Q
Q Q Q Q Q Q Q Q Q Q Q Q Q Q Q Q Q Q Q Q Q Q Q Q Q Q Q Q Q Q Q Q

† Solutions in the Appendix

3.3 GENERAL HINTS AND COMMENTS

In BASIC:

This is WRONG

This is RIGHT

Multiplication
is never implied

P = QR

R = S(T + U)

P = Q*R

R = S*(T + U)

Adjacent operators
are not permitted

X = 5* −V

Y = W ↑ −X

X = 5*(−V)

Y = W ↑ (−X)

Division by ZERO
not allowed

for V = 0

T = U/V

Never right!

Error message
can't divide by zero

for COS(B) = 0

A = C/COS(B)

(as above) BUT
exclude COS(B)
for value zero and
program may work.

Exponentiation
(raise-to-power)

PRINT 2 ↑ 6
is the same as
PRINT 2*2*2*2*2*2

Use brackets to clarify
thinking algebraically:
1. a = b/cxd
   is ambiguous, so use

A = B/(C*D) or
A = (B/C)*D

2. $p = \dfrac{q}{r-s}$

P = Q/R−S

P = Q/(R−S)

3.4 SOME FUNDAMENTAL CONCEPTS OF THE BASIC LANGUAGE

3.4.1 Number Formats

Numbers are either *constants* built into a program or they are *variables* read in from data, or entered at the keyboard in response to an INPUT command, while a program is running. In either case, numbers are represented in the following ways:

Examples

Integers (whole numbers)	$-13,\quad -1,\quad 0,\quad +2,\quad 32$
Real Numbers (decimal numbers)	$-19.,\quad -9.0,\quad +3.14,\quad 12.,\quad .0002$
Exponent Form (used when a number is greater than 999999 or less than -0.01)	$7.21631E+01$ $6.25-0E1$

3.4.2 Storage of Numbers

Numbers are most commonly stored to an accuracy of six significant figures as illustrated below.   ♪

3.4.3 Representations of numbers

Number	Stored as	Algebraic meaning
1.234569	1.23457	1.23457
9876543	9.87654E+05	9.87654×10^5
0.00123	1.23E−03	1.23×10^{-03}

Thus E+05 means *multiply* the number by 10^5
    E−03 means *divide* the number by 10^3

3.4.4

★ ★
★   ★
★   *The range of values allowed* is approximately 1E+38 to 1E−38. Values   ★
★   whose magnitude is smaller than 1E−38 are indistinguishable from zero.   ★
★   If no sign is attached to a number it is assumed to be positive.   ♪   ★
★   ★
★ ★

3.4.5 The Way BASIC Prints Numbers

	Example	First printing ↓position	Note
Positive numbers	3	3	A space preceeds the number
Negative numbers	−3	−3	A − sign preceeds the number
Numbers larger than 999999	2345234	2.34523E+06	The number is rounded to 6 significant figures

Variables have already been mentioned in Chapter 1. Data held in variables may be replaced many times during a program RUN, illustrated by the next example.

Example 3.1 Program FATSON

```
10 REM       p r o g r a m                    FATSON
100 PRINT "Give father's & son's heights (in cms)";
110 INPUT F,S
120 T = F  + S
130 PRINT "FATHER ";F;"  SON ";S," TOTAL";T
140 GOTO 100
150 END
RUN
Give father's & son's heights (in cms)? 100,200
FATHER   100    SON   200        TOTAL 300
Give father's & son's heights (in cms)? 197,163
FATHER   197    SON   163        TOTAL 360
Give father's & son's heights (in cms)? ↑Z

Interrupted at line 110
Ready:
```

When a program starts running, every variable must have an initial value. If a variable is without a value, RML 380Z BASIC makes it zero. It is however, a dangerous practice to assume this to be the case. It is good programming practice to allocate your own initial values as in:

Example 3.2 Program FACT

```
10 REM      p r o g r a m                FACT
100 PRINT "I will calculate factorials of all integers"
110 PRINT "          up to the maximum you give me now:";
120 INPUT N
130 LET C = 0
140 LET F = 1
150 PRINT "Number","Factorial"
160 LET C = C + 1
170 LET F = F * C
180 PRINT C ,F
190 IF C < N THEN 160
200 END
RUN
I will calculate factorials of all integers
          up to the maximum you give me now:? 5
Number          Factorial
 1              1
 2              2
 3              6
 4              24
 5              120

Ready:
```

The floating point equivalent of all numbers entered into the computer is stored in the corresponding location. Numbers may be entered in in any unambiguous and convenient way. Any of the following would be regarded as equivalent by BASIC.

$$-5 \qquad -.005E3 \qquad -5000E-3 \qquad -5.00$$

3.5 FUNCTIONS

A function is a pre-written program that can easily be used as part of another program at any stage. For example:

.
.
```
 99 INPUT  X
101 LET  Y  =  SQR(X)
```
.
.

will find the square root of any number INPUT during a RUN and store the result in Y. There is no need to tell the computer *how* to perform the square root operation since the function SQR(X) already exists in the BASIC interpreter.

Names of functions consist usually of three letters followed by an expression in parentheses which must be defined before the function is used in the program.

There are two types of functions:

(a) System Functions

(b) User Functions (Chapter 9).

3.5.1 System Functions

First here are two examples of system functions:

3.5.2 The Integer Function

```
10 LET  Y  =  INT(X)
```

If X is 13.9 Y is assigned the value 13
If X is −13.9 Y is assigned the value −14

A common requirement is that of rounding a number to the *nearest* integer as in:

Example 3.3 Rounding

                                                    Result
```
100 PRINT  INT(3.3333 + 0.5)              3
110 PRINT  INT(6.6666 + 0.5)              7
```

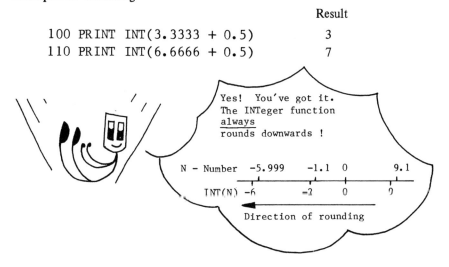

Yes! You've got it.
The INTeger function
always
rounds downwards !

N − Number −5.999   −1.1 0   9.1

INT(N) −6   −2   0   9

Direction of rounding

3.5.3 The RND Function and RANDOMIZE

Example	Description
10 PRINT RND(1)	Returns the next pseudorandom number in the range 0 to 1. RUN resets RND resulting in the same sequence each RUN. Differing positive arguments have no effect on the random number delivered.
20 PRINT RND(0)	The same value is returned as on the previous call.
50 RANDOMIZE	Sets the sequence to a random point.

The combination using RND(1) and RANDOMIZE is commonly found to be the most useful. While testing it is best to omit RANDOMIZE and hence always get the same sequence.

3.5.4 Table 3.2 Numeric Functions (Pre-defined by the BASIC system)

Function	Application	Description	
ABS(X)	10 LET Y = ABS(X)	Calculates the absolute value of X; $Y = |x|$	
ATN(X)	10 LET Y = ATN(X)	Calculates the arctangent of X; X in radians	††
COS(X)	10 LET Y = COS(X)	Calculates the cosine of X; X in radians	††
EXP(X)	10 LET Y = EXP(X)	Raises e to the power X; $Y = e^X$	†
INT(X)	10 LET Y = INT(X)	Assigns to Y the largest integer that does not exceed X	
LOG(X)	10 LET Y = LOG(X)	Calculates the natural logarithm of X	†††
RND(X)	10 LET Y = RND(X)	Produces a pseudo random number between 0 and 1	
SGN(X)	10 LET Y = SGN(X)	Determines the sign of X. Hence if: $\quad X < 0 \qquad Y = -1$ $\quad X = 0 \qquad Y = \ \ 0$ $\quad X = 0 \qquad Y = +1$	
SIN(X)	10 LET Y = SIN(X)	Calculates the sine of X; X in radians	††
SQR(X)	10 LET Y = SQR(X)	Calculates the positive square root of X	
TAN(X)	10 LET Y = TAN(X)	Calculates the tangent of X; X in radians	††

†   The symbol e represents the base of the natural (Naperian) system of logarithms. It is an irrational number whose approximate value is 2.718282. This value is returned by the relation:
$\qquad Y = e^X \quad$ when $\quad X = 1.0$

3.5.5 Two useful conversions

†† To convert
DEGREES to RADIANS

††† To convert
NATURAL to COMMON LOGS

```
10 LET D = 3.14159/180
20
  .
  .
200 Let Y = SIN(X*D)
```

```
25 LET C = .4343
  .
  .
  .
300 LET Y = LOG(X) * C
```

Note The exact value of PI is given by ATN(1)*4

3.6 USEFUL PRINT FUNCTIONS   †

Function	Application	Description
TAB(N)	10 PRINT TAB(N);X	Causes the value of X to be printed starting at position N on the line Left column is considered column zero TAB may only be used in a PRINT statement
SPC(X)	30 PRINT A;SPC(X);B	X extra spaces placed between A and B

3.7

Q Q Q Q Q Q Q Q Q Q Q Q Q Q Q Q Q Q Q Q Q Q Q Q Q Q Q Q Q Q Q Q Q Q Q

PROBLEMS

1. Write a program that will test the validity of the claims made by this book on page 56, with respect to the following:
   (Results should be printed under appropriate headings: e.g. X ABS(X))
   (a) Y = ABS(X)   use negative and positive values for X
   (b) Y = INT(X)   for X = 1.001, 2.9, −2.9, 2001
   (c) Y = EXP(X)   when X = 1
   (d) Y = RND(X)   print the first 10 random numbers for X = 1.
                      Repeat for X = 0
   (e) Repeat the question for (d) but include RANDOMIZE in the program.

2. Convert the numbers given in the random number sequence to numbers in the range 0 to 10. Include appropriate headings.

3. Construct your own common logarithm table from 1 to 100.

Q Q Q Q Q Q Q Q Q Q Q Q Q Q Q Q Q Q Q Q Q Q Q Q Q Q Q Q Q Q Q Q Q Q Q

†   See Chapter 6 – PRINTING

CHAPTER 4

Arrays and
FOR loops

LIST.

TABLE.

VECTOR.

MATRIX

4.1 ARRAYS

It is frequently necessary to refer to a whole collection of items at once. Such a collection, called an *array*, can hold a whole series of numbers or strings.

   A single list of items is known as a *one dimensional array* or *vector*. *A table of items* is known as a *two dimensional array* or *matrix*.

   Multi-dimensional arrays are allowed by some BASICs to a maximum of 255 elements. In practice however, the amount of memory space available restricts the upper limit. Only one and two dimensional arrays are considered in this book.   ♭

4.1.1 Array names are the same as those used for simple variables. Individual elements in the array are referred to by including a subscript or subscripts in the name, for example: T(3), OT(15), Things(3), PHIL(4,6).

   Some BASICs restrict array names to a single letter, limiting the number of arrays used in a program to 26. The same name may be used for an array as for a simple variable in that program. In practice this can be confusing.   ♭

An array is named and its size is set by:
(a) *Usage* if a vector has up to 11 elements or if a matrix is not greater than 11 × 11.
(b) *Declaration* using a dimension statement. The DIM statement may appear anywhere in a program before the array is used. For clarity it is usually placed at its head.   ♭

4.1.2

★ ★

★   ★
★   **The DIMension Statement**   ★
★   ★
★   The DIMension statement consists of a statement number and keyword   ★
★   DIM, followed by one or more array names separated by commas. Each   ★
★   array name is followed by brackets containing one or two integer   ★
★   constants separated by a comma if there is more than one. These   ★
★   integers define the size of the array. For example: ★
★   ★
★   ★
★   10 DIM A(20), A$(20)   ★
★   10 DIM B(2, 15)   ★
★   ★

★ ★

♭   Variations on a Theme (Appendix:) array sizes and names.

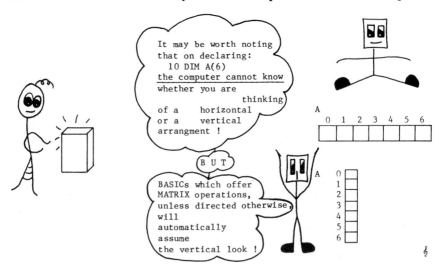

Although of little direct consequence at present, it should be appreciated that the statement:

```
30 DIM H(2,4), V(4,2)
```

causes space to be provided for 15 numbers, in both H and V. The computers with matrix operations 'view' these as shown below:

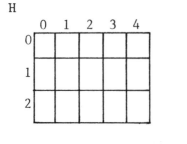

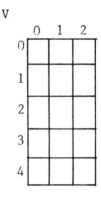

Assignment of a value to an array element may be by *direct reference:*

```
50 LET A(7) = 5
60 LET A(4) = X
70 LET Z(10) = Y↑3 - 2
80 INPUT X(2,5), A(5)
```

or by using a variable to indicate the position of an element in the array as in Example 4.1.

A *subscripted variable* is another name for an array element. All elements of an array are identifiable by using the array name followed by the subscript(s) in parentheses; (one for a vector; two for a matrix). Subscripts must be within the bounds of an array, as illustrated by:

Example 4.1 Program SUBSCRIP

```
10 REM      program   SUBSCRIP
20 DIM A(20)
30 LET C = 1
40 INPUT A(C)
50 LET C = C + 1
60 GOTO 40
70 END
```

Supposing your responses to the INPUTs were 5, 7, 11, 11, 13, 17, . . . 41, 43, 45. The storage area for this program would look something like this:

A	0	1	2	3	4	5	. . .	18	19	20
	0	5	7	11	11	13		41	43	45

The zero stored in A(0) was put there by BASIC. You may choose to use this zero or ignore it. The advisability of setting your own variable initial values has already been referred to in Chapters 1 and 3.   ¢

At first glance it appears that Program 4.1 could RUN on indefinitely. However when C = 21 the program RUN terminates with the *error message:*

Subscript out of range at line 40

4.1.3

★ ★

★   A **subscript** is an expression which is evaluated and truncated to the   ★
★   nearest integer in the range 0 to 65535. Subscripts must be within the   ★
★   bounds of the array.   ★
★   **In general ARRAYS** are expressed as: ★
★   A(m)   ★
★   B(m, n)   ★
★   m represents the rows   ★
★   n represents the columns   ★
★   In this sense every vector is a column vector, i.e.: a (m × 1) matrix.   ★
★   This fact is significant in matrix multiplication and in printing a vector.† ★
★   ★
★   *Note:* Element numbers and subscripts start at 0. The largest array size   ★
★   is limited by the available memory.   ¢ ★

★ ★

† MATRIX MULTIPLICATION: See Appendix.

¢ ARRAYS: See Variations on a Theme in Appendix.

Example 4.2   Program COMPLETE

```
100 REM                    PROGRAM         C O M P L E T E
120 REMEMBER, this program segment was written using information
130 REM        in the preceding pages of this book.
140 REM        A better method is one using FOR..NEXT loops described
150 REM        in the pages that follow.
160 REM  ----------------------------------------------------------
170 DIM A(9)
180 LET N = 1
200 PRINT "9 numbers please,   one on a line"
210 INPUT A(N)
220 LET N = N + 1
230 IF N > 9 THEN 250
240 GOTO  210
250 PRINT "You have successively entered these numbers into array A"
260 LET N = 1
270 PRINT A(N);
280 LET N = N + 1
290 IF N > 9 THEN 320
300 GOTO  270
320 REM = = = = = = = = = = = = = = = = = = = = = = = = = = = = =
340 REM            MODIFY PROGRAM COMPLETE
350 REM            =======================
370 REM     1.  Find the sum of the numbers in array A
380 REM     2.  Find their mean.
390 REM     3.  Print  sum and mean with suitable description
400 REM     4.  Print  the square of the seventh element in A
410 REM     5.  Print  the squares of all the numbers in A
420 REM     6.  The program above is rigid in that it always
425 REM         accepts only 9 numbers.  Modify it to accept up
430 REM         to 30 numbers.
435 REM     7.  Use a FOR-loop instead of the counter N=N+1.
450 REM = = = = = = = = = = = = = = = = = = = = = = = = = = = = =
470 END
RUN
9 numbers please,   one on a line
? 23
? -345
? 45.678
? -567.891
? 999999999
? .00000011
? 123467
? -4343
? 12
You have successively entered these numbers into array A
 23 -345  45.678 -567.891  1E+09  1.1E-07  123467 -4343  12
Ready:
```

4.2 REPETITION USING THE FOR . . . NEXT LOOP

Up to this point repetition has been caused by using a GOTO statement together
with a counter. Another form of repetition is a FOR . . . NEXT loop.

4.2.1

★ ★

The general form of a FOR . . . NEXT loop

FOR V = I TO E STEP S
.
.
NEXT V

FOR   marks the beginning of a loop

V   is a numeric variable, often referred to as the *controlling*
             variable

I   is the *initial value* ⎫   and may be any constant, variable
E   is the *end value*   ⎬   or expression of any complexity
S   is the *step value*   ⎭   provided that the FOR statement
                                         fits onto one line.

NEXT V   V must correspond to the same variable as the controll-
             ing variable. It marks the lower boundary. If it does not
             correspond to the controlling variable the error message
             NEXT without FOR results.

STEP S   May be omitted if the step is 1.

Note: When the number of repetitions specified by the FOR statement
have been completed the loop is abandoned and the statement following
the NEXT is obeyed. In this BASIC a FOR loop will always be executed
at least once, even when, for example, the end value is less than the
initial value with the STEP value positive. In some BASICs the loop
under these conditions is not executed at all.

If I, E, S are expressions or variables they are evaluated when the
loop is first entered and thereafter remain fixed. It is a good policy not
to attempt to change these values within the loop. Remember:

KEEP THE CONTROLS SIMPLE

★ ★

Some examples:

A variable may be used to indicate the position in an array.

```
100 FOR N = 1 TO 10
110 INPUT A(N), B(N, 2)
120 NEXT N
```

In the next example, statements between 100 and 150 will be executed 10 times, N taking the value 1, 2, 3 . . . 10. FOR always marks the beginning of a loop and NEXT the end of the loop.

```
100 FOR N = 1 TO 10
  .
  .
  .
150 NEXT N
```

The variable controlling the loop is automatically increased by 1 each time the loop is repeated, as Example 4.3 shows.

Example 4.3 Program DECISTEP

```
10 REM      program              DECISTEP
20    FOR J = 1 TO 2·STEP .1
30    PRINT "Come";
40    NEXT J
50 END
RUN
Come Come Come Come Come Come Come Come Come Come
Ready:
```

This is one of many variations on the FOR–NEXT loop.

4.2.3 The VALUE of the CONTROLLING VARIABLE on EXIT from LOOP
The best idea is for you to test this yourself for every new system you use. (It is assumed that the value referred to is that when the loop exit is 'natural'). Example 4.4 demonstrates the method of incrementation within the FOR/NEXT loop.

Example 4.4 Program LOOPVAL

```
10 REM     Program       L O O P V A L
20 REM
30    FOR V = 1 TO 7
40    PRINT V;
50    NEXT V
60 PRINT
65 PRINT
70 PRINT "On exit value of V is ";V
80 END
RUN
 1  2  3  4  5  6  7

On exit value of V is  8

Ready:
```

4.2.4 Nested Loops

One loop may be nested inside another. More complicated programs may require loops nested several deep. The depth of nesting permitted varies. A limit of about ten is usually more than adequate for any program.

Loops may never overlap, as illustrated by the next example.

Example 4.5   Illustrating correct loop nesting

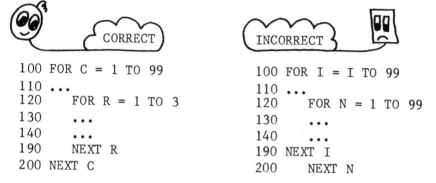

```
100 FOR C = 1 TO 99          100 FOR I = I TO 99
110 ...                      110 ...
120     FOR R = 1 TO 3       120     FOR N = 1 TO 99
130     ...                  130     ...
140     ...                  140     ...
190     NEXT R               190 NEXT I
200 NEXT C                   200     NEXT N
```

The multiplication table that follows is an example of nested loops.

Example 4.6   Program NESTING

```
100 REM          PROGRAM          N E S T I N G
110 REM
120 PRINT TAB(12); "M U L T I P L I C A T I O N     T A B L E"
130 PRINT
140 PRINT
150     FOR N = 1 TO 10
160     FOR J = 1 TO 5
170       PRINT (N * J),
180       NEXT J
190     PRINT
200     NEXT N
210 END

RUN
          M U L T I P L I C A T I O N     T A B L E
```

1	2	3	4	5
2	4	6	8	10
3	6	9	12	15
4	8	12	16	20
5	10	15	20	25
6	12	18	24	30
7	14	21	28	35
8	16	24	32	40
9	18	27	36	45
10	20	30	40	50

Ready:

4.3 USING FOR LOOPS TO LOAD AND REFERENCE AN ARRAY

The data input in the program below represents the heights and weights of five
people. These numbers could be used for a variety of statistical tests so although
only the average height and weight is calculated, the numbers are stored in an
array for ready access.

Example 4.7 Program AVEWTHT

```
90 REM        program        A V E W T H T
95 REM        Weights and Heights stored in array A
100 DIM A (2,5)
110 LET W = 0
115 LET H = 0
125 PRINT "Weight (pounds)";
130    FOR N = 1 TO 2
140       FOR P = 1 TO 5
150       READ A(N,P)
170       PRINT A(N,P);
180       REM         Sum weights and heights
190       IF N = 2 THEN 220
200       LET W = W + A(1,P)
210       GOTO 230
220       LET H = H + A(2,P)
230       NEXT P
235    IF N=2 THEN 250
240    PRINT
245    PRINT "Height (feet)   ";
250    NEXT N
260 REM        Average  weight and height
270 LET A1 = W/P
280 LET A2 = H/P
290 PRINT
295 PRINT
300 PRINT "Ave Weight:   ";A1
305 PRINT "Ave Height:   ";A2
310 DATA 120, 140, 160, 150, 110
320 DATA 5.5, 5.6, 5.8, 5.5, 5.5
350 REMarkable !
360 REM     Average height is less than least height
370 REM     Find the fault and correct it  + + + +
380 REM                                           +
400 END
RUN
Weight (pounds) 120   140   160   150   110
Height (feet)   5.5   5.6   5.8   5.5   5.5

Ave Weight:   113.333
Ave Height:   4.65

Ready:
```

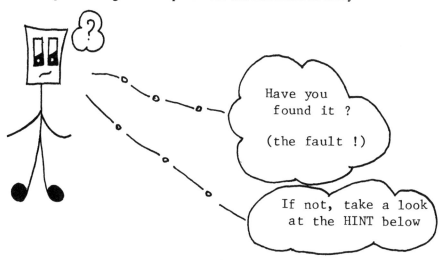

Hint: Check the value of P on exit from loop. (see example 4.4). Is this the value you want to divide by to find the average?

4.3.1 Illustrating the Happenings in Array A (ref. program 4.7)

```
120   DIM  A(2,5)
```
causes space to be reserved for 18 numbers.

```
200 FOR N = 1 TO 2
210 FOR P = 1 TO 5
220 INPUT A(N, P)
    —
    —
230 NEXT P
    —
240 NEXT N
```

Causes numbers in DATA to be read into A. At the start, when N = 1 and P = 1 the first number, 120, is placed in P(1, 1).

For the next round;
N becomes 1
P becomes 2
and 140 is read into A(1, 2).

A   P

                     2

N				
1	120	140			

This process continues. After the P = 5 round has been completed, control passes to the statement following NEXT P. When NEXT N is reached control goes to line 200. Now N = 2 and the next item of data is read into A(N, P), in this case A(2, 1)

A   P

                     1

N					
	120	140	160	150	110
2	5.5				

The final picture of the filled array is this:

A   P

	1	2	3	4	5
1	120	140	160	150	110
N 2	5.5	5.6	5.8	5.5	5.5

At any stage of the program any element of the array may be referred to. For example:

        PRINT A(2, 2),   A(2, 5)

causes

        5.6   5.5

to be printed.

To PRINT the contents of one row

```
FOR P = 1 to 5
    PRINT A( 1, P),
NEXT. P
```

the result:

120	140	160	150	110

To sum the contents of a column

```
LET   S = 0
FOR   N = 1 TO 2
    LET   S = S + A(N, 3)
NEXT  N
```

the result:

165.8

To PRINT the complete contents of the array

This has been done in example 4.7. See lines 130 to 250. The process is simplified when the summations are not made within the same loop. For example:

```
FOR N = 1 TO 2
FOR P = 1 TO 5
    PRINT A(N, P);
    NEXT P
    PRINT
NEXT N
```

Notice how the blank PRINT causes a new line to be started.

To access every second element in an array

e.g. Array $Z(30)$ is filled with values.
    To PRINT numbers stored in the even locations use:

```
FOR I = 2 TO 30 STEP 2
    PRINT Z(J)
NEXT I
```

4.4 CONDITIONAL EXIT FROM A LOOP

Sometimes it is necessary to exit from a loop before it terminates 'naturally'. This is illustrated by the next example.

Example 4.8   Program CONDEXIT

```
100 REM      p r o g r a m              CONDEXIT
110 REM      copes with up to 1000 numbers
120 DIM A(1000)
130 PRINT "PLEASE give me positive"
140 PRINT "numbers -ONE- on a line"
150 PRINT "End with a negative number"
160    FOR J = 1 TO 1000
170    INPUT A(J)
180    REM                          JUMP-OUT-HERE
190    REM                          when necessary !!
200    IF A(J) < 0 THEN 220
210    NEXT J
220 LET J = J - 1
230    FOR L = 1 TO J
240    PRINT A(L);
250    NEXT L
260 REM  !.......................................
270 REM  ! This program assembles the data into array A
280 REM  ! SUGGESTION:  Add to the program statements to
290 REM  !     1. PRINT the number of items in A.
300 REM  !     2. Calculate the mean and variance
310 REM  !        hint :- variance = Σ(X-X̄)²/(N-1)
320 REM  !     3. do your own thing
330 REM  !.......................................
340 END
RUN
PLEASE give me positive
numbers -ONE- on a line
End with a negative number
? 3
? 66
? 254
? -1
  3  66  254
Ready:
```

4.5

Q Q Q Q Q Q Q Q Q Q Q Q Q Q Q Q Q Q Q Q Q Q Q Q Q Q Q Q Q Q Q Q Q Q Q
Q   PROBLEMS   Q
Q   1(a) Use a FOR-loop to INPUT 10 numbers into array Z.   Q
Q   (b) PRINT a table headed NUMBER   N*N   N*N*N.   Q
Q   (c) PRINT the contents of the array backwards.   Q
Q   (d) PRINT every second number in the array starting with the first. Q
Q   2   And now for a traditional problem: Q
Q   Calculate the first 100 prime numbers and PRINT these out in Q
Q   5 columns.   Q
Q   3   Fill a two-dimensional array (5, 2) with random numbers scaled Q
Q   between 1 and 100. Under appropriate headings print, the total Q
Q   and mean of each column and the closest number to the mean for Q
Q   each column. Repeat these with reference to the whole array. Q
Q Q Q Q Q Q Q Q Q Q Q Q Q Q Q Q Q Q Q Q Q Q Q Q Q Q Q Q Q Q Q Q Q Q Q

CHAPTER 5
Strings and things

5.1 STRINGS DEFINED

Not only is a computer useful when working with numbers, but it is extremely valuable in manipulating text (sentences, words and characters). Words such as STRING and LITERAL STRING used to describe text are defined below.

5.1.1

★ ★

A String (or String Variable) is a sequence of characters. Every member of the character set, may form a string or part of a string. *The length of strings* varies from no characters, (called the null string), to 255 characters.

A Literal String is normally bounded by quotation marks. Its length depends on the space available on a line. Maximum length is ∮ approximately 120 characters. In DATA or INPUT statements† the quotation marks are optional, provided no commas, colons or leading spaces appear in the text. A comma terminates a string.

Names for Strings (sometimes called string variables) are similar to names for numbers‡ but with a dollar sign (**$**), as the last character of the name. e.g. **A$, B9$, HI$**

DIMensioning Strings *Simple strings* must not be dimensioned to reserve storage space for characters, unlike the requirements of many other BASICs.
String Arrays must be declared. 100 DIM AD$(20) reserves storage space for 21 strings, since arrays start from zero, each from 0 to 255 characters long.

A Subscripted String Variable such as T$(5) is itself a string. It is the sixth string in the array T$.

★ ★

The examples which follow illustrate a few primitive uses of strings, namely assignment of strings to string variables, and the storage of strings in the computer.

∮   See Appendix: Variations on a Theme
†   Data statements: see Chapter 7
‡   Names for numbers and strings: see Chapter 1

Example 5.1 Illustrating primitive uses of Strings

Example	Representation in the Computer	Comment

```
10 REM Program SUMMER
100 LET X$ = "Today it was summer in all of England !"
110 PRINT X$
120 END
RUN
"Today it was summer in all of England !"

Ready:
```

b)
```
1  REM Program ADD
10 PRINT "3+4+5 = ";3+4+5        3+4+5 =          String storage
20 END
RUN                              3  4  5          Number storage
3+4+5 = 12
```
Numbers between quotes are only literals!

```
Ready:
```

c)
```
10 REM Program Onand
20 LET A$ = "We could go "    A$  We could go    Strings are assigned
30 LET N$ = "ON"              N$  ON             to the associated
40 LET D$ = "and"             D$  and            named locations in
50 PRINT A$;                                     the computer.
60 PRINT N$;D$
70 GOTO 60
80 END
RUN
We could go ONandONandONandONand                 The RUN was stopped by
                                                 touching keys CTRL and Z
Ready:
```

Do you see why ONandONand ... is printed that way instead of ON and ON and ...? If you don't, consult chapter 6 on printing.

Example 5.2 goes a little further and attempts to join, or to use the correct term, concatenate, strings. Study the program and the RUN that follows.

Example 5.2 Program MEMORY3

```
100 REM  p r o g r a m    MEMORY3
110 LET P$="There was a young laddie named Peter, "
120 LET E$="Who was an incredible eater!"
130 LET H$="So when old Mother Hubbard "
140 LET C$="looked into her cupboard"
150 LET M$="It only contained a mosquita!!"
160 LET T$=P$+E$
170 LET S$=H$+C$
180 PRINT T$
190 PRINT S$
200 PRINT M$
300 END
RUN
```

```
No string space at line 170
Ready:
```

This program has failed only because insufficient memory space was allocated for it. The 100 character spaces automatically available to a program at the start have proved insufficient. More space can be made available by using the CLEAR command. This and other lines were added to the program MEMORY3 both to make it work and to improve the presentation of the RUN. In concatenating strings as in lines 160 and 170 of example 5.2, extra workspace must be provided.

105 CLEAR 500	reserves sufficient space.
106 PRINT "Fre-space";FRE(X$)	finds out the amount of remaining space.
107 LET U$="---------***---------"	used to improve appearance of the RUN.
108 PRINT U$;U$;U$	produces the first line printed in the RUN.

The content of lines 106 and 108 are included again at the end of the program the RUN of which is shown in example 5.3.

Example 5.3 Program MEMORY4

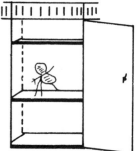

```
100 REM  p r o g r a m     MEMORY4
105 CLEAR 500
106 PRINT "Fre-space";FRE(X$)
107 LET U$="----------***----------"
108 PRINT U$;U$;U$
110 LET P$="There was a young laddie named Peter, "
120 LET E$="Who was an incredible eater!"
130 LET H$="So when old Mother Hubbard "
140 LET C$="looked into her cupboard"
150 LET M$="It only contained a mosquita!!"
160 LET T$=P$+E$
170 LET S$=H$+C$
180 PRINT T$
190 PRINT S$
200 PRINT M$
205 PRINT U$;U$;U$
210 PRINT "Fre-space";FRE(X$)
300 END
RUN
Fre-space 500
----------***--------------------***--------------------***----------
There was a young laddie named Peter, Who was an incredible eater!
So when old Mother Hubbard looked into her cupboard
It only contained a mosquita!!
----------***--------------------***--------------------***----------
Fre-space 383

Ready:
```

If at this point you are not happy with your understanding of strings, enter the program of example 5.3 into your computer and RUN it. Make the suggested modifications and RUN it again. Add your own variations. By 'talking' to a computer in this way your understanding will grow.

5.2

★ ★

CLEAR When BASIC is loaded into memory, space is automatically reserved for a program, the program data and also for 100 characters. Space for literal strings is included in the program space. Extra memory space is reserved via the CLEAR command. e.g. CLEAR 2000 reserves storage space for up to 2000 characters and clears all variables and arrays. If the number is omitted the storage area remains unchanged but all variables and arrays are cleared. On loading BASIC the reserved space remains constant unless it is reset by using CLEAR or BASIC is reloaded. CLEAR should appear at the head of a program before DIM.   †

If a program runs out of string space during execution, the program stops and the *error message;*
'No string space' is displayed.

FRE The current amount of free string space is found by typing:
PRINT FRE(X$)
and free memory space is found by typing:
PRINT FRE(X)
These two statements are informative and do not alter X$ or X. X$ and X are simply 'dummy' names. Reserved space can be altered repeatedly using the CLEAR command until the available free memory is quite small.

★ ★

Besides the definitions of strings and commands which reserve space for strings, BASIC has several inbuilt functions for handling strings. For a start it is frequently useful to know how many characters there are in a string. The LENgth of a string is used in a variety of ways including the lighthearted, as in the next example.

†   Workspace: is the area of temporary storage of program and data.

Example 5.4 Program FREDDIE

```
100 REM       Program   F R E D D I E
110 LET F$ = "Little Freddie was a clown!"
120 PRINT F$; LEN(F$); "foot tall ... oh my!"
130 END
RUN
Little Freddie was a clown! 27 foot tall ... oh my!

Ready:
```

5.3

★★★★★★★★★★★★★★★★★★★★★★★★★★★★★★★★★★★★★★★
★ The LEN function   ★
★ LEN(L$) gives the number of characters, or LENgth, of the string L$. ★
★ *Note:* Spaces and punctuation marks are also counted as characters by ★
★ the computer.   ★
★★

It is sometimes necessary to extract parts of strings. The functions which
follow provide the tools for doing this.

Example 5.5 Program CANCAN

Function   Example   Resulting RUN

```
          10 REM       Program    CANCAN
          20 LET L$="------------------------------"
          30 LET D$="She can can-can as only she can"
          40 PRINT D$                          She can can-can as only she ca
          50 PRINT "         * o *"                     * o *
          60 PRINT L$                          ------------------------------
LEFT$     70 PRINT LEFT$(D$, 7)                She can
          80 PRINT
          90 PRINT L$                          ------------------------------
MID$      100 PRINT MID$(D$, 16)                as only she can
          110 PRINT MID$(D$, 8, 8)             can-can
          120 PRINT
          130 PRINT L$                         ------------------------------
RIGHT$    140 PRINT RIGHT$(D$, 12)             only she can
          150 PRINT L$                         ------------------------------
          160 END
                                               Ready:
```

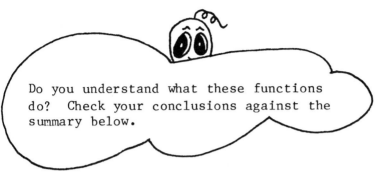

Do you understand what these functions do? Check your conclusions against the summary below.

5.4

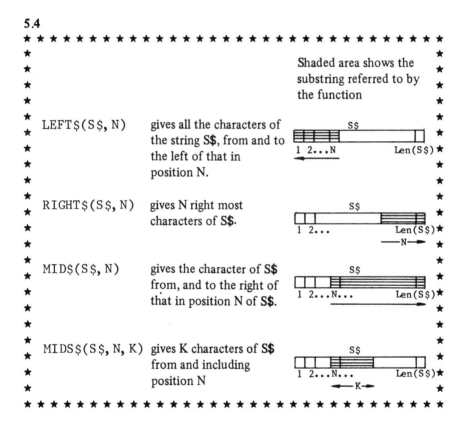

Shaded area shows the substring referred to by the function

LEFT\$(S\$, N)   gives all the characters of the string S\$, from and to the left of that in position N.

S\$
1 2...N   Len(S\$)

RIGHT\$(S\$, N)   gives N right most characters of S\$.

S\$
1 2...   Len(S\$)
                    —N—

MID\$(S\$, N)   gives the character of S\$ from, and to the right of that in position N of S\$.

S\$
1 2...N...   Len(S\$)

MIDS\$(S\$, N, K)   gives K characters of S\$ from and including position N

S\$
1 2...N...   Len(S\$)
                    —K—

The example that follows illustrates one application of these functions. It is also an example of good programming practice as in providing a trap for words too long for the purpose of the program.

Example 5.6 Program ALLSUBS

```
10 PRINT "Program     A L L S U B S"
20 PRINT "             gives all substrings of a word with up to 10 characters"
30 PRINT "             A word of more than 10 characters is ignored"
40 PRINT "Your word";
50 INPUT W$
60 LET L = LEN(W$)
70 IF L > 10 THEN 40
80 PRINT TAB(L+15); "has these substrings:"
90 PRINT "---------------------------------------------------------------------"
100 LET L = LEN(W$)
110 LET L1 = L
120   FOR K = 1 TO L
130     FOR J = 1 TO L1
140       PRINT MID$(W$, K, J);"   ";
150     NEXT J
160   PRINT
170   LET L1 = L1 - 1
180   NEXT K
190 END
RUN
Program     A L L S U B S
             gives all substrings of a string with up to 10 characters
             A string of more than 10 characters is ignored
Your word? archives
                         has these substrings:
---------------------------------------------------------------------
a    ar   arc   arch    archi   archiv   archive   archives
r    rc   rch   rchi    rchiv   rchive   rchives
c    ch   chi   chiv    chive   chives
h    hi   hiv   hive    hives
i    iv   ive   ives
v    ve   ves
e    es
s

Ready:
```

(cloud) GOT IT? Printing of all substrings is controlled by lines 100–180

A question asked by some is that of how frequently a word, or character occurs in a given text. The next program, CSEARCH, does this for any character input while it is running.

Example 5.7 Program CSEARCH

```
100 REM                                      program    C S E A R C H
110 DIM B(100)
120 LET S$="The Carrion Crow is a solitary bird. "
130 LET S$ = S$ + "It is usually found flying alone or in pairs."
140 PRINT "(NOTE:   CAPITAL and small letters are treated as distinct characters)"
150 PRINT "Choose a character";
160 INPUT L$
170 IF LEN(L$) = 1 THEN 200
180 PRINT "only    O N E    character please"
190 GOTO 160
200 PRINT "Character", "Position"
210 PRINT "---------------------"
220 REM  C - counts the occurrences of chosen character
230 REM  B - is the array of position markers (1), of the character
240 LET C = 0
250   FOR L = 1 TO LEN(S$)
260   IF MID$(S$, L, 1) <> L$ THEN 300
270   B(L)=1
280   PRINT L$, L
290   C = C + 1
300   NEXT L
310 PRINT S$
320   FOR N = 1 TO LEN(S$)
330   IF B(N) <> 1 THEN 350
340   PRINT TAB(N-1);"↑";
350   NEXT N
360 PRINT
370 PRINT "The FREQUENCY of occurrence of  ";L$; " is ";C/LEN(S$) * 100; " %"
380 END
RUN
(NOTE:   CAPITAL and small letters are treated as distinct characters)
Choose a character? r
Character      Position
---------------------
r              7
r              8
r              14
r              29
r              34
r              72
r              80
The Carrion Crow is a solitary bird. It is usually found flying alone or in pairs.
   ^^       ^           ^       ^                              ^          ^
The FREQUENCY of occurrence of  r  is  8.53659  %

Ready:
```

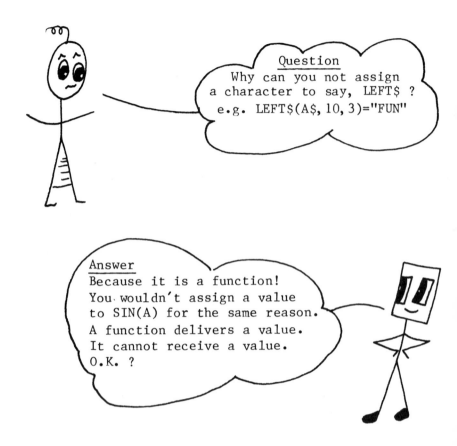

Question
Why can you not assign
a character to say, LEFT$?
e.g. LEFT$(A$, 10, 3)="FUN"

Answer
Because it is a function!
You wouldn't assign a value
to SIN(A) for the same reason.
A function delivers a value.
It cannot receive a value.
O.K. ?

One last example on strings demonstrates their usefulness in certain types of graphical work. The method used in example 5.8 is known as the line buffer method. First a character array is declared. For example, 130 DIM L$(40). This reserves space for 40 strings each of length 255 characters. The string buffer, **L$**, is however used as though it were a one dimensional array, making the buffer just 40 characters long. The rest of the method is explained by the program ROMANBUF and the summary of the line buffer method that follows.

Example 5.8 Program ROMANBUF

```
100 REM     p r o g r a m          ROMANBUF
110 REM        uses the  LINE BUFFER  method to produce the
120 REM        ROMAN NUMERAL  8
130 DIM L$(40)
140 REM    First fill the buffer, L$, with spaces
150    FOR L = 1 TO 40
160    LET L$(L) = " "
170    NEXT L
180 PRINT "-----------------------------------------"
190 REM    Set start positions, K and J, for the 'V'
200 LET K = 6
210 LET J = 16
220    REM    The  FOR N / NEXT N loop controls loading and printing
230 REM    of the buffer
240    FOR N = 1 TO 6
250    REM    Load characters for this line into buffer
260    LET L$(K)="5"
270    LET L$(J)="5"
280    LET L$(21)="6"
290    LET L$(27)="7"
300    LET L$(33)="8"
310    REM    Next positions for the 'V'
320    LET K=K+1
330    LET J=J-1
340      FOR N1 = 1 TO 40
350      PRINT L$(N1);
360      REM    The buffer is cleared ready to receive the next line
370      L$(N1) = " "
380      NEXT N1
390    PRINT
400    NEXT N
410 PRINT "-----------------------------------------"
420 END
RUN
-------------------------------------------
    5         5     6     7     8
    5         5     6     7     8
     5       5      6     7     8
      5     5       6     7     8
       5 5          6     7     8
        5           6     7     8
-------------------------------------------
Ready:
```

5.5 SUMMARY OF THE LINE BUFFER METHOD

Step	Action	Line from Example 5.8
1	Clear the buffer.	150 to 170
2	Put all you want printed on the current line into the buffer.	260 to 300
3	Print the line.	340, 350, 380
4	Clear the buffer.	370
5	Return to the start of the cycle.	Via 400
		start again at 240
.	Continue until done!	

The string functions that follow are included last and without detailed explanation. While it is generally true to say that these are not used as frequently as the functions looked at so far, there are those who find these invaluable tools in their programmer's kit.

5.6

★ ★

Function	Application	Description
ASC("T")	40 LET B=ASC("T")	B is given the value 84, the ASCII code for the letter T.
	50 LET C=ASC("POT")	C is given the value 80, the numerical equivalent of 'P', the first letter of the string. For 'P', 80.
CHR$(N)	60 PRINT CHR$(N)	CHR$ returns the ASCII character of the specified numeric code. N is a number in the range 0 to 255. For N = 122, Z is printed. CHR$ is the inverse of ASC.
VAL(W$)	70 LET A$ = "3.3" 80 LET B = VAL(A$) 85 LET C=VAL("none") 90 LET D=VAL("5.6.7")	VAL returns the number (W$) represented as a string or as part of a string. In this example 3.3 is assigned to B. C takes the value zero for character(s). D takes the value 5.6.
STR$(N)	10 LET E$=STR$(N)	STR$ returns a string representing the given number, N.
	20 LET F$=STR$(7.9)	F$ is assigned '7.9'. A leading space is inserted if the number is positive and a minus sign if it is negative. STR$ is the inverse of VAL.

★ ★

5.7

Q Q Q Q Q Q Q Q Q Q Q Q Q Q Q Q Q Q Q Q Q Q Q Q Q Q Q Q Q Q Q Q Q

PROBLEMS

1. Modify example 5.1c so that the program will end after printing out 6 repeats of the sequence.

2. Using the line buffer as in example 5.8 write a program to print the Roman numeral IV (four). If you feel a little more adventurous get your program to print out the Roman numeral X (ten). Try other Roman numerals.

3. In writing a program to produce the Roman numeral 8 the RUN sometimes looks like this:

```
-------------------------------------
    5          5      6    7    8
    55         55     6    7    8
    555        555    6    7    8
    5555     5555     6    7    8
    55555  55555      6    7    8
    55555555555       6    7    8
-------------------------------------
```

Can you give a reason for this obvious fault in shading round the V?

4. Using the CLEAR command reserve enough string space for this program. Assign the sentence 'Round the ragged rocks the rugged rascal ran.' to R$. Using the string functions extract and print the words of the sentence one per line.

   Search for and count the number of occurances of the letter r.

   Extract the first and last words of the sentence and concatenate these to read 'ran Round' when printed out.

5. Program a secret CODER that will translate and print any message you input into a number code. For example in the first instance the code should be A is 1 B is 2 ... Z is 26.

   Extend the program to decode and print a message input in 'number code'. Develop your own variations.

Q Q Q Q Q Q Q Q Q Q Q Q Q Q Q Q Q Q Q Q Q Q Q Q Q Q Q Q Q Q Q Q Q

CHAPTER 6
Printing

If you have been working steadily through the book up to this point you will already be familiar with several aspects of the versatile PRINT statement. This chapter draws together the scattered information and adds to it.

6.1

★ ★

The PRINT Statement

The PRINT statement causes the computer to output information, usually to a screen or to a printer. Numeric and character (string) items are listed following the word PRINT. A COMMA or a SEMICOLON is used to separate items.

A separator after the last item inhibits a new line. If there is space on the current line, items of the next PRINT statement will be printed on that line.

PRINT followed by no further characters produces a blank line. If the previous PRINT line ended with a comma or semi-colon it cancels out their effect. A general form of the PRINT statement is:

line number PRINT item separator item separator . . .
item: constants, variables, expression, strings or TAB
separator: , or ;

★ ★

6.1.1 Examples of PRINT Statements

Item	Example
constants	10 PRINT 30, 9.91, −.5,
literals	20 PRINT "Hello"
variables	30 PRINT B, A(N), C(99), K(N+1), S(2*N), P2
string variables	40 PRINT S$, U$(15), P$(N)
expressions	60 PRINT X, X↑2, X↑3
	70 PRINT 4 * U1 + 6 * V1
	80 PRINT Y; LOG(Y)
	90 PRINT SQR(ABS(B*B−4*A*C))

6.2 The COMMA

All items separated by a comma are output in zones 14 character positions wide. The item following a comma will be printed at the start of the next print zone. Two adjacent commas (see line 220 in the next example) cause a zone to be skipped.

Example 6.1 Program COMMAZONE

```
100 REM      Program      C O M A Z O N E
110 LET RU$ = "0123456789012345678901234567890123456789012345678901234567890123456789"
120 LET RD$ = "1    Start    2    of    3    zone    4    indicators 5"
130 LET L$ = "----------------------------------------------------------------------"
140 PRINT L$
150 PRINT 55, 77, 99
160 PRINT -11, -22, -33
170 PRINT L$
180 PRINT RU$
190 PRINT RD$
200 PRINT L$
210 PRINT "Mount Kilimanjaro", "Snowdon", "Nelsonskop"
220 PRINT 19340,, 3560, 6027, "feet"
230 PRINT L$
240 END
RUN
---------------------------------------------------------------------
 55            77            99
-11           -22           -33
---------------------------------------------------------------------
01234567890123456789012345678901234567890123456789
1    Start    2    of    3    zone    4    indicators 5
---------------------------------------------------------------------
Mount Kilimanjaro          Snowdon       Nelsonskop
 19340                     3560          6027        feet
---------------------------------------------------------------------

Ready:
```

The number of printed items per line depends on the types of items and on the width of the screen or printer. If there are more items than will fit on one line these appear on the next line where output is directed to a screen. Where the output is directed to a printer, the print head may print on the spot at the end of the line! ♩

♩   Reminder: The symbol ♩ implies there are Variations on a Theme in BASICs at this point. Please refer to the appendix.

Information is always printed left justified in each zone as you may have observed in example 6.1. One position is allowed for the sign of a number. If the number is positive the + sign is suppressed, if negative the − sign is printed in the first position of the zone. The use of COMMAs in a print line gives an easy way to print columns of information. The next illustration illuminates these points.

0	14	28	Start of zones
−12	−.01	−99	negative numbers
12	.01	99	positive numbers
words	words	words	characters

6.3 THE SEMICOLON

A more compact result is obtained by using a semicolon as the separator. If the items are *characters* they are printed in a continuous stream. In other words items are printed without any space between them. *Numeric items* are printed allowing for the sign of the number and one space between each item. These features are illustrated by the next example.

Example 6.2 Program PACKED

```
100 REM          Program   P A C K E D
110 PRINT
120 PRINT 1;2;3;4;5;6;7;8;9
130 PRINT -1;-2;-3;-4;-5;-6;-7;-8;-9
140 PRINT "--------------------------"
150 PRINT 12;23;34;45;56;67;78
160 PRINT 123;345;6789;98765;321
170 PRINT "--------------------------"
180 PRINT "Words";"Words";"Words";"Words";"  etc"
190 END
RUN

 1  2  3  4  5  6  7  8  9
-1 -2 -3 -4 -5 -6 -7 -8 -9
--------------------------
 12  23  34  45  56  67  78
 123  345  6789  98765  321
--------------------------
WordsWordsWordsWords   etc

Ready:
```

The spacing between PRINT items differs from system to system. Consult the appendix and your computer manual for details.

The next example shows up the contrast between printing the same sets of data twice, first using the comma to separate items, and secondly the semicolon.

Example 6.3 Program PARTERS

```
100 REM        program          P A R T E R S
110 LET   R$ ="Rain"
120 LET   S$ ="Spain"
140 LET   P$ ="Plain"
150 LET   I$ ="inches"
160 LET   R1 = 30
170 LET   R2 = 40
180 LET   L$ ="*-------------*-------------*------------
185 PRINT
190 PRINT L$
210 PRINT R$, S$, P$, "COMMA spacing"
220 PRINT R1,R2
225 PRINT S$,R$,R1,R2
230 PRINT L$
240 PRINT R$;S$;P$;"SEMICOLON spacing"
250 PRINT R1;R2
255 PRINT S$;R$;R1;R2
260 PRINT L$
300 END
RUN


*-------------*-------------*------------*
Rain           Spain         Plain         COMMA spacing
  30             40
Spain          Rain           30            40
*-------------*-------------*------------*
RainSpainPlainSEMICOLON spacing
 30  40
SpainRain 30   40
*-------------*-------------*------------*

Ready:
```

You may have noticed that not all the data in the program appears in the RUN. This is often the case. Only that required in the RUN was selected for the PRINT statements.

6.4 TAB and SPC

Where a more varied layout is wanted the instructions TAB and SPC are used. These may only be used as part of PRINT or LPRINT statements. LPRINT causes the results to appear on the printer provided the link to the computer has been set up.

6.4.1

★ ★

The TAB command

The TAB command has a similar role to the tabulate on a typewriter. It causes the screen cursor or printhead to move to the indicated column. Columns are numbered starting from zero.

Example: PRINT A;TAB(25);B when A = 7, B = −9 the results are:

```
  7                        −9
  |                        |
  01234 ...                25        position
```

Note the space that preceeds the 7 is printed in position zero, (first column). The − preceding the 9 is printed in position 25, (column 26).

If a TAB command indicates a position prior to the present position of the screen cursor or printhead it is ignored.

If the position indicated by the TAB command is greater than the number of positions allowed on that line (255), or if it is negative, the error message *Illegal function* is given.

A comma following a TAB has no effect on positioning.

★ ★

Example 6.4 Program TABBIE

```
100 REM        Program        T A B B I E
110 REM        uses TAB control to position print items.
120 PRINT
130 PRINT "N";TAB(10);"N*N";TAB(30);"SQR(N)";TAB(40);"N"
135 LET L$ = "----------------------------------------
140 PRINT L$
150   FOR N = 1 TO 5
160   PRINT N;TAB(10);N*N;TAB(30);SQR(N);TAB(40);N
170   NEXT N
180 PRINT L$
200 END
RUN
```

N	N*N	SQR(N)	N
1	1	1	1
2	4	1.41421	2
3	9	1.73205	3
4	16	2	4
5	25	2.23607	5

Ready:

6.4.2

★★
★   ★
★ **The SPC command**   ★
★ causes extra spaces to be printed between two items in addition to a   ★
★ space following the first item and the space or minus sign before the   ★
★ second.   ★
★   ★
★ example   30 PRINT A;SPC(5);B   ★
★   ★
★★

6.5 OTHER COMMANDS AND FUNCTIONS

Command/Function		Example
POS	The POS function returns the current position of the screen cursor in columns numbered from zero. The argument must be zero. POS can be used with other arguments to indicate the printhead position for example. Check your own machine manual for details.	50 LET P = POS(0)
LPOS	As POS but returns the position of the printhead on the device accessed by the L commands (e.g. LPRINT). The argument is a dummy.	60 P = LPOS(0)
WIDTH	When BASIC starts, the screen width is considered to be infinite. The WIDTH command sets the logical width of the screen such that BASIC automatically begins a new line after the specified number of characters have been output. WIDTH 0 returns BASIC to initial state. The requested width must lie within the range 15 to 255, or be zero.	10 WIDTH 40 WIDTH 20
LWIDTH	As WIDTH, but sets the logical width of the printer.	10 LWIDTH 72 LWIDTH 80
?	The symbol ? may be used as a synonym for PRINT. However, its use in programs does not improve their readability! It is often convenient to use in 'calculator-mode,' for in inspecting the value of a variable in an example. A fuller explanation follows.	?A, B, C
LVAR	LVAR lists the values of all the simple variables, on the console.	LVAR
LLVAR	The value of all simple variables are printed on the printer.	LLVAR
LVAR #10	LVAR #10 lists the values to the OUTPUT FILE (See Chapter N)	LVAR #10

Generally #10 can be added to the above instructions to send to the output file.

6.6 BASIC USED IN DIRECT MODE

6.6.1 BASIC can be used as a simple calculator

BASIC can be used as a simple calculator by typing PRINT (or the equivalent ? symbol) followed by the item or items to be PRINTed. BASIC statements without a line number are obeyed immediately. Direct-mode is most useful for testing individual lines of a program, and for discovering the value of variables at the end of a program RUN.

General Examples

```
PRINT(5*(80-32))/9
PRINT 99
PRINT"MICRO";380
```

Instant Result

```
26.6667
99
MICRO  380
```

Direct mode is very useful when trying to trace the reason for a program failure. This is demonstrated in example 6.5. Here the values of the variables after a program RUN are found in two different ways; by using PRINT followed by the variable names, or by using LVAR.

Example 6.5 Program VARIABLE

```
100 REM      p r o g r a m              VARIABLE
110 REM      will fail.   To find the value of the variables
120 REM      on failure use either BASIC CALCULATOR mode, PRINT,
130 REM                       or the command LVAR
140 LET D = 3.14159/180
150   FOR N = 0 TO 360 STEP 15
160   LET S = SIN(N*D)*30
170   LET T = 30+S
180   PRINT TAB(T);"*"
190   NEXT N
200 END
RUN
```

```
                              *
                                    *
                                  *
                                       *
                                         *
                                          *
                                           *
                                            *
                                           *
                                          *
                                         *
                                       *
                                   *
                                 *
                           *
                        *
                     *
                  *
              *
          *
      *
  *
```

```
Illegal function at line 180
Ready:
PRINT D, N, S, T
 .0174533        270          -30            -3.8147E-06
```

Ready:
LVAR
D= .0174533
N= 270
S=-30
T=-3.8147E-06

> Use LVAR after any RUN especially if the program is failing. It is a most useful aid to finding the fault(s).

Ready:

Why does the program fail?
What is the reason for the error message at the end of the RUN?
If you can't answer these questions check the Solutions.

6.7

QQQQQQQQQQQQQQQQQQQQQQQQQQQQQQQQQQQQ

PROBLEMS

1. Input 10 numbers into array A. Print these numbers using the semi-colon as a separator. Print 2 blank lines. Print the 10 numbers using the comma to separate items and to give 5 numbers per line in the RUN.

2. With the aid of the TAB function print the numbers input in question 1 sloping down the page diagonally from left to right.

3. Print the headings SIN(X) and COS(X) starting in positions 20 and 35 respectively. Print a dotted line below the headings. Print the values of SIN(X) and COS(X) in columns below the appropriate headings for X = 10, 20, 30, 45, 90.

4. Write a program to print a frame similar to the one surrounding these questions.

5. This program should print the heading:

number   square root   cube root   fourth root

One number at a time should be input and printed under 'number'. The values named in the heading should be calculated and printed in the appropriate columns, (each 14 character positions wide). Your program should accept positive values only and terminate if a value less than 0 is input.

6. Print the first hundered numbers exactly divisible by 7. Print seven numbers on a line so that your output is in neat columns.

QQQQQQQQQQQQQQQQQQQQQQQQQQQQQQQQQQQQ

CHAPTER 7
Reading data

7.1 INCLUDING DATA IN A PROGRAM

At times it is cumbersome and inconvenient to assign data to variables directly using a LET statement, or through an INPUT statement. This is particularly true where large numbers of items are required. The alternative offered by BASIC is to use the combination of the READ *and* DATA *statements.*

Data required by the program is recorded on DATA statements and activated by appropriate READ statements. The general forms of these statements are:

7.1.1

★★
★   ★
★   The DATA Statement   ★
★   DATA item, item, item . . .   ★
★   item: numeric-constant (i.e. no expressions)   ★
★   string-constant   ★
★   unquoted-string   ★
★   separator: , (comma) but no comma after the last item of the   ★
★   statement. If there is a comma at the end of a data line ★
★   BASIC picks up a zero or null.   ★
★   ★
★   The READ Statement   ★
★   READ item, item, item, . . .   ★
★   item: numeric-constant   ★
★   string-constant   ★
★   unquoted-string   ★
★   separator: , (comma) but no comma after the last item of the   ★
★   statement   ★
★   ★
★★

Example 7.1 Program SEGMENT

```
100 REM     Program segment     SEGMENT
110 DATA "This is a valid data item"
120 DATA "Lines 110 to 150 also contain only valid DATA items"
130 DATA 33
140 DATA .5, 9, 11, .2, 13, .3, -1, -1
150 DATA "Lark", "Sparrow", "Lammegeiger"
160 DATA And this is an unquoted string,and this the next unquoted string
170 REM >>*   The READ statements below read all the given DATA items   *<<
180 READ D1$,D2$
190 READ N
200    FOR J = 1 TO 10
210    READ M1,M2
220    IF M1 < 0 THEN 240
230    NEXT J
240 READ B1$, B2$, B3$
250 READ U1$, U2$
260 REM >>*             Here endeth the program-segment          *<<
```

The READ statement assigns the numeric or string value in the DATA to a variable it names. The DATA statement itself is a non-executable statement. DATA held in such statements must be brought into use in the program via a READ statement. If during execution a program reaches a DATA statement the statement is skipped and it proceeds to the next line.

Any number of DATA statements may be included anywhere in a program. It makes a program clearer however if all the DATA statements are grouped together near the beginning or end of the program. Irrespective of where the statements are in a program BASIC arranges them in one queue. The first item of data is assigned to the first variable named in the first READ statement. The remaining items in the queue are assigned to subsequent variables in the READ statements. The data in example 7.1 would therefore be queued like this:

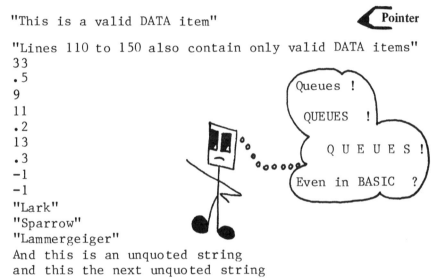

```
"This is a valid DATA item"                    Pointer

"Lines 110 to 150 also contain only valid DATA items"
33
.5
9                          Queues !
11
.2                         QUEUES  !
13
.3                         Q U E U E S !
-1
-1                         Even in BASIC  ?
"Lark"
"Sparrow"
"Lammergeiger"
And this is an unquoted string
and this the next unquoted string
```

Data items are collected into a single sequence as illustrated above, rather than two separate ones for numeric DATA and for string DATA. At the start of a program run BASIC sets a pointer pointing at the first item in the data sequence. This item is assigned to the first variable in the first READ statement. The pointer is moved on to the next item in the sequence. String data is assigned only to string variables and numeric data to numeric variables. The next program illustrates this point.

Example 7.2 Program RECTIFY

```
100 REM           program        R E C T I F Y
110 READ A, A$
120 PRINT A, A$
130 DATA "All", 1, "because", 2, "chemistry", 3, "doesn't", 4
140 END
RUN
Syntax error at line 130
Ready:
```

The syntax error indicated in the RUN at line 130 is an example of BASIC's response when the type of data does not correspond to the variable type named in the relevant READ statement. What is needed to correct the situation?   †

Line 130 holds more data than is used in the program. This is acceptable. The reverse, however, is not. BASIC will complain if there is too little data, with the error message:

Out of data at line n   (n = line number)

The next program shows a correct matching up of data and variable types. It also demonstrates a way to deal with unwanted data in the DATA statements. Compare the READ and DATA lines together with the PRINT results.

Example 7.3 Program PEARTREE

```
100 REM           program        P E A R T R E E
110 DIM L$(5)
120 READ A, B, T$, P$, PT$, A$
130 PRINT TAB(30);A;" ";T$
140   FOR N = 1 TO 5
150     READ L$(N)
160     PRINT TAB(45);L$(N)
170   NEXT N
180 PRINT TAB(55); B;" ";P$
190 DATA 2, 1, "Turtle doves"
200 DATA Partridge, Pear Tree, a
210 DATA "    *", "   *-*", "  **-**"
220 DATA "***-***", "    -"
230 END
RUN
                        2  Turtle doves
                                *
                               *-*
                              **-**
                             ***-***
                               -
                                              1  Partridge

Ready:
```

†   See Solutions in Appendix.

Sometimes it is convenient to READ the same DATA again. This is done using the RESTORE statement.

7.2

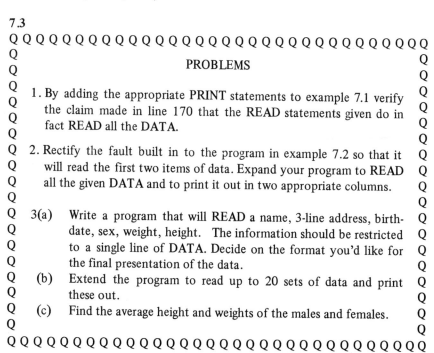

★ ★
★   ★
★   **The RESTORE statement**   ★
★   ★
★   RESTORE   reinitialises the DATA pointer. In the first case the ★
★   RESTORE 200   pointer is reset to the beginning of the DATA. In the ★
★   second the pointer is reset to the first item of DATA in ★
★   line 200.   ★
★   ★
★ ★

RESTORE can be particularly useful in conjunction with subroutines containing sets of data — (see chapter 9).

7.3

Q Q Q Q Q Q Q Q Q Q Q Q Q Q Q Q Q Q Q Q Q Q Q Q Q Q Q Q Q Q Q Q Q Q Q Q
Q   Q
Q   PROBLEMS   Q
Q   Q
Q   1. By adding the appropriate PRINT statements to example 7.1 verify   Q
Q   the claim made in line 170 that the READ statements given do in   Q
Q   fact READ all the DATA.   Q
Q   Q
Q   2. Rectify the fault built in to the program in example 7.2 so that it   Q
Q   will read the first two items of data. Expand your program to READ   Q
Q   all the given DATA and to print it out in two appropriate columns.   Q
Q   Q
Q   3(a)   Write a program that will READ a name, 3-line address, birth-   Q
Q   date, sex, weight, height. The information should be restricted   Q
Q   to a single line of DATA. Decide on the format you'd like for   Q
Q   the final presentation of the data.   Q
Q   (b)   Extend the program to read up to 20 sets of data and print   Q
Q   these out.   Q
Q   (c)   Find the average height and weights of the males and females.   Q
Q   Q
Q Q Q Q Q Q Q Q Q Q Q Q Q Q Q Q Q Q Q Q Q Q Q Q Q Q Q Q Q Q Q Q Q Q Q Q

CHAPTER 8
Program control

8.1 CONTROL – (BRANCHING AND LOOPING)

The control statements   GO TO and .

IF . . . THEN . . .

have been introduced in chapter 1. To recap:

8.1.1 Unconditional control

The GO TO statement causes a change in the natural progression of a program. Execution of the program is transferred unconditionally to the specified line number.

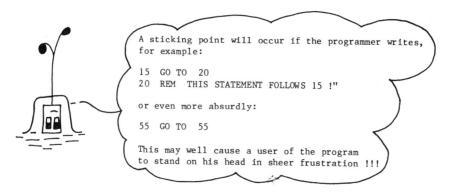

A sticking point will occur if the programmer writes, for example:

```
15  GO TO  20
20  REM  THIS STATEMENT FOLLOWS 15 !"
```

or even more absurdly:

```
55  GO TO  55
```

This may well cause a user of the program to stand on his head in sheer frustration !!!

A further bit of trouble is encountered in the next program segment:

```
60 PRINT "This is an endless loop"
70 GO TO 60
```

When executed these lines result in:
This is an endless loop
This is an endless loop
This is an endless loop

Remember touching ⎡CTRL⎤ ⎡Z⎤ will break this cycle by stopping the execution of the program.

8.1.2 Conditional control

The IF . . . THEN statement causes control to be transferred to some other specified point in the program only if a given condition is met Otherwise, the statement following the IF . . . THEN is obeyed next.

When comparing two variables they must be of the same type, numeric or string. When making comparisons using IF . . . THEN . . ., use one of the following relational operators.

8.1.3

★ ★

★ **RELATIONAL**	**OPERATORS**	♩ ★
★ >	is greater than	★
★ <	is less than	★
★ >=	is greater than or equal to	★
★ <=	is less than or equal to	★
★ =	is equal to	★
★ <>	is not equal to	★

★ The two-character operators may be written as =>, =< or > < without ★
★ change of meaning. ★

★ A relational operator compares two items. The result of the operation is ★
★ either −1 or 0 depending on whether the relationship between them is ★
★ true or false. ★

★ ★

8.1.4 Variations on IF . . . THEN . . . ELSE

In the special case where the IF statement governs an unconditional transfer of control using GOTO, e.g.

```
10 IF A=2 THEN GOTO 100
```

either 'THEN' or 'GOTO' may be omitted. The forms: ♩

```
10 IF A=2 THEN 100
10 IF A=2 GOTO 100
```

are permissible, and have an equivalent effect to the previous example.

ELSE   ```10 IF A=2 THEN PRINT B ELSE PRINT C```   ♩

If the Boolean expression following the IF keyword is:

FALSE	TRUE
and an ELSE clause is present, the ELSE clause is executed.	the THEN clause is executed and the ELSE clause is skipped.
An ELSE *clause* extends from ELSE to the end of the line.	*A* THEN *clause* extends from THEN to ELSE if present or to the end of the line if not.

Illustration

```
10    IF    A - 2    THEN    PRINT    B    ELSE    PRINT    C
```

        IF clause   THEN clause   ELSE clause

♩   Variations on a Theme in the Appendix.

It should now be evident that either the THEN clause, or the ELSE clause, or both, may include a compound statement, that is a series of statements separated by colons.

The following example should clarify the behaviour of

IF . . . THEN . . . ELSE.

Example 8.1 Program ITELSE

```
100 REM    program         ITELSE
110 REM    illustrating the behaviour of    IF...THEN...ELSE...
130 PRINT "This program collects numbers(N) into two categories"
140 PRINT "when N < 50          N*N is printed"
150 PRINT "when N >= 50         LOG(N) is printed"
160 PRINT "..................................................."
170 LET C = 0
180 LET L = 0
200 PRINT "Input positive numbers"
210 PRINT "Terminate with a negative no."
220 PRINT
230 PRINT "N","N*N","LOG(N)"
235 PRINT "---------------------------------------------------"
240 INPUT N
250 IF N < 0 THEN 280
260 IF N >= 50 THEN LET G=G+1:PRINT,,LOG(N) ELSE LET L=L+1:PRINT,N↑2
270 GOTO 240
280 PRINT
290 PRINT "You input ";L; "number(s) < 50, and ";G; "number(s) >= 50"
330 END
RUN
This program collects numbers(N) into two categories
when N < 50          N*N is printed
when N >= 50         LOG(N) is printed
.................................................
Input positive numbers
Terminate with a negative no.
```

N	N*N	LOG(N)
? 32		
	1024	
? 111		
		4.70953
? 49.9		
	2490.01	
? -1		

You input 2 number(s) < 50, and 1 number(s) >= 50

Ready:

8.2 LOGICAL OPERATORS

More complicated sets of relationships can be set up and the truth or otherwise of series of relations tested with the use of the:

LOGICAL OPERATORS: AND   OR   NOT

Such statements could be, for example:

```
30 IF X = A  AND  Y < B  THEN  333

55 IF X = A   OR  Y < B  THEN  100

90 IF X > A  AND  X > B  THEN  500
```

Line 90 sets up boundary conditions for X. This is often needed when evaluating a function and/or in graphical work. The statement in line 90 could be made to test for values outside the range −20 to 20. When such values are found they are either suppressed or recorded on the boundary, as illustrated.

Logical operations result in the following:

8.2.1

★ ★

Logical Operators on Numbers

OPERATOR	RESULT
AND	TRUE if both operands are TRUE
	FALSE if either is FALSE
OR	TRUE if either operand is TRUE
	FALSE if both are FALSE
NOT	TRUE if the operand is FALSE
	FALSE if the operand is TRUE

★ ★

In the computer the above are represented as   TRUE   −1
                                                     FALSE   0

You might wonder what happens if you apply   AND   OR   NOT   to numbers other than   −1   and   0   (that is, TRUE or FALSE).
−− If it does not concern you skip to 'Logical Operators on Strings'. −−

8.2.2 Logical Bitwise Operations

Example

Such comparisons are dealt with in what is known as LOGICAL BITWISE OPERATIONS. This means that the numbers are converted into their 16 bit binary equivalents and compared bit by bit. The result of each bit comparison is kept and accumulated in a register. When the comparison is complete the number is converted back to decimal and the appropriate result appears on the screen if that is the requirement.

A = 26   -> | 0 | 0 | 1 | 1 | 0 | 1 | 0 |

AND

B = 3   -> | 0 | 0 | 0 | 0 | 0 | 1 | 1 |

A AND B   -> | 0 | 0 | 0 | 0 | 0 | 1 | 0 | -> 2

For further information consult *Extended BASIC Version 5* (for Disc Systems), Research Machines' Reference Manual, or possibly the equivalent for other computers).

8.2.3 Logical Operations on Strings

A relation between strings is decided by the ASCII values of the first differing character. Thus 'AARDVARK' is considered to be less than 'ATOM'.

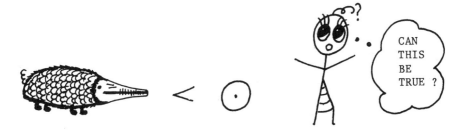

At first glance, some comparisons give surprising results, which are not so surprising on further reflection. For example: 'ADAM4' > 'ADAM10' ! If you don't see why this is so re-read the first sentence in this section (Logical Operators).

Many people seem to shy away from using Logical Operators, as if they are difficult ! Why don't YOU write a short program NOW, which includes the use of a logical operation ? You'll see for yourself how straight forward it is. What is more, you will discover how useful it is to operate logically !

Computers are often used to solve algebraic equations that cannot be solved by elementary methods. We shall consider such an example now, noting the application of the control statements GO TO and IF . . . THEN . . ., and the use of the function ABS.

8.2.4

Question: Compute the roots of the equation: $X1 = (10 - 3X^2)^{.2}$

We shall discover the roots of the equation by a repeated trial and error method (an iterative procedure).

First a guess is made for the value of X and this is substituted in the right hand side of the equation. A new value for X is thus calculated, (X1). Now substitute this new value for X into the right hand side of the equation and obtain a new value for X again.

Continue in this way until the number of iterations you specified have been completed, or until successive values of X have become sufficiently close. At this stage it is said that the method has converged. Before writing a program the symbols must be defined:

X   is the value substituted to the RHS of the equation. (It is guessed and INPUT to start with).
X1 the newly calculated value of X.
I   counts the number of iterations.
N   is the number of iterations you intend to permit.

Note: The program below will fail if the bracketed part of line 210 turns out to be a negative quantity. Do you know why? If not FIND OUT!!   †

† Solutions.

Example 8.2 Program ITERATE

```
100 REM        Program    ITERATE
110 REM     To compute the roots of an equation
120 REM  Method :- Trial and error
130 REM     or          Iterative
140 REM                  Method
150 PRINT "Please give your value for X"
160 INPUT X
170 PRINT "How many trials do you want ?"
180 INPUT N
190 PRINT
200 LET I = 1
210 LET X1 = (10-3 * X ↑2)↑.2
220 PRINT "I =";I,"X1 =";X1
230 IF ABS(X-X1) < .001 THEN 280
240 IF I = N THEN 290
250 LET X = X1
260 LET I = I + 1
270 GOTO 210
280 PRINT "After";I;"iterations the final answer is X =";X
290 GOTO 320
300 PRINT "Computation has not converged after";I;"iterations
310 PRINT "Last value of X =";X1
320 END
RUN
Please give your value for X
? .25
How many trials do you want ?
? 30

I = 1        X1 = 1.5789
I = 2        X1 = 1.20315
I = 3        X1 = 1.41423
I = 4        X1 = 1.3195
I = 5        X1 = 1.36719
I = 6        X1 = 1.34444
I = 7        X1 = 1.35558
I = 8        X1 = 1.35019
I = 9        X1 = 1.35281
I = 10       X1 = 1.35154
I = 11       X1 = 1.35216
After 11 iterations the final answer is X = 1.35154

Ready:
```

The flow of a program is easily traced using the method of drawing in forward flow on the right hand side of a program, and backward flow on the left.

8.3

When you cannot trace a fault in a program, list it to a printer and find in the flow of the program as above. 90% of the time you will trace your mistake without asking anyone for help.

Q Q Q Q Q Q Q Q Q Q Q Q Q Q Q Q Q Q Q Q Q Q Q Q Q Q Q Q Q Q Q Q Q

Q   Extend example 8.2 to include a test for a negative quantity.   Q
Q   When a negative quantity is detected a message should be conveyed to   Q
Q   the user and he/she should be given the option of guessing another   Q
Q   value for X without having to exit from the current RUN.   Q

Q   Have you observed from the RUN of 8.2 how the values for X become   Q
Q   closer and closer?   Q

Q   Convergence is not always obtained. Try running the program with   Q
Q   different guesses for X. You should be given a clear message when   Q
Q   convergence does not occur.   Q

Q Q Q Q Q Q Q Q Q Q Q Q Q Q Q Q Q Q Q Q Q Q Q Q Q Q Q Q Q Q Q Q Q

8.4 END and STOP

As mentioned in chapter 1, a program may have many ENDs, but in good programming practice a program has only one END — the very last statement. The computer stops executing the program when the END statement is reached (and obeyed).

There may be several places in a program when you wish to tell BASIC to stop work on your program. This can be done by using GO TO 99, if 99 labels END; or an IF . . . THEN 99. Alternatively the statement STOP is provided.

★ ★

★   **STOP**   ★
★   The STOP statement terminates the program instantly. It may appear   ★
★   several times, and anywhere in a program.   ★

★ ★

The use of STOP is demonstrated in the trivial example 8.3.

Example 8.3 Program CAMRIDGE

```
100 REM          Program       CAMRIDGE
110 PRINT "Have you been to Cambridge ";
120 INPUT N$
130 IF N$ = "NO" THEN 170
140 IF N$  = "YES" THEN 190
150 PRINT "Only replies of YES or NO are acceptable"
160 STOP
170 PRINT "That is fortunate  !"
180 GOTO 220
190 PRINT "How unfortunate! Did you not know "
200 PRINT "O X F O R D  is  'The Place'"
210 PRINT "--------------------------"
220 END
RUN
Have you been to Cambridge ? NO
That is fortunate  !

Ready:
RUN
Have you been to Cambridge ? Never heard of the place
Only replies of YES or NO are acceptable

Interrupted at line 160
Ready:
RUN
Have you been to Cambridge ? YES
How unfortunate! Did you not know
O X F O R D  is  'The Place'
--------------------------

Ready:
```

8.5 A MULTI-WAY SWITCH (Computed GO TO)

8.5.1

★ ★
★   ★
★   ON X GO TO a, b, c . . . $\oint$ ★
★   ★
★   X is an expression which is calculated and rounded down to the nearest ★
★   integer.   ★
★   ★
★   a, b, c, d, . . . is a list of statement numbers found within the program. ★
★   ★
★   If the value of X is 1, BASIC uses the first statement number in the list; ★
★   control is sent to a. If X is 2 control goes to b, and so on.   ★
★   ★
★   If X is negative, zero or greater than the number of statement numbers ★
★   listed, control passes to the statement following the ON X GO TO . . . ★
★   statement.   †   ★
★   ★
★ ★

The computed GO TO is a powerful and neat tool in your programmers toolbox. Use it as much as you can. It is often the short-cut and in fact the best-cut!!!

This multi-way switch is used in program example 8.4 the program for the question below:

Question:
Write a program that will find the area of any given shape. For a start it should be programmed to calculate the area of a triangle, a rectangle, a circle, and a cylinder. The program should allow the user to request, one-by-one, any number of calculations to be done! Use the most efficient methods you know in writing this program.

Notice the straight-forward flow of the program in 8.4.

---

†   For a slightly more complicated use of ON X GO TO . . . see program LADSNAKE, Chapter 16.

Example 8.4 Program CALCULA

```
100 REM              Program    CALCULA
120 PRINT "    +  +  +      Area  Calculator    +   +   +"
140 PRINT "    1.  Triangle               2.  Rectangle"
150 PRINT "    3.  Circle                 4.  Cylinder"
170 PRINT "    Type the number of your choice"
190 INPUT X
200 ON X GOTO  230,320,400,420
210 PRINT X; "  is not an option    -    BYE"
220 STOP
230 PRINT "      *   *    area  of  triangle   *   * "
240 PRINT
250 PRINT "Give lengths of the three sides"
270 INPUT L1, L2, L3
280 LET S = .5 * (L1 + L2 + L3)
290 LET Z = SQR(S * (S - L1) * (S - L2) * (S - L3))
300 PRINT "Area of triangle is ";
310 GOTO   550
320 PRINT "      *   *    area  of  rectangle   *   *"
330 PRINT
340 PRINT "Give breadth and length "
360 INPUT L, B
370 LET Z = L * B
380 PRINT "Area of rectangle is ";
390 GOTO   550
400 PRINT "      *   *    Area  of  circle   *   *"
410 PRINT
420 PRINT "Give radius"
440 INPUT R
450 LET Z = 3.14159 * R * R
460 IF X = 4 THEN 490
470 PRINT "Area of circle is";
480 GOTO   550
490 PRINT "      *   *    area  of  cylinder   *   * "
500 PRINT
510 PRINT "Give length"
520 INPUT D
530 LET Z = 2 * Z + 2 * R * 3.14159 * D
540 PRINT "Surface area of cylinder is";
550 REM      flow merges here
560 PRINT Z
570 PRINT
580 PRINT "Another  go  ?        type   Y   or    N"
600 INPUT A$
610 IF A$ = "Y" THEN 140
620 PRINT
630 PRINT "And so  ...  on to other things  ...  farewell  !!"
640 END
```

```
RUN
        +    +    +      Area  Calculator      +    +    +
        1.  Triangle                       2.  Rectangle
        3.  Circle                         4.  Cylinder
        Type the number of your choice
? 1
           *    *    area  of  triangle    *    *

Give lengths of the three sides
? 3,4,5
Area of triangle is  6

Another  go  ?           type   Y    or     N
? Y
        1.  Triangle                       2.  Rectangle
        3.  Circle                         4.  Cylinder
        Type the number of your choice
? 4
Give radius
? 3
           *    *    area  of  cylinder    *    *

Give length
? 10
Surface area of cylinder is 245.044

Another  go  ?           type   Y    or     N
? N

And so  ...  on to other things  ...  farewell  !!

Ready:
```

8.6 THE EXCHANGE OF VARIABLES

```
Q Q Q Q Q Q Q Q Q Q Q Q Q Q Q Q Q Q Q Q Q Q Q Q Q Q Q Q Q Q Q Q
Q                                                                  Q
Q   Given that you have a program in which variables A and B are used,   Q
Q   you arrive at a point when you wish to exchange the value of A for that   Q
Q   of B and vice versa. Write a suitable program segment to do this. An   Q
Q   explanation follows BUT BEFORE you look at it have a go at solving   Q
Q   this for yourself.                                             Q
Q                                                                  Q
Q Q Q Q Q Q Q Q Q Q Q Q Q Q Q Q Q Q Q Q Q Q Q Q Q Q Q Q Q Q Q Q
```

A SOLUTION   CONCEPT

A SOLUTION	CONCEPT
START	A: 3 B: 7
LET W = A	W: 3
LET A = B	A: 7
LET B = W	B: 3
FINISH	W: 3 A: 7 B: 3

This 'exchange technique' is frequently used in problems involving SORTING. Try the problem below before consulting the solution on the next page.

```
Q Q Q Q Q Q Q Q Q Q Q Q Q Q Q Q Q Q Q Q Q Q Q Q Q Q Q Q Q Q Q Q
Q                                                                  Q
Q   Write a program to arrange numbers into ascending order. The data for   Q
Q   the first round is:                                            Q
Q    5,  15,  −25,  0,  500,  −5,  35,  −35,  −500,  .05,  −15, −.05, 25   Q
Q                                                                  Q
Q Q Q Q Q Q Q Q Q Q Q Q Q Q Q Q Q Q Q Q Q Q Q Q Q Q Q Q Q Q Q Q
```

Example 8.5 Program SORT (A Solution)

```
100 REM                   Program    SORT    (for ascending order)
120 DIM N(100)
130 PRINT " ---------- Numbers in original order ----------"
150   FOR I = 1 TO 100
160   READ N(I)
170   IF N(I) > 9999 THEN 200
180   PRINT N(I);
190   NEXT I
200 PRINT
210 LET T = I-1
220 REM     T numbers have been read in.
230 REM     The exchange process is repeated
240 REM     once after the order is correct.
250 LET F = 0
260   FOR L = 2 TO T
270   IF N(L) => N(L-1) THEN 330
280   REM         Exchange N(L) and N(L-1)
290   LET W = N(L)
300   LET N(L) = N(L-1)
310   LET N(L-1)= W
320   LET F = 1
330   NEXT L
340 IF F > 0 THEN 250
350 PRINT
360 PRINT " ---------- Numbers in sorted order ------------"
380   FOR M = 1 TO T
390   PRINT N(M);
400   NEXT M
410 DATA 5, 15, -25, 0, 500, -5, 35, -35, -500, 5, -15, -.05, 25, 99999
420 END
RUN
    ---------- Numbers in original order ----------
  5  15 -25  0  500 -5  35 -35 -500  5 -15 -.05  25

    ---------- Numbers in sorted order ------------
 -500 -35 -25 -15 -5 -.05  0  5  5  15  25  35  500
Ready:
```

Note:

1. In the above program F has been used as a flag to indicate whether or not an exchange has taken place during any run through the list. When F is 0 on exit from the FOR/NEXT loop (line 340), the sort is complete.

2. There are many different ways of sorting. Section II presents further ideas and examples on the subject.

8.6.1 A problem with FOUR LETTERS!!

This problem requires that any given sequence of four 'unique' letters be re-arranged repeatedly until all possible combinations have been made. A good program should make the problem simple! It should allow the user to INPUT a 4-letter sequence. It should test for the correct number of letters given. If necessary an error message should be printed followed by an invitation to try again. Finally the original word and all the combinations of the letters should be printed.

A Solution is offered below. Your solution may be a better one, so try that first, before reading further.

Q Q Q Q Q Q Q Q Q Q Q Q Q Q Q Q Q Q Q Q Q Q Q Q Q Q Q Q Q Q Q
Q　　　　　　　　　　　　　　　　　　　　　　　　　　　　　　　Q
Q　The problem of example 8.6 has some serious loopholes. Can you find　Q
Q　these? If you do, extend the program to deal with them. If you cannot　Q
Q　see ways to improve the program consider the questions below.　Q
Q　　　　　　　　　　　　　　　　　　　　　　　　　　　　　　　Q
Q　1. Modify the program so that an error message will be given to the　Q
Q　　　user if he INPUTs a character other than a letter.　Q
Q　2. Include a test that will ensure that each of the four letters INPUT is　Q
Q　　　unique to the four.　Q
Q　　　　　　　　　　　　　　　　　　　　　　　　　　　　　　　Q
Q　In each of the above the user should be given the chance to try again.　Q
Q　This is what is attempted in the program 8.7.　Q
Q Q Q Q Q Q Q Q Q Q Q Q Q Q Q Q Q Q Q Q Q Q Q Q Q Q Q Q Q Q Q

Example 8.6 Program ANAGRAM

```
100 REM     Program     ANAGRAM
110 DIM W$(50)
120 REM This program asks for a word of four letters and prints all the anagrams
130 PRINT " Please input a word of 4 different letters";
140 INPUT W$
150 IF LEN(W$) = 4 THEN 190
160 PRINT "Your word :";W$;" does not contain 4 letters.        Try again"
170 PRINT
180 GOTO   130
190 PRINT "Your word is  :  "; W$
200 PRINT
210 FOR N = 1 TO 4
220 FOR J = 1 TO 4
230 IF N = J THEN 330
240 FOR K = 1 TO 4
250 IF J = K THEN 310
260 IF N = K THEN 310
270 IF MID$(W$, N, 1) = MID$(W$, J, 1) THEN 360
280 LET L = 10 - (N + J + K)
290 PRINT TAB(17);
300 PRINT MID$(W$, N, 1); MID$(W$, J, 1); MID$(W$, K, 1); MID$(W$, L, 1),
310 NEXT K
320 PRINT
330 NEXT J
340 NEXT N
350 GOTO 370
360 PRINT
370 PRINT
380 PRINT "These are all the combinations of the letters in   ";W$
390 END
RUN
 Please input a word of 4 different letters? TIME
Your word is  :  TIME

                    TIME        TIEM
                    TMIE        TMEI
                    TEIM        TEMI
                    ITME        ITEM
                    IMTE        IMET
                    IETM        IEMT
                    MTIE        MTEI
                    MITE        MIET
                    METI        MEIT
                    ETIM        ETMI
                    EITM        EIMT
                    EMTI        EMIT

These are all the combinations of the letters in    TIME

Ready:
```

Example 8.7 Program ANAMOD 119

```
100 REM       Program       ANAMOD
110 DIM W$(50)
120 REM This program asks for a word of four letters and prints all the anagrams
130 PRINT " Please input a word of 4 different letters";
140 INPUT W$
150 IF LEN(W$  ) = 4 THEN 200
160 PRINT "Your word :";W$;" does not contain 4 letters.     Try again"
170 PRINT
180 GOTO  130
190 REM              Now check that each character is a letter
200 FOR C = 1 TO 4
210 LET A$ = (MID$(W$, C, 1))
220 IF ASC(A$) < ASC("A") OR ASC(A$) > ASC("Z") THEN 250
230 NEXT C
240 GOTO  270
250 PRINT "The character ";A$;" is not a letter"
260 GOTO  130
270 PRINT "Your word is  :  "; W$
280 PRINT
290 REM                   test for non-unique letters
300 FOR T = 1 TO 3
310 LET A = T + 1
320 FOR S = A TO 4
330 IF MID$(W$, T, 1) = MID$(W$, S, 1) THEN 510
340 NEXT S
350 NEXT T
360 FOR N = 1 TO 4
370 FOR J = 1 TO 4
380 IF N = J THEN 480
390 FOR K = 1 TO 4
400 IF J = K THEN 460
410 IF N = K THEN 460
420 IF MID$(W$, N, 1) = MID$(W$, J, 1) THEN 510
430 LET L = 10 - (N + J + K)
440 PRINT TAB(17);
450 PRINT MID$(W$, N, 1); MID$(W$, J, 1); MID$(W$, K, 1); MID$(W$, L, 1),
460 NEXT K
470 PRINT
480 NEXT J
490 NEXT N
500 GOTO 550
510 PRINT
520 PRINT "You have failed to obey instructions"
530 PRINT MID$(W$, T, 1); "  is not unique in  ";W$;".     Try again"
540 GOTO 130
550 PRINT
560 PRINT "These are all the combinations of the letters in    ";W$
570 END
RUN
```

```
 Please input a word of 4 different letters? TIDE
Your word is  :  TIDE
```

TIDE	TIED
TDIE	TDEI
TEID	TEDI
ITDE	ITED
IDTE	IDET
IETD	IEDT
DTIE	DIEI
DITE	DIET
DETI	DEIT
ETID	ETDI
EITD	EIDT
EDTI	EDIT

```
These are all the combinations of the letters in    TIDE

Ready:
```

8.7

QQQQQQQQQQQQQQQQQQQQQQQQQQQQQQQ
Q
Q　　　　　　　　　　　PROBLEMS　　　　　　　　　　　　Q
Q　1(a)　Write a program to read in numbers of value from 101 to 500.　Q
Q　　　　If a number lies outside this range an error message should be
Q　　　　given.
Q　(b)　Find the average of these numbers. PRINT all numbers above
Q　　　　average under a suitable heading. PRINT the average and the
Q　　　　quantity of numbers equal to the average.
Q　2. This program should allow one number to be INPUT. The user may
Q　　　then select one of the given operations to be performed on X (the
Q　　　INPUT number), via square root, square, cube, fourth power, factorial.
Q　　　The output should include the name of the process used, the value of
Q　　　X, and the result of the operation. After any one process has been
Q　　　performed the user should be given these options:
Q　　　i. exit from the program.
Q　　　ii. another operation on the same X may be selected.
Q　　　iii. a new number may be INPUT with the same possibilities as the
Q　　　　first number.
Q　3. Factors. A number should be INPUT and all its factors found. PRINT
Q　　　the number and each of its factors once. Modify the program so that
Q　　　each factor is printed as many times as it occurs.
Q　4. Write a program that will read in two lists of numbers, A and B,
Q　　　having 10 and 15 numbers respectively. PRINT out a list of all
Q　　　numbers common to both A and B.
Q　5. Using your data from question 4 write a program to PRINT every
Q　　　second element in A and every third element in B. PRINT the sums
Q　　　of the corresponding elements in the new lists.
Q　6. INPUT the following information into two one dimensional arrays.
Q　　　S (Small Animal Identity number) and W (Weight of said animal in
Q　　　grams)

Q　　　S　(I)　1,　5,　8,　9,　19
Q　　　W　(I)　5.1,　4.8,　9,　5.5,　8.3

Q　　　Print out a table of the animals' identity number and weight, headed
Q　　　appropriately. Select one of the animals by its identity number,
Q　　　e.g. 9, and program the following to appear in your output:
Q　　　　'9 appeared today, after 5 weeks of absence.
Q　　　　weight 5.5, shows a gain of .55 grams'
Q　　　The 5.5 should be printed as a result of reference to the array.
Q　7. Compute the sum of the series　$1 + 1/2 + 1/3 + \ldots 1/10$
Q　8. INPUT a number N and compute N!　$(4! = 4 \times 3 \times 2 \times 1)$
QQQQQQQQQQQQQQQQQQQQQQQQQQQQQQQ

CHAPTER 9

Functions and subroutines

9.1 USER FUNCTIONS – DEFining a Function

To avoid repeatedly programming the same calculations you may define your own *single statement functions.* To do this use:

9.1.1

★★

The DEF Statement

This is of the form:

DEF FNA(B) = C   where

FN   is the prefix.
A   is a variable name chosen to identify the function.
B   is a valid variable name used as a dummy argument.
C   is a numeric expression which is to be evaluated each time the function is called.

Note:

1. *B is local to the function* and is distinct from the variable B which might be used elsewhere in the program. The dummy variable can be thought of as a marker to indicate to BASIC where to insert the corresponding argument from the function call.

2. A user defined function may be called from anywhere in a program but before it is called it must have passed through the flow of program execution. It is however, good programming practise to group all function definitions together and place them near the beginning of a program. This contributes towards a tidy and easy-to-read program.

3. A function cannot be defined in immediate mode.

★★

Examples of function definitions are shown below:

Example 9.1 Program FUNCTION

```
100 REM     program     FUNCTION
110 DEF FNS(X) = X*X
120 LET A = 5
130 LET B = FNS(A)
140 LET C = FNS(4)
150 PRINT B, C
160 END
RUN
  25            16

Ready:
```

Example 9.2 Examples of functions

```
10 DEF FNA(X) = X↑3 + 2*X↑2 - 3*X + 4

20 DEF FNX(N) = INT(SQR(Q)) + LOG(Q) * 10

30 DEF FNN(D) = RND(0) * 10
```

To evaluate a function it is necessary to refer to the function name elsewhere in the program, as in Example 9.3.

Question:
Dimensions of circular fishpond, lawn, path are as shown on diagram. Calculate the area of lawn to be turfed; and the area of path to be laid to gravel.

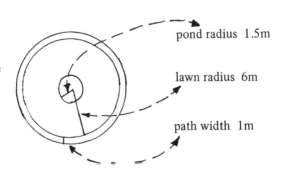

pond radius 1.5m

lawn radius 6m

path width 1m

Example 9.3 Program CFNA

```
100 REM                    Program CFNA
110 DEF FNA(R) = 3.14159 * R * R
120 PRINT "Input :- Radii of pond & lawn, width of path"
130 INPUT F, L, W
140 LET T = FNA(L) - FNA(F)
150 LET P = FNA((L + W)) - FNA(L)
160 PRINT
170 PRINT "Area of : turf  "; T; "square metres"
180 PRINT "          path  "; P; "square metres"
190 END
RUN
Input :- Radii of pond & lawn, width of path
? 1.5,6,1

Area of : turf    106.029 square metres
          path     40.8407 square metres

Ready:
```

> Compare the programming methods used in examples 9.3 and 9.4 which do you think is the better approach?

Example 9.4 Program CFNANO

```
100 REM            Program            CFNANO
110 PRINT "Input:-   Radii of pond & lawn,   width of pa
120 INPUT F, L, W
130 LET T = 3.14159 * L * L - 3.14159 * F * F
140 LET P = 3.14159 * (L + W) * (L + W) - 3.14159 * L *
150 PRINT "Area of :  turf  ";T;"square metres"
160 PRINT "           path  ";P;"square metres"
170 END
RUN
Input:-   Radii of pond & lawn,   width of path
? 1.5,6,1
Area of :  turf    106.029 square metres
           path     40.8407 square metres

Ready:
```

9.2 SUBROUTINES

It is often desirable to repeat a set of instructions at various points within the same program. When this is the case the relevant lines of program may be formed into a subroutine which may be referenced from anywhere within the program. Whereas a function consists of one line only, and returns one value, a subroutine may have many lines and be used to determine one or many numeric and/or string variables.

A subroutine is a section of a program that is entered by a GOSUB statement (GO SUB is equivalent), and must be left via a RETURN statement. The RETURN statement causes the control to return to the statement immediately following the GOSUB which sent it to the subroutine.

While executing a GOSUB command, BASIC notes its location. Program execution is then transferred to the specified line number which is usually the start of the routine.

9.2.1

Structure of a Subroutine

1. The first line may be any statement. It is good practice to make this a REMark which identifies the purpose of the subroutine.
2. Exit from a subroutine should be via . . . RETURN statement.
3. There may be several RETURN statements in subroutine.
4. The last statement of a subroutine must be a RETURN statement.

```
Example:  900 REM   SUBROUTINE STD. DEVIATION
          910
           –
          960 RETURN
          970
           –
          990 RETURN
```

Note: A subroutine may be called many times.
There may be several subroutines.
One subroutine may call another or itself (recursion).

9.2.2 Using Subroutines

Example 9.5 A Single Subroutine

Something makes me think this program ain't gonna work the way it should!

```
100 DIM F(15)
110
  -
  -
160 GOSUB 500
170
180
  -
  -
220 GOSUB 500
225
  -
  -
  -
500 REM SUBROUTINE READ, PRINT
  -
  -
  -
590 RETURN
800 DATA 1.5,2., 3,5, 2.1, 1.1, ....
900 END
```

WHY? will it fail ???

r e a s o n r e a s o n r e a s o n r e a s o n r e a s o n r e a s r

e   After the last GOSUB has been obeyed control of the program is   e
a   returned to line 225. The statements that follow are obeyed in the   a
s   usual manner. Thus at line 500 the subroutine will be entered illegally   s
o   without the direction of a GOSUB statement. When execution reaches   o
n   590 RETURN the program fails with error message: n
r
e   `LINE 590   RETURN without GOSUB at line 590`   r
a   The way to guard against this is to insert: e
    a
s   `499 STOP`   s
o   or   o
n   `499 GO TO 800`   n
r   If the subroutines are all clustered at the end of the program, (and this   r
e   is generally a good idea), place the STOP in the statement immediately   e
a   before the subroutine starting at the lowest line number.   a

r e a s o n r e a s o n r e a s o n r e a s o n r e a s o n r e a s r

Example 9.6 Many Subroutines

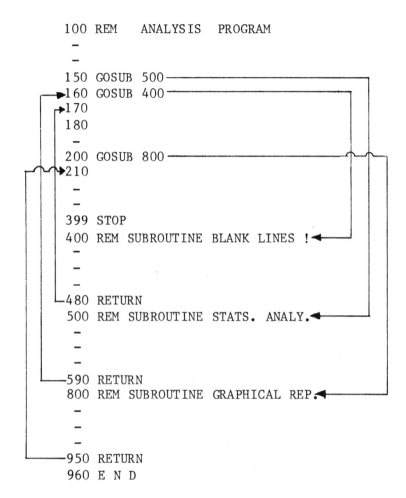

```
100 REM    ANALYSIS  PROGRAM
-
-
150 GOSUB 500
160 GOSUB 400
170
180
-
200 GOSUB 800
210
-
-
399 STOP
400 REM SUBROUTINE BLANK LINES !
-
-
-
480 RETURN
500 REM SUBROUTINE STATS. ANALY.
-
-
-
590 RETURN
800 REM SUBROUTINE GRAPHICAL REP.
-
-
-
950 RETURN
960 E N D
```

Example 9.7 Calling a Subroutine from within another Subroutine

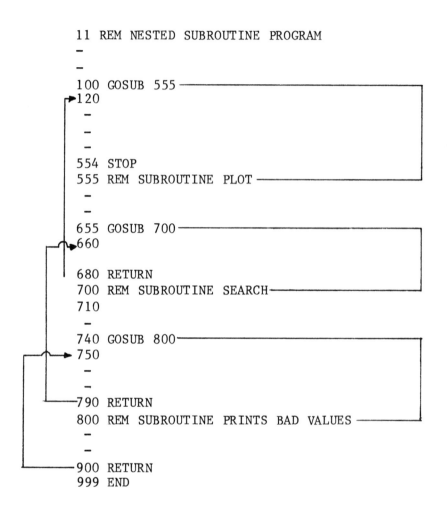

```
11 REM NESTED SUBROUTINE PROGRAM
-
-
100 GOSUB 555
120
-
-
-
554 STOP
555 REM SUBROUTINE PLOT
-
-
655 GOSUB 700
660

680 RETURN
700 REM SUBROUTINE SEARCH
710
-
740 GOSUB 800
750
-
-
790 RETURN
800 REM SUBROUTINE PRINTS BAD VALUES
-
-
900 RETURN
999 END
```

Example 9.8 Entering a Subroutine at Different Points (Program SUBENTRY)

```
100 REM              Program      SUBENTRY
110 REM
120 REM      multiple entry to subroutine
130 REM
140 LET X = 1
160 PRINT "Display when  x = "; X
170 PRINT
180 ON X GOSUB  290, 300, 310
190 LET X = X + 1
210 PRINT "================================="
220 IF X < 4 THEN 160
240    FOR J = 1 TO 3
250    GOSUB  310
260    NEXT J
270 STOP
280 REM  Subroutine   c o l o u r s
290 PRINT "red"
300 PRINT "    white"
310 PRINT "          blue"
320 RETURN
330 END
RUN
Display when  x =   1

red
    white
          blue
=================================
Display when  x =   2

    white
          blue
=================================
Display when  x =   3

          blue
=================================
          blue
          blue
          blue

Interrupted at line 270
Ready:
```

9.2.3 Error Checks Before Chicken Dispatch!

The program below demonstrates a simple use of a subroutine. First a description of the data is read and printed. The program then reads the data checking each item to determine whether or not it lies within the range $1 < x < 6$. The subroutine ERROR is used to print an error message whenever a value lies outside of this range.

Example 9.9 Program ERRCHECK

```
100 REM                          Program        ERRCHECK
120 DIM A(25), T$(50)
130 REM                chicken   weights
150 LET F = 0
160 READ T$
170 PRINT   T$
180 PRINT   "========================================="
190   FOR C = 1 TO 25
200     READ A(C)
210     IF A(C) > 1 AND A(C) < 6 THEN 230
220     GOSUB   250
230     NEXT C
240 STOP
250 REM              Subroutine    Error
260 PRINT
270 IF F = 1 THEN 350
280 PRINT
290 PRINT A(C); "  is a ridiculous weight for a chicken'
300 PRINT
310 PRINT TAB(4);
320 PRINT "c  h  e  c  k      this batch  before  dispatch
330 LET F = 1
340 RETURN
350 PRINT " ***    Another    E R R O R   !"
360 PRINT TAB(6); "when last did you dispatch a "
370 PRINT TAB(6); "chicken weighing "; A(C); " pounds ?
380 RETURN
390 DATA "Batch number  5              date   12.7.81"
400 DATA 3, 2.2, 5.1, 4.2, 3.4, 3.5, 3.6, 4, 2.9, -4.1,
410 DATA 2.5, 2.9, 3, 3.8, 3.4, -5.2, 4.1, 3.8
420 DATA 10.5, 3, 4, 3.9, 3, 4
430 DATA 4.2, 4.4, 4.5, 3.9, 3.9, 3.9
440 END
```

```
RUN
Batch number   5              date   12.7.81
=========================================
```

-4.1   is a ridiculous weight for a chicken

   c h e c k   this batch before dispatch

  ***   Another   E R R O R   !
      when last did you dispatch a
      chicken weighing -5.2 pounds ? ?

  ***   Another   E R R O R   !
      when last did you dispatch a
      chicken weighing 10.5 pounds ? ?

Interrupted at line 240
Ready:

9.3 THE COMPUTED GOSUB

★ ★

ON X GOSUB a, b, c . . .

X is an expression which is calculated and rounded to the nearest integer.
a, b, c, d . . . is a list of the statement numbers at the head of the subroutines.
When the value of X is 1 control of the program is passed to the first subroutine in the list. If X is 2 control goes to b and so on.
RETURN behaves in the same way as in GOSUB.
If X is negative, zero or greater than the number of statement numbers listed, control passes to the statement following the ON X GOSUB . . . statement.

★ ★

The computed GOSUB is not unlike its relative, the computed GO TO (Chapter 8).

In the program segment below all the options in the ON X GOSUB . . . statement are indicated.

Example 9.10 Program Segment using ON . . . GOSUB

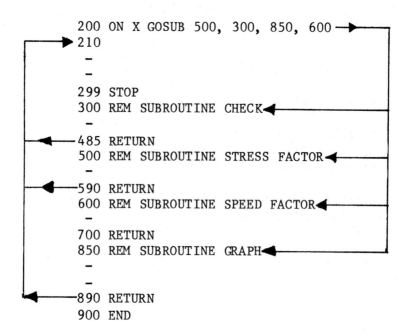

9.4

Q Q Q Q Q Q Q Q Q Q Q Q Q Q Q Q Q Q Q Q Q Q Q Q Q Q Q Q Q Q Q Q Q Q Q
Q   Q
Q   PROBLEMS   Q
Q   Read 20 numbers (N), from DATA.   Q
Q   Use subroutine CHECK to determine whether or not a number lies in   Q
Q   the range 32–312.   Q
Q   Two more subroutines should print messages when: Q
Q   (a) A number is less than 32   Q
Q   'Item at N degrees is FROZEN'   Q
Q   (b) A number is greater than 312   Q
Q   'Item at N degrees is FRAZZLED'   Q
Q   Numbers in the desired range are included in array T. If a number is less   Q
Q   than 32, zero (0) is assigned and if greater than 312, 999 is assigned.   Q
Q   Print the original numbers and the numbers in T.   Q
Q Q Q Q Q Q Q Q Q Q Q Q Q Q Q Q Q Q Q Q Q Q Q Q Q Q Q Q Q Q Q Q Q Q Q

CHAPTER 10
Graphics

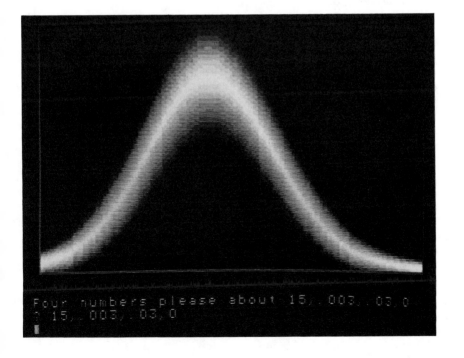

10.1 INTRODUCTION

By and large graphics is a relatively recent extension to BASIC. As yet there is little, if any, adopted standardisation making graphics one of the most machine-dependent features of BASIC.

The reader should note that although some graphics principles are presented all specific examples have necessarily been developed on a RML 380Z micro-computer and are unlikely to RUN on other computers. Those not working on a RML 380Z are strongly recommended to consult the literature specific to their computers.

Note: Unless stated to be 'general' all reference is to RML 380Z graphics. There are three distinct graphics modes:

Graphics mode	Resolution	'Display' Reference
1. Line-by-line, or 'character-based', graphics	(40 × 24)	1 to 40 and 1 to 24
2. Low Resolution Graphics (LRG)	(80 × 60)	0 to 79 and 0 to 59
3. High Resolution Graphics (HRG) which subdivides into:		
Medium Resolution Graphics (MR)	(160 × 96)	0 to 159 and 0 to 95
High Resolution Graphics (HR)	(320 × 192)	0 to 319 and 0 to 191

The following conventions are adopted throughout this book:

    HRG – implies both HR and MR Graphics
    HR   – implies High Resolution Graphics mode
    MR   – implies Medium Resolution Graphics mode

Line-by-line graphics is the most portable as, unlike the other modes, it does not require any special graphics features to be built into the computer. Programs included in this mode may in fact run on your computer with few or no changes.

10.2 LINE-BY-LINE, OR 'CHARACTER-BASED' GRAPHICS

First take a look at the graphics used in earlier chapters.

Chapter	Example	
5	5.8	Program ROMANBUF
5		Summary of Line Buffer Method
6	6.5	Program VARIABLE – a function plot using TAB
8		Logical Operators used to define boundary conditions

Another illustration of line-by-line graphics is program DENSITY, example 10.1. This example of a density plot displays the typical characteristic of achieving the visual impression of varying concentrations of the data. The simple technique of plotting using characters of different densities can be surprisingly effective. (The cover of this chapter shows the RUN of the MR version of this skew-Gaussian, the program of which is Example 10.8).

Notes on program DENSITY

line 130   Characters to be used for the plot are stored in D$
line 240   A character is selected for plotting
line 150   The function describes a bell-shaped (skew-Gaussian) curve
line 170   The values to be INPUT are to represent the characteristics of 'the bell'

    X1 height
    X2 breadth
    X3 coefficient of skewness
    X4 position

Example 10.1 Program DENSITY

```
100 REM          Program      D E N S I T Y  by Steve Thomas
110 DIM D$(10)
120    FOR I = 1 TO 5  :REM  Plot characters read in
130    READ D$(I)
140    NEXT I
150 DEF FNX(X) = X1 * EXP(-X2 * (X - 50) ↑ 2 + X3 * X + X4) + 2
160 PRINT "4 numbers please (about 30,.01,.01,0)"
170 INPUT X1, X2, X3, X4
180    FOR X = 30 TO 60 :REM  The plot
190    LET Y = FNX(X)
200    LET Y1 = INT(SQR(Y))
210    PRINT TAB(Y - Y1 - 1);
220      FOR Y2 = -Y1 TO Y1
230      LET Y3 = ABS(Y2) / Y1 * 5 + 1
240      PRINT D$(Y3);
250      NEXT Y2
260    PRINT
270    NEXT X
280 DATA "*","+","-",",","","."
290 END
RUN
4 numbers please (about 30,.01,.01,0)
?  30,.01,.01,0
*
 *
 *
 -*-
  -*-
   -*-
    -*-
      ,+*+,
       ,+*+,
        ,+*+,
         ,-+*+-,
          ,-+*+-,
           .,-+*+-,.
            .,-+*+-,.
             .,-+*+-,.
              .,-+***+-,.
               .,-+***+-,.
                .,-+***+-,.
                 .,-+***+-,.
                  .,--+***+--,.
                   .,--+***+--,.
                    .,--+***+--,.
                     .,--+***+--,.
                    .,-+***+-,.
                   .,-+***+-,.
                  .,-+***+-,.
                 .,-+***+-,.
                .,-+*+-,.
               .,-+*+-,.
              .,-+*+-,.
             ,-+*+-,
```

Ready:

10.3 LOW RESOLUTION GRAPHICS

10.3.1 Know Your Screen

Before attempting graphics work familiarise yourself with the facilities of your computer. The RML 380Z screen can, in TEXT mode, display 24 lines of 40 (or 80) characters each.

In the *special graphics mode* the screen looks like:

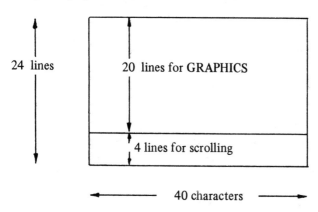

Character cell

Each character cell can be divided into 6 'square' dots. Each dot can be set to on or off individually. The 'on-dots' are either grey or white. Two dots within the same character cell must be the same shade.

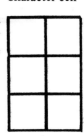

The top 20 lines of the screen can therefore be treated as an array of dots. Each dot is black, grey or white

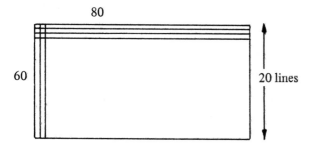

10.3.2 Graphic Commands

★ ★

The GRAPH command

GRAPH 1   clears the top 20 lines of text and sets the text scroller
GRAPH   to use only the bottom 4 lines

GRAPH 0   restores the full screen scroller

GRAPH 2   opens screen for use of PEEK and POKE

GRAPH 3   restores screen to normal state

If in GRAPH N, N is negative or greater than 3 the program execution halts with the error message: Illegal Function

The TEXT command

TEXT restores the scroller to all 24 lines on the screen. It is equivalent to, though faster than GRAPH 0.

The PLOT command

PLOT X, Y, Z is used for plotting points, characters and strings on the screen anywhere in the top 20 lines. *The first two arguments* are the X and Y co-ordinates of the item to be plotted. *The third argument, Z,* is the item to be plotted.

(a) When Z is a string it is displayed at the co-ordinates X, Y.
     e.g. PLOT 28, 27, "ATTENTION!" causes ATTENTION! to appear in the middle of the screen.

(b) When Z is a number or a numeric expression, a point or a character is plotted.
     when $Z = 0$ the point is switched off
                 $Z = 1$ the point is grey
                 $Z = 2$ the point is white
     when $3 <= Z <= 255$ the specified ASCII character is plotted. Each character occupies one character cell, of six points.   †

An error message

Illegal function occurs if values of X or Y are less than 0 or more than 127, or if the value of Z is greater than 255.
Program execution stops.
If $79 < X <= 127$ or
   $59 < Y <= 127$
the information is off the 'visible' screen.

The Screen

(79,59)

(0,0)

(c) If Z is omitted BASIC uses the last specified value, or 0 initially

★ ★

†   See Appendix The ASCII code

Type in and RUN program CHARSET:

Example 10.2 Program CHARSET

```
1 REM        program      CHARSET
10 GRAPH
20    FOR I = 0 TO 15
30       FOR J = 0 TO 31
40          PLOT J*2, I*3, I*32 + J
50       NEXT J
60    NEXT I
70 TEXT
80 END
```

Observations

The RUN of this program should display the character set and halt with the message:

Illegal function at line 40

Insert a TRACE to discover why this has failed. For example:

31 PRINT J*2, I*3, I*32+J

Did you notice the third argument? Its final value of 256 is outside the given range 0–255, hence the failure.

Now type in and RUN program SINPLOT

Example 10.3 Program SINPLOT

```
10 REM        program              SINPLOT
15 GRAPH
20    FOR X= 0 TO 79
30    PLOT X,    25*SIN(X/10)+26,2
40    NEXT X
50 TEXT
60 END
```

The run of this program should end tidily after plotting a sine curve.

10.3.3 More GRAPHICS commands

```
* * * * * * * * * * * * * * * * * * * * * * * * * * * * * * * * * *
*                                                                  *
*   LINE X, Y, I                                                   *
*   Line causes a straight line to join the last point plotted, or the endpoint   *
*   of the last line drawn, to the specified position.            *
*   when   I = 0 the line is black                                 *
*          I = 1 the line is grey                                  *
*          I = 2 the line is white                                 *
*          I > 2 the line is drawn in characters                   *
*                                                                  *
* * * * * * * * * * * * * * * * * * * * * * * * * * * * * * * * * *
```

Now RUN Example 10.4 or a modified version, on your computer.

Example 10.4 Program RECTANG

```
10 REM program   R E C T A N G
20 GRAPH
30   FOR N = 1 TO 2
40     FOR I = 2 TO 4
50       READ A,B
60       PLOT A,A,I
70       LINE B,A
80       LINE B,B
90       LINE A,B
100      LINE A,A
110    NEXT I
120   NEXT N
130 DATA 10,49,20,59,30,69
140 DATA 15,20,5,15,25,25
160 END
```

Observation

Six rectangles are drawn rather rapidly. If you want to observe the drawing process in more detail
slow the program down by adding

```
105 FOR W = 1 TO 200 :NEXT W
```

For an even slower RUN increase the end value beyond 200, to say, 2000.

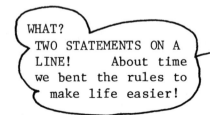

WHAT? TWO STATEMENTS ON A LINE!   About time we bent the rules to make life easier!

Have some fun
Change the values on line 40 so that I
is greater than 2 some of the time and
then all of the time. Your rectangles
should now be constructed of interesting
characters!
One such run is recorded in Fig. 10.1

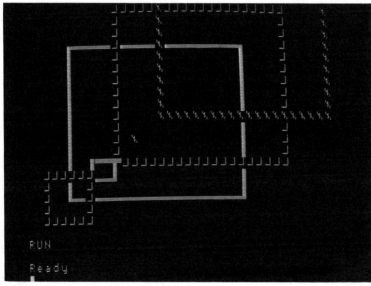

Figure 10.1 Photograph of VDU screen showing one RUN of program
RECTANG modified.

10.3.4

★ ★
★   **POINT** gives the intensity of a specified point on the screen.   ★
★   e.g. **B = POINT (20, 30)**   ★
★   Both arguments must lie in the range 0 to 127. If the point contains an   ★
★   ASCII character that character is returned. If the point is a graphics   ★
★   character 0, 1 or 2 is returned (for off, grey, white).   ★
★   ★
★   **POINTS** returns the value of the character stored at the specified point ★
★   on the screen. For non graphics characters the same value as for **POINT** ★
★   is returned. A graphics character will be returned as a number in the   ★
★   range 128-255   ▲
★ ★

LRG can be used to good effect in producing visual aids such as HISTOGRAMS.
One such example is HISTOGRM in Example 17.2.

10.4 HIGH AND MEDIUM RESOLUTION GRAPHICS   ♭

As the name implies, High Resolution Graphics (HRG) can be used to produce pictures of fine definition. HRG is a relatively recent extension of BASIC and in order to use it, software support packages are needed as well as additional 'hardware'.   †

The RML 380Z HRG may be in as black and white and/or in colour. This is dependent on which of the available graphics boards are implemented on a particular microcomputer. In this book considerations are geared mainly to black and white. The word colour, when used, refers to different shades of grey, from and including, black to white. 'Real colour' is a trivial extension of 'black and white colour'!

High Resolution (HR) and Medium Resolution (MR) graphics includes the plotting of points, lines, and rectangular blocks at a number of intensities. The illumination of pictures may be changed instantly or gradually by changing the intensity, or by altering the brightness-value of particular intensities in the memory. Moving pictures are made by dividing the graphics memory into up to eight logical views and displaying these in succession.

The possibilities offered by HRG seem endless and half a chapter on graphics can hardly do justice to the subject. Here a summary of the commands and selected programs and explanations are presented.

A section on Cartesian and polar co-ordinate systems is included, as well as some discussion on scaling factors, particularly in relation to combining Low Resolution Graphics with Medium Resolution or High Resolution graphics, for example in labelling pictures.

First meet the two, by now 'famous', characters in this book, as drawn in MR Graphics. There is nothing difficult in producing such pictures. A few calls to the routines RESOLUTION, GRAPH, PLOT, LINE, FILL, CLEAR and TEXT and there you have it!

---

† Please consult: *Research Machines High Resolution Graphics Reference Manual* for more details, or the equivalent manuscript for your computer.
♭ See Variations on a Theme in the Appendix.

**Figure
10.2**

**Figure
10.3**

10.4.1 Summary of High Resolution Graphics Routines
Each routine is presented in the form in which it is used. They will best be understood by working through the programs which follow, and developing programs of your own.

The name of the routine must be in capital letters, surrounded by quotation marks, and followed by a comma. The parameters must be separated by commas. Items in [ ] can be omitted.

ROUTINE & CALL	PURPOSE	PARAMETERS

1. CALL "RESOLUTION", R, B	Initialises the system. It must come before other HR or MR graphics routine calls.	R – resolution to be used
		R=0 high resolution (HR) (319, 192)
		R=1 medium resolution (MR) (160,96)
		
		B – number of bits per pixel
		  In HR 1 or 2
		  In MR 1, 2 or 4
		If B is less than the maximum, multiple views of graphics memory are possible.

2. CALL "PLOT", X, Y [, I]	Plots point at X, Y, intensity I on current page and view.	I – Intensity of the point.
		Value for I depends on the number of bits/pixel.
		If 1 bit/pixel I is 0–1
		   2 bit/pixel I is 0–3
		   4 bit/pixel I is 0–15
		If I < 0 its absolute value is exclusive ORed (XOR) with the old contents of the pixel.
		If I > 15 no point plotted but 'pen' moves to X, Y
		(see LINE) I defaults to last value specified.

3. CALL "LINE", X, Y, [, I]	Draws a line from 'pen' position to X, Y.	X, Y – co-ordinates of the end-point of the line. I – same meaning as for PLOT. 'pen' position – the last value for X, Y given in a PLOT or LINE call.
4. CALL "FILL", X1, Y1, X2, Y2 [, I]	Fills the rectangle specified by the points X1, Y1 and X2, Y2. X2 > X1 Y2 > Y1 essential	(X1, Y1) (X2, Y2) I has the same meaning as for PLOT and LINE

Call	Description	Parameters
CALL "PLOT" …	… physical brightness N.	N – in the range 0–255. If all parameters are omitted the default settings are used. (See PLOT).
CALL "COLOUR", R, G, B		R – red in range 0–7 G – green in range 0–7 B – blue in range 0–3
6. CALL "SETCOL", I, N	Similar to colour except that this call is delayed until a call to view is made. Enables the setting up of non-standard views and allows a rapid change of all the colours.	As for COLOUR
7. CALL "VIEW" [, P]	Transfer colour changes specified by SETCOL to the colour look-up table.	P (should be omitted in HRG) specifies MR page on which to effect the changes.
8. CALL "UPDATE" [, P], V	Specifies which page and view will be written to by subsequent calls to: PLOT, LINE, FILL.	P – the page which will be written to. (P should be omitted for only one page). V – the view to be written to. There can be 2 or 4 views, which can be written to or, displayed independently, if the number of bits/pixel is less than the maximum.
9. CALL "DISPLAY" [, P], V	Specifies which page and view is to be displayed.	P – should be omitted in HR mode.
10. CALL "CLEAR"	Clears the current page and view.	
11. CALL "OFFSET", X, Y	Co-ordinates of bottom left-hand corner of screen are changed from 0, 0 to X, Y.	X, Y – the new co-ordinates of bottom left-hand corner.
12. CALL "GLOAD", A CALL "GSAVE", A	Loads a picture from BASIC cache memory at address A into the HR memory, and vice versa. Picture is in current resolution. In MR, uses page selected by UPDATE.	

10.4.2 Glossary of Terms unexplained in the Summary

PIXEL − A picture element. It is the smallest unit of the screen whose intensity and brightness can be changed under program control, in the given graphics mode. (The size of the pixel is really its physical dimension. This is not to be confused with the number of bits which are used to describe its intensity (the pointer to the colour look-up table). See Table 10.1.

COLOUR LOOK-UP TABLE − a table in memory (part of the hardware) where each of the possible 16 intensities is a pointer to a brightness value which determines the actual 'colour' of the pixels. The brightness value in the look-up table may be changed at any time. This affects the colour of points, lines, and rectangles which have already been plotted. See tables 10.4 and 10.5.

PAGE − Two separate pages of graphics memory (two separate pictures) are available in medium resolution.

VIEW − By restricting the number of bits/pixel it is possible to have more than one picture on each page. These 'logical' pages are called views. See Table 10.2 and 10.6.

Table 10.1 Showing Relationships between Graphics-Type, Pixels, and Intensities

Type	Bits/Pixel	CALL	Intensities represented as combinations of bits	Max No. Intens.
HR	1	CALL "RESOLUTION", 0, 1	0 or 1	2
HR	2	CALL "RESOLUTION", 0, 2	0 0 or 0 1 or 1 0 or 1 1 *gives a choice of 4 colours (shades of grey)*	4
MR	4	CALL "RESOLUTION", 1, N for N = 1 to 4	0 0 0 0 or 0 0 0 1 — (for N=1) 0 0 1 0 or 0 0 1 1 (for N=2) 0 1 0 0 or 0 1 0 1 or 0 1 1 0 or 0 1 1 1 1 0 0 0 or 1 0 0 1 or 1 0 1 0 or 1 0 1 1 (for N=4) 1 1 0 0 or 1 1 0 1 or 1 1 1 0 or 1 1 1 1	2 4 16
LR	8	PLOT, X, Y, I	0 0 0 0 0 0 0 0 or .... or 0 0 0 0 0 1 0 0 .... or .... or .... or .... or .... 1 1 1 1 1 0 0 0 or .... or 1 1 1 1 1 1 1 1	256

You may find the next table (Table 10.2) helpful in sorting out the relationships between the different calls, pages and views.

Table 10.2 A Bird's Eye View of the Relationships Between HRG Calls, Pages, Views — in a 'likely' order of use
(adapted from 'Computer Graphics Course Notes' by Frank Pettit)

```
CALL "RESOLUTION",R,B
```

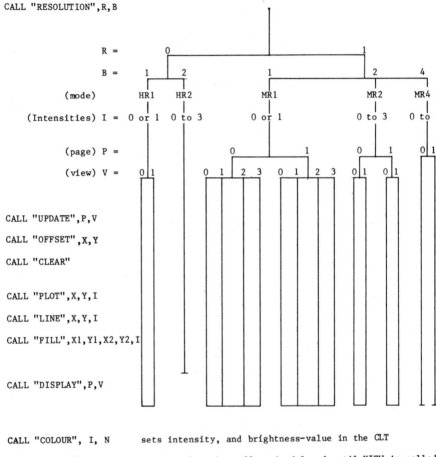

```
CALL "UPDATE",P,V

CALL "OFFSET",X,Y

CALL "CLEAR"


CALL "PLOT",X,Y,I

CALL "LINE",X,Y,I

CALL "FILL",X1,Y1,X2,Y2,I


CALL "DISPLAY",P,V
```

CALL "COLOUR", I, N	sets intensity, and brightness-value in the CLT
CALL "SETCOL", I, N	as for colour but effect is delayed until VIEW is called
CALL "VIEW",P	transfers SETCOL values to the Colour Lookup Table(CLT)
CALL "COLOUR"	restores the default values in the CLT
CALL "COLOUR",I,R,G,B	(for 'real-colour') sets values for red, green, blue

10.4.3 Some Examples and Explanations

Here is a program to get you started. Type it into your computer followed by RUN and see what happens.

Example 10.5 Program LINE

```
1 REM              program  L I N E
2 GRAPH            :REM clears screen of text
3 REM              scrolling limited to 4lines
10 CALL "RESOLUTION",0,1
20 CALL "PLOT",0,0,3
30 CALL "LINE",90,150
400 TEXT           :REM full screen available
401 REM            for text scrolling
500 END
```

What happened? Was your line drawn on top of existing text? If so:

clear the screen of text by holding CTRL while typing L or type PUT 12.

The line remains on the screen.

CALL "CLEAR" removes the picture. Type RUN. Your screen should resemble:

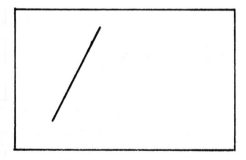

Figure 10.4 RUN of Example 10.5

If nothing happened or if an error message appeared check:

1. Are RESOLUTION, PLOT and LINE all in capitals?
2. Are these surrounded by quotes and followed by a comma?
3. Are there typing errors e.g. wrong spelling?
   Correct errors and RUN again.
4. Are you using the right version of BASIC?

Note on the program
Line 10 CALL "RESOLUTION", 0, 1 sets the graphics display to HR, with 1 bit/pixel and clears the HR memory.

This program is very limited in its usefulness! To make it more general and flexible the co-ordinates of points to be plotted and lines to be drawn will be READ as DATA. By adding 2 more points to the data and returning to the original point a triangle can be drawn, as in:

Example 10.6 Program 3LINES

```
1 REM            program  3 L I N E S
2 GRAPH          :REM clears screen of text
3 REM            scrolling limited to 4 lines
10 CALL "RESOLUTION",0,1
14 READ I
15 READ X,Y
20 CALL "PLOT",X,Y,I
22    FOR J = 1 TO 3
25    READ X2,Y2
30    CALL "LINE",X2,Y2
40    NEXT J
200 DATA 3,0,0    :REM Intensity,X,Y
210 DATA 90, 150 , 180,0, 0,0
400 TEXT          :REM full screen available for scrolling
500 END
```

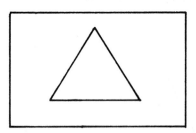

Figure 10.5
Diagram of the RUN

Example 10.7 Program 2rt2tr

```
100 REM             program  2 r t 2 t  r
150 GRAPH           :REM clears screen of text
200 REM             scrolling limited to 4 lines
250 CALL "RESOLUTION",0,1
300 READ I
305 GOSUB 340       :REM R E C T A N G L E
306 GOSUB 340       :REM T R I A N G L E
308 GOSUB 642       :REM S H A D I N G
310 READ I
312 GOSUB 340
314 GOSUB 340
320 GOSUB 642
338 GOTO 800
339 REM --------------------------------
340 REM        subroutine read,plot,line
350 READ X,Y
400 CALL "PLOT",X,Y,I
450    FOR J = 1 TO 3
500    READ X2,Y2
550    CALL "LINE",X2,Y2
600    NEXT J
640 RETURN
641 REM --------------------------------
642 REM        subroutine  shading
643 READ X1,Y1,X2,Y2
644 CALL "FILL",X1,Y1,X2,Y2,I
648 RETURN
649 REM --------------------------------
650 DATA 3,0,0     :REM Intensity,X,Y
700 DATA 90, 150 , 180,0, 0,0
750 DATA 50,0,  50,80,  130,80,  130,0     :REM Rectangle1
760 DATA 50,0,  130,80  :REM fill
765 DATA 0            :REM Intensity
770 DATA 50,80
775 DATA 130,80,  90,0,  50,80  :REM Triangle 2
780 DATA 70,80, 70,40,  110,40,  110,80
782 DATA 70,40,  110,80
800 TEXT             :REM full screen available for scrolling
850 END
```

Figure 10.7 RUN of Example 10.6

Does your screen look
like this?

10.4.4 Slowing down a program RUN

QQQQQQQQQQQQQQQQQQQQQQQQQQQQQQQQQQQ
Q   Q
Q Perhaps this picture was drawn at a speed that left you behind. Q
Q *To slow down the drawing process* include a third subroutine— Q
Q e.g.   Q
Q   Q
Q   790 REM Subroutine   Q
Q   792 FOR N= 1 to 100: NEXT N   Q
Q   794 RETURN   Q
Q   Q
Q and call this at relevant points in the program. This will help you to see Q
Q what is happening!   Q
QQQQQQQQQQQQQQQQQQQQQQQQQQQQQQQQQQQ

Table 10.3 Summary of Commands to clear the screen of text and/or graphics

Commands for text (All characters)	Commands for clearing 'pictures' in HRG	Description
GRAPH or GRAPH 1		Clears the screen of text and sets the bottom 4 lines for scrolling.
TEXT or GRAPH 0		Restores full screen to scrolling.
CTRL L or PUT 12		Clears screen of text.
	CALL "CLEAR"	Clears current page and view of 'pictures'.
	CALL "RESOLUTION", R, B	Clears the high resolution memory. R $-$ 0 or 1 B $-$ 0, or 3

All the above except CTRL L may be used in immediate mode or may be embedded within a program. CTRL L may only be used in immediate mode.

10.4.5 The CALL to RESOLUTION

When a call to RESOLUTION is made, for example:

       CALL "RESOLUTION", 0, 1   (HR1)
or   CALL "RESOLUTION", 1, 4   (MR4)

certain relationships between the screen and the memory are automatically set up. These are extended if one or more of the following calls are made:

       CALL "PLOT", X, Y, I
       CALL "LINE", X, Y, I
       CALL "FILL", X1, Y1, X2, Y2, I

The argument I is sometimes referred to as the intensity, or brightness, or colour of the resultant point, line, or rectangle. I has also been called the 'plotted' intensity on the screen. In reality I *is a pointer* to a table on the graphics board called the *Colour Lookup Table*. In the table are restored the actual brightness-values of each intensity. With each brightness there is an associated 'colour'; or white, shade of grey or black.

A lot of confusion has arisen in the 'loose' use of the terms colour, brightness, and intensity. In the interests of clarity the following conventions are adopted.

CALL "COLOUR", I, N

Intensity: (I)   the pointer reference to the Colour lookup table

Brightness (value): (N)   number in the Colour lookup table representing an 'actual' colour

Colour: the 'actual' colour corresponding to the brightness number — white, through shades of grey, to black as seen on the screen. (Or if using 'real-colour', the 'real' screen colour!)

Examples of these relationships are summarised in Tables 10.4 and 10.5.

10.4.6 Examples of the COLOUR LOOKUP TABLE

Table 10.4   The COLOUR LOOKUP TABLE for HR2
(CALL "RESOLUTION", 0, 2)

INTENSITY (I) (pointer to the lookup table)	BRIGHTNESS (N) (default values)	COLOUR (as displayed)	Potential 'new' brightness range achieved by: CALL "COLOUR", I, N
0	0	black	0-255
1	64	dark grey	0-255
2	128	light grey	0-255
3	255	white	0-255

Table 10.5 The COLOUR LOOKUP TABLE for HR4.

(CALL "RESOLUTION", 1, 4)

INTENSITY (I) (pointer to the lookup table)	BRIGHTNESS (N) (default) values	COLOUR (as displayed)	Changing the brightness by:	FOR N = 0 TO 255 CALL "COLOUR", 1, N NEXT N
			'New' brightness value	Range of 'New' displayed colour
0	0	black	0–255	black to white
1			0–255	black to white
.			. . .	. . .
.			. . .	. . .
		shades of grey	all intensities may have the brightness levels changed in the range 0 to 255.	
.			. . .	. . .
.			. . .	. . .
14			0–255	black to white
15	255	white	0–255	black to white

10.4.7 Modifying the Displayed Intensity

By suitably altering the values of I you may:

10.4.7.1 Erase (or 'turn off') a picture by:
10.4.7.1.1 Replacement

A picture is overwritten by plotting on top of it with the same intensity as that of the background.

Type these lines into your computer and RUN:

```
10 CALL "RESOLUTION",0,2
20 CALL "PLOT",0,0,3
30 CALL "LINE",90,90
```

You should see a white line drawn from (0, 0) to (90, 90). Erase the line by plotting a black line on top of it.

```
40 CALL "PLOT",0,0,0
50 CALL "LINE",90,90
```

If you cause this line to cross a grey background by including the line:

```
15 CALL "FILL",20,20,60,60,2
```

and introduce a pause:

```
35 INPUT "To continue type a number";A
```

RUN the program again. You should see a black line through a grey square.

10.4.7.1.2 Exclusive OR Plotting (XOR)

This takes place when the intensity argument is negative. To see the difference in screen results make these changes to the existing intensities:

```
20 CALL "PLOT",0,0,-3
40 CALL "PLOT",0,0,-3
```

and RUN. This time when the original line is replotted the square remains intact!

XOR plotting is used for drawing data provisionally and then 'turning it on' at the appropriate moment. Program GUITARI is a FUN example which uses XOR mode. RUN it and see for yourself!   †

Example 10.8 Program GUITARI

```
10 REM              program        GUITAR1
20 CALL "RESOLUTION",0,2
30 CALL "CLEAR"   :PUT 12
35 PLOT 35,35,"A little 1-string band"
40 I = 2
50 GOSUB 170            :REM rectangles
60 GOSUB 170            :REM rectangles
70 I=3
80 GOSUB 210            :REM WAIT
90   FOR K = 1 TO 100
100   RESTORE 320
110   READ X,Y
120   GOSUB 240            :REM LINES
140   I = -I              :REM XOR plot
150   NEXT K
160 STOP
170 REM SUB                 DRAW RECTS
180 READ X1,Y1,X2,Y2
190 CALL "FILL",X1,Y1,X2,Y2,I
200 RETURN
210 REM  Subroutine          WAIT
220   FOR W = 1 TO 200:NEXT W
230 RETURN
240 REM subroutine           LINES
260 CALL "PLOT",X,Y,I
270 READ XS, YS
280 CALL "LINE",XS,YS,I
290 RETURN
300 DATA 0,50,60,57
310 DATA 60,35,110,70
320 DATA 10,54,100,54
400 END
```

† (For more details see Chapter 2 of Research Machines High Resolution Graphics Manual.)

10.4.7.2 Fade a picture up or down

Program COLFADE provides an example.

Line 30   The intensity in the CALL to FILL is set, and hence is plotted, at 2.

Line 70   A CALL is made to "COLOUR", 2, Q. The brightness-value of intensity 2, is changed as Q cycles from 0 to 255. The screen undergoes colour changes as you will observe when you RUN COLFADE.

Example 10.9 Program COLFADE

```
10 REM        program COLFADE
20 CALL "RESOLUTION",0,2
22 ON BREAK GOTO 200
25 PUT 12
30 CALL "FILL",50,50,150,150,2
40 CALL "PLOT",0,0,-3
50 CALL "LINE",200,200
60 INPUT A
65   FOR Q = 0 TO 255
70   CALL "COLOUR",2,Q
80   NEXT Q
90 GOTO 65
200 PUT 12
210 CALL "CLEAR"
```

10.4.7.3 Select portions of pictures
Segments of pictures written at different intensities may be faded or erased while a program is running. Impressive effects may be achieved using this idea. Over to you!

ATTENTION If you are using 'real-colour' experiment using the CALL:

CALL "COLOUR", I, R, G, B

10.4.8 Elementary Maths Section

10.4.8.1 Scaling (general)

Scaling is the technique of adjusting data so that it can be conveniently represented graphically within a defined area. For example:

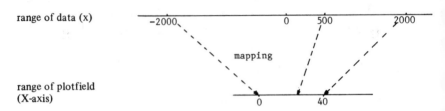

Figure 10.7 Illustraing one-dimensional scaling

A common method of determining and using a scaling factor

Example (Fig. 10.7)

1. Find the minimum and maximum data-values (Dmin, Dmax)   —2000, 2000
2. Find the minimum and maximum plotfield values. (Fmin, Fmax)   0, 40
3. Scaling factor:

$$S = \frac{Fmax - Fmin}{Dmax - Dmin} \qquad\qquad S = \frac{40 - 0}{2000 - (-2000)}$$

$$S = 0.01$$

4. For value x in the data, the value X in the plot field is:

$$X = S * (x - Dmin) \qquad\qquad X = S*(500-(-2000))$$

$$X = 25$$

    The scaling factors for the X and Y axes may be independent of each other resulting in a change in the X, Y ratio. If a common (dependent) scaling factor is used the resultant mapping of data to the plotfield is linear.

    For the 380Z scaling is necessary when more than one graphics mode is to be used to produce one screen-display. For example, LRG may be used to label axes, or to place words onto a HRG display.

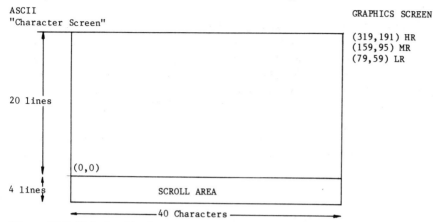

Figure 10.8 Relationships between the Graphics Screens of the 380Z

To simplify the figures, the extreme upper right co-ordinates can be thought of as:

(320,192) HR
(160,96)   MR
(80,60)   LR

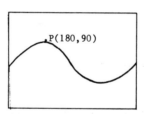

Say, for example, the above graph was plotted in MR and you want to 'write' P(180,90) in the relevant position on the screen. You might adopt the following sequence of steps:

(a) A position on the MR screen is denoted by the co-ordinates (X, Y).

(b) The scaling factors needed to convert to the equivalent LR screen-point are:

$$XS = 80/160 \quad YS = 60/96$$

(c) The reference co-ordinates for plotting this point are thus:

$$X = X * XS \quad \text{and} \quad Y = Y * YS$$

(d) To label this point in LR use PLOT X, Y, "P(180,90)"

(e) RUN.

(f) Your result may be slightly off target. Adjust the scaling factors XS, YS and RUN again. (Trial and error method!).

(g) Once you arrive at 'standard' scaling factors, life in front of a VDU is easy! But be warned, HRG is hazardously addictive!

The above method is used in program GUITAR1. (See Example 10.8)

An example in labelling axes is program HISTOGRM, (See Example 17.2).

10.4.8.2 WINDOWING – (using OFFSET)
The VDU screen, (the visible screen), is in fact only a window into a vast potential memory space, (the virtual screen), which can be used for mapping. Normally, in HR for example, the co-ordinates of the bottom left the VDU screen are (0,0) and the top right (319,191). The potential space on the 'virtual screen' is in the approximate range −32000 to 32000 in both directions.

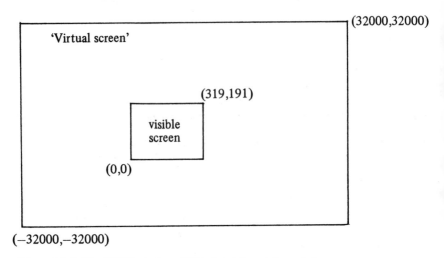

Figure 10.9 The VDU window (HR) (not drawn to scale)

By making CALLS to OFFSET the window can be moved around the 'virtual screen'.

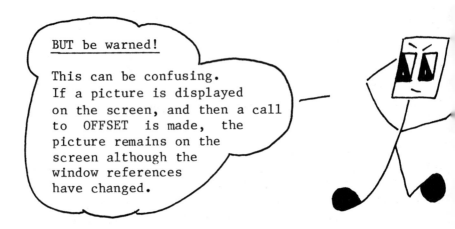

Program MWINDOW is a good illustration of this very point. RUN it. You could be in for a surprise!

Example 10.10 Program MWINDOW

```
10 REM            program      MWINDOW
20 CALL "RESOLUTION",0,1
30 CALL "CLEAR" :PUT 12
40    FOR T = 1 TO 2
50    N = 100
60    A = COS(180/N) : B=SIN(180/N)
70    R=100
80    X=R  :Y=0
90    CALL "PLOT",X,Y
100      FOR I = 1 TO N
110      X0=A*X - B*Y
120      Y = A*Y + B*X
130      X = X0
140      CALL "LINE",X,Y,3
150      NEXT I
160    INPUT"to continue type a number";W
170    CALL "OFFSET",-140,-100
180    NEXT T
190 END
```

QQQQQQQQQQQQQQQQQQQQQQQQQQQQQQQQQQQQQQQ
Q   Q
Q   Add one line to this program so that the first picture is removed from   Q
Q   the screen before the second one is plotted.   Q
QQQQQQQQQQQQQQQQQQQQQQQQQQQQQQQQQQQQQQQ

Using OFFSET effectively enables the programmer to move around the 'VIRTUAL screen' and to examine its contents on the 'VISIBLE screen'

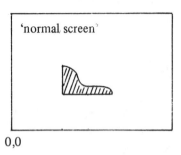

0,0

Example CALL 'OFFSET', −50, −50

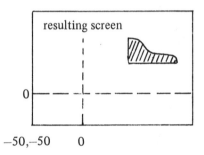

−50,−50   0

10.4.8.3 Some tools useful to graphics

10.4.8.3.1 A Straight Line

general equation: $Y = mX + c$

where the slope is: $m = \dfrac{Y2 - Y1}{X2 - X1}$

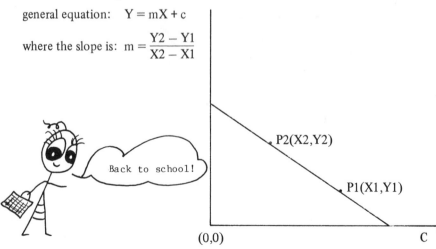

10.4.8.3.2 A Circle

10.4.8.3.3 Cartesian Rectangular Co-ordinates

general equation: $X^2 + Y^2 = R^2$

    or: $Y = \pm\sqrt{R^2 - X^2}$

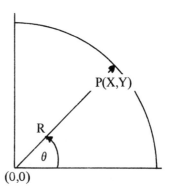

In practice it is often more convenient to work with polar-co-ordinates.

10.4.8.3.4 The Polar Co-ordinates

general equation: $\cos^2\theta + \sin^2\theta = 1$

    or: $r\cos^2\theta + r\sin^2\theta = r$

general co-ordinates:

    $x = r\cos\theta \; ; \; y = r\sin\theta$

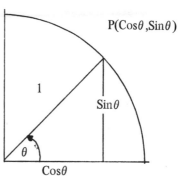

10.4.8.3.5 The screen is a Cartesian screen
The screen is a Cartesian screen and the graphics routines are based on this system. Every point on the screen is addressable using Cartesian co-ordinates.
    It is sometimes necessary to convert non-rectangular co-ordinates in order to plot.

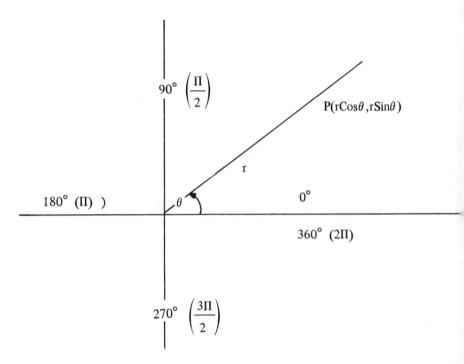

Whence: $x = r \cos \theta$ $y = r \sin \theta$

Figure 10.11 The screen

10.4.8.4 Drawing polygons and circles

These are most efficiently plotted using a method in which SIN and COS only evaluated once. The algorithm for a polygon/circle of radius R basically:

```
X=R: Y=0: CALL "PLOT",X,Y
FOR I=1 TO N
XO = A*X - B*Y
Y = A*Y + B*X
X = XO
CALL "LINE", X,Y
NEXT N
```

where $A = \cos(2\pi/N)$ and $B = \sin(2\pi/N)$
         N = number of sides (large for a circle).

10.4.8.5 A trigonometrical reminder

180 degrees = PI radians

Remember

The computer always
works with radians
and not degrees.
If you need HELP
with this conversion
consult chapter 3.

10.4.9 Animation
Apparent 'movement' on the screen can be achieved by building up pictures on successive pages and views in memory (using UPDATE) and then DISPLAYing these in turn. Table 10.6 shows that at most 8 pictures can be stored at any one time. (MR1)

Table 10.6 Showing relationships between graphics modes, pages and views

GRAPHICS MODE	CALL	RANGE OF INTENSITY	VIEWS	PAGES
HR2	CALL "RESOLUTION", 0,2	0-3	0 only	0 only
HR1	CALL "RESOLUTION", 0,1	0,1	0,1	0 only
MR4	CALL "RESOLUTION", 1,4	0-15	0 only	0,1
MR2	CALL "RESOLUTION", 1,2	0-3	0,1	0,1
MR1	CALL "RESOLUTION", 1,3	0-1	0,1,2,3	0,1

10.4.9.1 Clearing a view
While displaying one view another may be cleared invisibly in the 'background'. This is useful when 'building' and displaying many pictures in succession. A conveneient way to clear a complete view, for example:

        CALL "UPDATE", 1
        CALL "CLEAR"

The next program, 8PAGES, uses all eight PAGEs in MR1.

Example 10.11 Program 8PAGES

```
1 REM   program 8PAGES  by Steve Thomas
10 DEF FNX(A)=40*COS(A)     :REM The X and Y co-ordinates
20 DEF FNY(A)=40*SIN(A)
25 PUT 12
30 CALL "RESOLUTION",1,1
40 CALL "OFFSET",-80,-48    :REM Centralise the circle
50 LET PI=3.14159
60    FOR T=0 TO 127
70    LET A=T*PI/64              :REM To get an angle in range 0 to 2pi
80    CALL "UPDATE",T AND 1, (T AND 7)/2 :REM To place successive points
90    CALL "PLOT",FNX(A),FNY(A),1        :REM on different pages and views
100   NEXT T
110   FOR I=1 TO 100
120     FOR V=0 TO 3
130       FOR P=0 TO 1
140         CALL "DISPLAY",P,V
150       NEXT P
160     NEXT V
170   NEXT I
180 END
```


Illuminating the rotating circle!

To the program 8PAGES add the line:


```
135 CALL "COLOUR",1,(I*7 AND 127) + 128
```


and RUN!

Strategical use of colour adds variety and interest to graphical displays.

Q Q Q Q Q Q Q Q Q Q Q Q Q Q Q Q Q Q Q Q Q Q Q Q Q Q Q Q Q Q Q Q Q Q Q
Q   Q
Q Plot a second circle within the existing one so that they will rotate in Q
Q opposite directions. Q
Q   Q
Q Q Q Q Q Q Q Q Q Q Q Q Q Q Q Q Q Q Q Q Q Q Q Q Q Q Q Q Q Q Q Q Q Q Q

The next program is a modification and extension of Program 8PAGES. Before running it try to visualise the screen throughout the RUN.

Example 10.12 Program THEFAIR

```
1 REM   program THEFAIR  by Steve Thomas
30 CALL "RESOLUTION",1,1
40 CALL "OFFSET",-80,-48
50 LET PI=3.14159
60   FOR T=0 TO 127
70   LET A=T*PI/64
80   CALL "UPDATE",T AND 1, (T AND 7)/2
82   LET D=1
85     FOR S=5 TO 45 STEP 5
90     CALL "PLOT",S*COS(D*A),S*SIN(D*A),1
92     LET D=-D
95     NEXT S
100  NEXT T
110  FOR I=1 TO 100
120    FOR V=0 TO 3
130      FOR P=0 TO 1
140        CALL "DISPLAY",P,V
150      NEXT P
160    NEXT V
170  NEXT I
180 END
```

10.4.10 Concluding remarks

This chapter is only a brief introduction to graphics and not a comprehensive coverage of all there is to be known. Hopefully, by this stage you are brim-full of ideas on how to bring the graphics screen to life, and add your personal contribution to this relatively new and expanding field. Here is one final program (HDENSE2), the RUN of which is on the chapter cover.

Example 10.13 HDENSE2

```
100 REM        program     HDENSE2   by Steve Thomas
110 CALL "RESOLUTION",1,4
120 DEF FNX(X) = X1*EXP(-X2*(X-50)↑2+X3*X+X4)+2
130 PRINT "Four numbers please about 15,.003,.03,0"
140 INPUT X1,X2,X3,X4
145 PUT 12
150   FOR X = 0 TO 160
160   LET Y = FNX(X/2+20)
170   LET Y1 = SQR(Y)*4
180     FOR Y2 = -Y1 TO Y1
190     LET Y3 = 15-ABS(Y2)/Y1*15+1
200     CALL "PLOT",X,Y+Y2,Y3
210     NEXT Y2
220   NEXT X
300 END
```

10.5

QQQQQQQQQQQQQQQQQQQQQQQQQQQQQQQQQQQQQQQ
Q   PROBLEMS   Q
Q   Q
Q   **A challenge**   Q
Q   Q

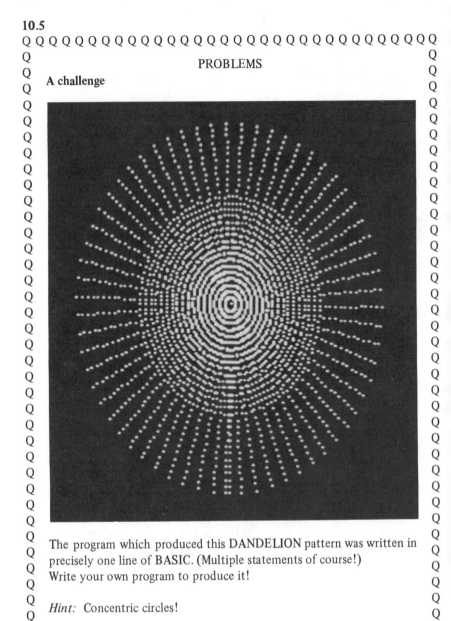

The program which produced this DANDELION pattern was written in precisely one line of BASIC. (Multiple statements of course!) Write your own program to produce it!

Hint: Concentric circles!

QQQQQQQQQQQQQQQQQQQQQQQQQQQQQQQQQQQQQQQ

CHAPTER 11

Filing

*

A FILE IS

an area

for storage

and retrieval

of information

*

The information

may be data

or

a program

*

11.1 INTRODUCTION

There are about as many different filing systems as there are computers on the market, so don't forget to consult the literature specific to your computer if you are not using a Research Machines 380Z (BASICSG Version 5.0). The file handling commands available on this computer are described in the following pages.   ♩

When large sets of data are involved it is particularly worth using files. They allow manipulation of larger amounts of data in a shorter time than is possible with the more familiar practice of inputting and outputting via a keyboard and a screen. Files also enable data and results to be preserved, for example, on disc.

Data files are organised sequentially. This means that the entire file must be read in order to read the last item of data.

Only one input and output file may be selected concurrently.

Multiple Files may be selected in turn.

Most of the commands used in conjunction with data files have already been met, chiefly in chapters 2 and 6. Here they are extended to redirect their input or output to the file channel. A channel is specified by a hash (#) followed by the channel number.

11.2 EXAMPLES OF POSSIBLE CHANNEL SPECIFICATIONS

For INPUT commands		For OUTPUT commands	
#0	keyboard	#0	screen
#10	file	#2	printer
		#10	file

Example: PRINT #10,a,b,c, "Finished" causes the values of a, b, c, and the word Finished to be printed to the output file.

Note: The channel specification follows immediately after the keyword and is separated from further items by a comma. The channel specification defaults to zero in all the commands which accept this specification, with the exceptions of CREATE, OPEN, CLOSE.

Many of the commands can alternatively be preceded by L. This indicates the printer device. Such commands must not be followed by a # specification. The summary below is followed by explanations and examples.

♩   See Variations on a Theme in the Appendix.

11.3 GENERAL FILE HANDLING COMMANDS

Note: RENAME and ERASE, as described in Chapter 12, are also useful here.

Command	Example	Purpose
CLOSE	CLOSE #10	Closes the output file. The output buffer is emptied, the disc directory is updated. *Warning:* If this step is omitted the file will be lost. *Note:* The BYE and CREATE commands both automatically close the output file if necessary.
CREATE	CREATE #10, "FOXI" CREATE #10, E$	CREATEs the specified file and makes it ready for output. If the file already exists, the message: File exists—replace (Y/N): is given. If Y or y is typed at the console, the old copy of the file is erased and the new file is created. Otherwise the program halts. If the disc directory is full, the message: Directory full is given. The file must be erased or the disc changed before retrying. *Remember* to give the RESET command after changing a disc.
LOOKUP	A=LOOKUP("FOXI")	Allows program to determine whether a file exists. (See the examples 11.3 at the end of this summary). LOOKUP returns −1 if the file exists, 0 if it doesn't or if the file specification is malformed. *Warning:* If an attempt is made to open a non-existent file, an error results. To prevent this use LOOKUP first.
OPEN	OPEN #10, "COUNTY" OPEN #10, C$	Opens a data file for reading and the filing system is initialised. If the specified file is non-existent the error message: File not found is produced and program execution stops.

The above commands merely set up files for input or output. The following section describes the commands used for reading from and writing to files.

11.4 INPUT AND OUTPUT COMMANDS

Command	Example	Purpose
INPUT	INPUT #10, C$, C	Data is input from a file. It is exactly analogous to INPUT from the console. If there is more than one data item per line they *must* be separated by commas. Error Messages given are: *Invalid input − if data is invalid *Extra lost − if too many items per line However, no question mark prompts are produced even if insufficient items are given − under these circumstances BASIC merely reads another line from the file. The form: INPUT #10, "Prompt"; A is not allowed. If no file has been opened the error message produced is: No input file If the end of the file is reached the error message is: Illegal EOF

Command	Example	Purpose
INPUT LINE	INPUT LINE #10,A	Exactly the same as the normal INPUT LINE command, except that the data is taken from the file and not from the console. If no file is OPEN, the error message given is: No input file If the end of the file is reached without an ON EOF, the error message given is: Illegal EOF
GET		A single character input routine, which returns the ASCII value of the next character from the selected input stream. Console input may be timed, allowing interactive response without halting the program. The function may be provided with zero, one, or two arguments. The examples below should clarify its purposes.
	A = GET()	Read next character from keyboard. GET waits indefinitely for this single character input.
	B = GET(100)	Wait 1 second for 1 character. The delay is measured in centiseconds (hundredths of a second).
	C = GET(#0)	Read next character from keyboard.
	D = GET(#0,100)	Wait 1 second for a character from keyboard. If no character is available by the end of the given time 0 is returned.
	E = GET(#10)	Read next character from file.
	F = GET(-1)	Waits for whatever time was left over from the last GET.
	G = GET(-2)	Returns the remaining time.
	H = GET(0)	Test keyboard, return character or zero.
GET$	A$ = GET$(#10) B$ = GET$(123)	Next sequential byte returned as a string of length zero or one.

With both GET and GET$, no special note is taken of any control character, including CTRL C and CTRL Z. This means that CTRL Z is not recognised as a console interrupt during a GET from the console, or as end of file from the file channel. EOF results if the physical end of file is reached.

Command	Example	Purpose
PRINT	PRINT #10,Z	The same as the normal form of PRINT introduced in Chapter 6, except that the characters are sent to the file. If no file is CREATEd, the error message given is: No output file Other messages given are: No disc space if the disc is full Directory full if the directory is full Write error if the disc is full or if there is a hardware malfunction.
PUT	PUT 13, "Hello" PUT #10,A$	Outputs the elements of the list of arguments, (numeric or string expressions separated by commas) to the selected channel. A numeric expression represents the ASCII value of a single byte; a string is output character by character. Examples of PUT are:
	PUT 12	Clears the screen
	PUT #10, "HELLO"	Outputs HELLO to the file. As with all commands which output to a file, the error messages given are: No output file No disc space Directory full Write Error

Command	Example	Purpose
DIR	DIR #10	These commands behave exactly as described in
	DIR #2,"*.*"	Chapters 12 and 2, for DIR and LIST.
LIST	LIST #10,25-99	
LVAR	LVAR #10	LVAR and TRACE have been described in Chapters
	LVAR #2	6 and 12 except that their output is sent to a file. If
		no file has been CREATEd, the error message is:
TRACE	TRACE #10,1	No output file
	TRACE #2,0	See Chapters 2,6 and 12 for further details.

11.5 INPUT CONTROL COMMANDS

Command	Example	Purpose
ON EOF	ON EOF GOTO 299	Causes control to be transferred to the specified line number if end of file is found using GET, INPUT or INPUT LINE. Otherwise, the error message: Illegal EOF would be given. See Example 11.4.
	ON EOF	Restores BASIC to its original state whereby end of file causes an error.
EOF	EOF	Causes BASIC to react as if the end of file had been reached. This will either cause transfer of control to a line number specified by an ON EOF command, or cause an error message. Neither the author of this book nor the author of the BASIC can find a use for this command, but it is included here for the sake of completeness.

11.6 OUTPUT CONTROL COMMANDS

Command	Example	Purpose
NULL	NULL #10,3,0	See page 337.
LNULL		The example causes each RETURN/LINE FEED sent to the file to be followed by three ASCII NULs.
POS	A = POS(10)	Returns the position of the 'printhead' of the channel
	B = POS(2)	specified by the argument. The examples assign the cursor position of the file to A and the printer head position to B.
QUOTE	QUOTE #10,0	Sets the 'quote character' on the specified channel to
	QUOTE #10,34	be the character whose ASCII value is the second argument, or 34 by default. The quote character affects output of PRINT. If it is zero, then output is normal. Otherwise, all strings are enclosed in the quote character, and commas separating multiple items on a line are output literally instead of causing columnar output.
WIDTH	WIDTH #10,132	Sets logical width of a line so that BASIC
LWIDTH		automatically begins on new line after the specified number of characters have been output. The example sets the logical width of the output file to 132.

With the definitions and descriptions of the file handling commands available to us, we will now take a look at ways in which those commands usefully operate together.

11.7 A NOTE ON CHANNEL NUMBER 10 – THE FILE CHANNEL

OUTPUT to a file and INPUT to a file are two different operations which are done using the same channel number. They can be represented diagrammatically thus:

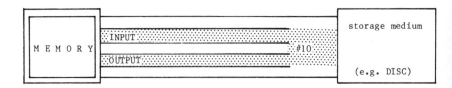

A further note on channels

CREATE #10, "FILENAME" makes the association between channel 10 and the file to be written to.

CLOSE #10 breaks this association and updates the directory

OPEN #10, "FILENAM1" makes the association between channel 10 and a file for reading.

OPEN #10, "FILENAM2" breaks the association with the channel and FILENAM 1 and makes it with FILENAM2.

11.8 To OUTPUT Information to a File

11.8.1 If the file is a new file or to be erased and treated as new:

If file does not exist   If file already exists

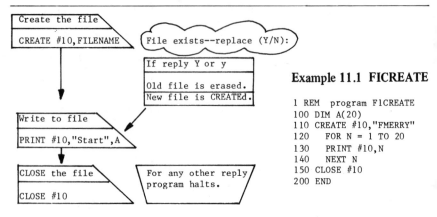

Example 11.1 FICREATE

```
1 REM   program F1CREATE
100 DIM A(20)
110 CREATE #10,"FMERRY"
120   FOR N = 1 TO 20
130     PRINT #10,N
140     NEXT N
150 CLOSE #10
200 END
```

11.8.2 If the file exists and data is to be added (appended):

If the file exists   Ref. to Example 11.2

DISC	Open file for reading	310
	OPEN #10,"FMERRY"	
MEMORY		
Data from FMERRY	Read stored information into memory	
	INPUT #10,B(N) or GET #10	360
appended data	Add to this information in memory	400-420
	Send the merged information to the file for storage.	
data to FMERRY	PRINT #10,B or PUT #1 LVAR #10	
CLOSE FMERRY	LIST #10	

Example 11.2 Program F2OPEN

```
299 REM                   PROGRAM F2OPEN
300 DIM B(100)
310 OPEN #10,"FMERRY"      :REM 20 nos.have been written to FMERRY by F1CREATE
350   FOR N = 1 TO 20
360   INPUT #10,B(N)       :REM 20 nos. read from FMERRY into array B
370   NEXT N
400   FOR J = 21 TO 50     :REM 30 nos. added to array B
410   LET B(N) = N↑2
420   NEXT J
440 CREATE #10, "FMERRY"   :REM Open the file to be written to
450   FOR N = 1 TO 50
460   PRINT #10,B(N)
470   NEXT N
500 CLOSE #10              :REM Close the file which has been written to
550 END
```

11.9 The LOOKUP check – does this file exist?

Reminder LOOKUP(A$) returns 0 if the file does not exist
                                     −1 if the file exists

Example 11.3 Program FILOOKUP

```
1 REM                PROGRAM F1LOOKUP
10 INPUT "give filename:"; F$
20 IF LOOKUP(F$)<> 0 THEN 50
30 PRINT "There's no such file  -  "
40 GOTO 10
50 OPEN #10,F$
70 ?"I found your file!"
100 END

RUN
give filename:? UTOPIA
There's no such file  -
give filename:? FMERRY
I found your file!

Ready:
```

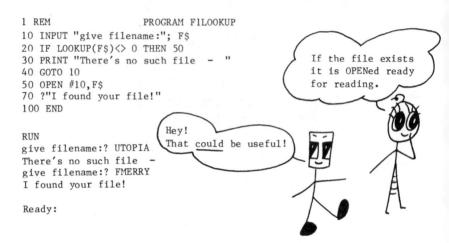

If the file exists it is OPENed ready for reading.

Hey! That could be useful!

11.10 To Avoid Reading Past the End of a File

ON EOF sets a flag within BASIC; as soon end of file is reached, BASIC jumps to the specified line number. Thus example 11.2 could be made more flexible by modifying the lines shown in example 11.4.

Example 11.4 Program FONEOF

```
100 REM          program segment FONEOF
340 ON EOF GOTO 400
350    FOR N = 1 TO 50
360    INPUT #10,B(N)     :REM 50 nos. read from FMERRY into array B
370    NEXT N
400    FOR J = N-1 TO 50 :REM the remainder of array A is filled
```

11.11 To Halt a Program Run Temporarily

Use A = GET(). See Example 18.2.

11.12 A Note on the Size of Files

Essentially they may be as big as needed, limited by the amount of space on the disc in units of 1K (1024 bytes).

On one side of a 5″ floppy disc there are:

- 40   tracks each of size 2K giving a potential total storage space of 80K, of which
- 3   tracks are reserved for the operating system,
- 1   track is kept for the directory, leaving
- 72K for general usage. Typically some of this will be used by BASIC, TXED (EDIT), etc.

On one side of an 8″ floppy disc there are:

- 77   tracks each of size 3.25K giving a potential total space of 250.25K of which
- 2   tracks are reserved for the operating system
- 1   track for the directory, leaving
- 241K for general use, as above.

It is worth noting that the following facilities are *NOT* offered in current versions of R.M.L standard BASIC though found in other BASICs:

RANDOM ACCESS   REWIND   APPEND   &

11.13

Q Q Q Q Q Q Q Q Q Q Q Q Q Q Q Q Q Q Q Q Q Q Q Q Q Q Q Q Q Q Q Q

PROBLEMS

1. Automatic Cheque Stubs

Write a program to store and retrieve the following information on a file (or files), (use FRAMEMOD, example 14.1 as a controlling structure) the date, all debits and credits, the running total of your personal finances. It should also record the type of purchase. Your program should allow you to extract:

       all transactions on a given date

       all transactions of a kind

       all credits and debits.

It should automatically warn you if you go into the red!!

Extend these suggestions to suit your own requirements.

2. Write an **automatic addressbook** program, that will store, alphabetically by surnames, addresses and telephone numbers in a file. The program should be capable of inserting new entries in the correct places. It should give you the address and telephone number of any name on request.

       Vary the program so that by giving a telephone number the program supplies the persons name and address.

       To make the program efficient do not allow the search to go beyond the relevant point in the alphabet.

Q Q Q Q Q Q Q Q Q Q Q Q Q Q Q Q Q Q Q Q Q Q Q Q Q Q Q Q Q Q Q Q

CHAPTER 12

EDIT and some miscellaneous commands

12.1 EDIT

A BASIC program may be edited using two different methods:

12.1.1 Making an alteration whilst still on a line by using the DELETE (DELT) key to 'rub out' what is there. Type in the new character or characters.
For example:

101 REAF A,█

Touch DELT 4 times   101 REA█

Type in correction D and continue   101 READ A,█

12.1.2 Using the EDIT command

EDIT brings into operation the line editor which may be used to alter, insert, or delete any characters on any line of a program. For example, if we were developing the program of Example 12.1 and decided to edit line 300, on typing EDIT 300 and RETURN, that line is copied into the edit buffer. Commands to alter this line may now be given. When alterations to the line are completed it is copied back into the program.

Example 12.1

```
100 REM   program NOTRIGHT
300 DAT 1,8"Nuts"
400 END
```

Learning to use the EDIT command can prove difficult at first, particularly as most of the commands do not reflect the typed characters, and some cause no change at all on the screen. However familiarity with even a few commands does speed up program development. In the table below a detailed account of an edit on line 300 is given.

The best way to become familiar with these EDIT commands is to try them out for yourself. Why not type line 300 into your workspace and follow the line by line edit guide below? Type in the commands, in Table 12.1, in the column headed Action (TYPE). The following subset of commands are used in this edit:

EDIT 300   — to bring line editor into operation.
L   — to look at the line.
space   — to move one space to reveal next character on right.
n(space)   — to move n(spaces) to reveal up to the nth character on right.
Fx   — to find first x on the line.
I   — to insert.
ESC   — to escape from Insert mode.
RETURN   — to return edited line to program.

Note: Once in the line editor, typing RETURN gets you out of it.

Edit keeps a pointer within the buffer. Normally only the characters to the left of it are displayed on the screen. But beware, this picture is sometimes confused when, for example, the DELT key is used.

The CURSOR, the small square (or line on some VDUs), indicates where you are. It sits on the exact spot where a character may be deleted or inserted. Multiple commands may be given on a line, for example in point 3   FT(space) implies: type F, then T and finally, a space. The keys typed, in order, for a complete concise edit looks like this:

EDIT300   RETURN   300
L   300 DAT 1,8"Nuts"
F(space)IA(esc)F"I,RETURN   300 DATA 1,8,"Nuts"

Table 12.1 A sample edit

	Human		Computer	
	Aim	Action(TYPE)	Response as reflected on screen	Line as recorded in edit buffer
1	EDIT line 300	EDIT300 RETURN	300 ∎	300 DAT 1,8 "Nuts"
2	See whole line	L	300 DAT 1,8 "Nuts" 300 ∎	300 DAT 1,8 "Nuts"
3	Move to position after T.	3 (space) or FT (space)	300 DAT∎ or 300 DA∎ 300 DAT∎	300 DAT 1,8 "Nuts" 300 DAT 1,8 "Nuts"
4	Insert A	IA	300 DATA∎	300 DATA 1,8 "Nuts"
5	Escape from Insert mode	esc	300 DATA∎	300 DATA 1,8 "Nuts"
6	Insert ',' after 8	F8(space)	300 DATA 1,8∎ 300 DATA 1,8,∎	300 DATA 1,8 "Nuts" 300 DATA 1,8, "Nuts"
7	Leave line editor as no further edit required	RETURN	300 DATA 1,8, "Nuts" ∎	300 DATA 1,8, "Nuts"

Having completed a 'Sample' edit now take a look at other edit commands available to you. Several of the commands may be repeated from 1 to 255 times by typing the required number before the command. The number typed does not reflect on the screen as you may have noted in typing in lines 3 and 6 in Table 12.1. In the following description of the edit command n is used to represent the required number of repeats. (In jargon terms n is the numeric argument).

12.1.3 Summary of Edit Command

Command/
Example   Purpose

Command/Example	Purpose
EDIT n	Line n is copied into the edit buffer and the pointer is set to the first position after the line number.
RETURN	The line to the right of the pointer is typed out and the original line is replaced by the edited version. This is the normal way to end an edit session.
ESC	Terminates any command sequence. In particular it ends an Insert.
n(space)	Typing the space bar once moves the cursor once to the right. The character it steps over can be seen. n(space) moves the (pointer) 6 spaces to the right revealing the 6 next characters.
n DELT	The reverse of (space), it moves the cursor back n characters. In Insert mode typing DELT n times deletes n characters from the buffer. DELT will not move cursor past the line number.

WARNING — the following commands will not work whilst in Insert mode. To leave Insert mode type ESC , then give your command.

12.1.4 In Edit Mode

Command   Example   Purpose

Command	Example	Purpose
A	A	The current edit is abandoned. The edit buffer is refilled from the original line in the program. The pointer is reset to beginning of the line. (This command is useful if an edit has become confused).
nD	D 5D	n characters following the pointer are deleted. The deleted characters appear between back slashes (\) (or between some other symbol such as (/) or (1/2)).
nFc	Fz 3F9	Finds the nth occurrence of the character c. The cursor is moved 'on top' of c. The cursor moves to the end of the line if there is no occurrence of c, or if n is greater than the number of times c is found on that line.
H	H	Everything to the right of the pointer is deleted. Insert mode is entered. See command I for details of Insert mode.

Command	Example	Purpose
I	I	Insert mode is entered and can be used to delete or replace faulty text. (Line numbers cannot be changed.) Characters typed following the I are entered directly into the buffer. This includes DELT which removes characters to the left of the cursor position. ESCape ends the insert mode. RETURN leaves the EDIT and updates the line.
nKc	KZ 5KO	Kills (or deletes) all characters from the pointer up to but not including the nth occurrence of c. The cursor appears in the first position to the left of the character.
L	L	The whole line can be looked at. The line to the right of the pointer is typed out. The pointer is returned to the beginning of the line.
Q	Q	Edit is abandoned without implementing the changes made.
nR	R 3R	Replace the n characters in the buffer following the pointer, by n characters from the keyboard.
X	X	The pointer is moved to end of line and Insert mode entered. This is useful for appending to a line.
nDELT	DELT 8DELT nDELT	The reverse of (space), it moves the cursor back n characters. In Insert mode these will be deleted from the buffer. DELT will not move cursor past the line number.

At this point you may feel you don't understand EDIT at all. If so, act on the words Lewis Carroll put into the mouth of the Dodo when he replied to Alice's question 'What is a Caucus-race?'

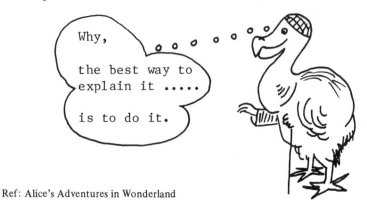

Ref: Alice's Adventures in Wonderland

12.2 SOME MISCELLANEOUS COMMANDS

12.1.1 General Purpose Commands

Most of the following commands are normally used without line numbers, in direct mode. However, some commands, such as ERASE and RENAME, are often used with programs.

File specifications are necessary for several of the commands described. These are, for example:

> LOAD "DRAWING"   Filenames must be enclosed
>   in quote-marks.
>
> ERASE F$ †

The filename may optionally be preceded by the name of a disc unit (A to D), followed by a colon, for example:

> SAVE "B:GRAPH"

If no reference is given to a disc unit, the one selected when BASIC was loaded is assumed.

The filename may be extended by three characters preceded by a full stop, for example:

> RESONATE.BAS

If omitted .BAS is assumed.

Command	Example	Purpose
CONT	CONT CONTINUE	Resumes program execution after CTRL Z has been typed, or after a STOP instruction has been executed.
DELETE	DELETE 100 DELETE 20-80 DELETE 25- DELETE -80	Deletes line 100. Deletes from line 20 to line 80. Deletes from line 25 to the end. Deletes lines up to line 80.
DIR	DIR	Lists directory on the screen of all files on the disc which have the extension .BAS.
	DIR "C:*.*"	Lists directory of all .BAS files on drive C. Also valid for drives A, B and D.

†   See Chapter 11 for details on files.

Command	Example	Purpose
ERASE	ERASE "CH1"	Erases the specified file. No error message is given if the file does not exist.
FSAVE	FSAVE "CLIMA"	FSAVE acts like SAVE (described below) except that the program is saved in internal format. (See example later in this chapter.)
LLIST	LLIST	Similar to LIST but listings are to the printer.
	LLIST 15	Lists line 15.
	LLIST 15-90	Lists from line 15 to line 90.
	LLIST 15-	Lists line 15 onwards.
	LLIST -90	Lists up to and including line 90.
LLVAR	LLVAR	The same as LVAR except that output goes to the printer device. (See chapter 6.)
LOAD	LOAD "BIRDIE" LOAD "B:GEOG.BAS" LOAD N\$	Loads a program from disc into memory overwriting any pre-existing program. LOAD must be followed by the name of the program in quotation marks, or a variable string. When the loading operation is complete BASIC gives the message: Ready: If the program name cannot be found in the directory the message displayed is: File not found If it is in the wrong internal format the message given is: Wrong internal format.
LOAD?	LOAD? "RECTANG"	Is used to verify that the file on the disc and that in memory are the same. It only works on internal format files. Attempts to LOAD? ASCII format files generates the error message: Can't verify ASCII files. If files are the same the message given is: Ready:

Command	Example	Purpose
		Otherwise BASIC gives the message: Files different. The file in memory remains unchanged.
LOADGO	LOADGO "TETRA"	Loads and executes the program.
	LOADGO "SPIN", 150	Loads and executes program from specified line number. If filename is missing the error message given is: Missing file name LOADGO clears all variables and user-defined functions.
MERGE	MERGE "CIRC"	File on disc (CIRC) is combined with lines of program already in memory. Incoming lines with the same numbers as those already in memory replace these. Use the RENUMBER command to move existing line numbers out of the way before merging with an existing file on disc. Internal format (FSAVEd) files cannot be merged. An attempt to do so results in the error message: Can't MERGE internal files.
MERGEGO	MERGEGO "SQU" MERGEGO "QUA", 200	This is a combination of the LOADGO and MERGE commands already described. The specified file is merged into the program in memory and executed from the lowest line number unless a higher number is specified.
PRINTER	PRINTER 4, 6	Refer to RML Systems manual for details. Alternatively, consult the manufacturer's instructions if you are working on a different computer.
RENAME	RENAME "NEWFILE", "OLDFILE"	The existing "OLDFILE" is given the new name, "NEWFILE". If the OLDFILE.BAS is not found the error message given is: File not found. If the NEWFILE.BAS already exists BASIC prompts File exists—replace (Y/N) Type Y to rename.

Command	Example	Purpose
RENUMBER	RENUMBER	All line numbers and internal references such as GOTO 99, are adjusted.
	RENUMBER 1000	RENUMBER may be followed by two arguments.
	RENUMBER 500, 20	The first is the startpoint for renumber-
	RENUMBER , 50	ing and the second, the interval. If either is omitted the default value of 10 is used. Line numbers in REMarks are not affected.
RESET	RESET	Issue this command after changing a disc because the computer will not allow you to write to a changed disc. Data files currently open for input and output will be discarded. If you try to write to a changed disc the error message given is: BDOS ERROR ON B: R/O If in difficulty consult Research Machines BASICSG Manual.
SAVE	SAVE "SPIRALS"	Program is saved on disc.
	SAVE "B:SPIRALS"	When BASIC has completed saving the
	SAVE "C:LISS.BAS"	program — the message 'Ready:' is given. Before issuing a SAVE command, *check* that there is a disc in the selected unit. If a disc has been changed since starting BASIC give the RESET command before the SAVE command. Failure to do this results in the error message: BDOS Read Only error (see RESET).
TRACE	TRACE 0	The line numbers, enclosed in angle
	TRACE #10, 1	brackets, of all statements executed whilst the tracing is enabled, are output. The last or only argument in the TRACE command is evaluated. If it is zero tracing is turned off. Otherwise it is enabled.
LTRACE	LTRACE	As for TRACE but the output is sent to the printer.

12.2.2 Error Handling

Command	Example	Purpose
ON ERROR	ON ERROR GOTO 500	Normally BASIC prints an error message when an error occurs. Where it is preferable to control what happens in the event of an error, ON ERROR may be used to specify the line which should be executed next. An error cancels the ON ERROR switch, so a second error will cause BASIC to print the error message. The form ON ERROR cancels the effect of a previous ON ERROR GOTO . . . and normal BASIC error handling resumes.
RESUME	RESUME	Causes program execution to be resumed after an error has been trapped by ON ERROR. BASIC returns to the statement that caused the error. (WARNING: Take care not to create an infinite loop when using RESUME). If RESUME is encountered and no ON ERROR trap was set the error message given is: RESUME without error and execution stops.
ERR	LET B=ERR	Returns the number of the most recent error. For details of what the error numbers mean consult: Research Machines Extended Basic Version 5 Reference Manual.
ERL	LET A=ERL	Returns the number of the line on which the most recent error occurred. WARNING: BASIC does not RENUMBER a line which is being compared with ERL, for example: IF ERL = 200 THEN . . .
ERROR	ERROR ERROR 3	Causes BASIC to act if an error had occurred. The message given is: Unknown error unless a specified and valid error number is given.

Command	Example	Purpose
ON BREAK	ON BREAK GO TO 200	Traps an attempt to interrupt a running program with CTRL Z from the keyboard, and redirects program execution to the specified line.

12.2.3 Note on Internal Format
To store a program or data in internal format means that it is stored in a form more convenient to the computer. The loading of such a file is significantly faster.

12.2.4 Machine and ASSEMBLY LANGUAGE SUPPORT
There are a number of features in BASISGSG that allow the user direct access to the 380Z computer during the execution of a BASIC program. The use of these is not a normal part of programming in BASIC, but rather an extension to language.

A detailed description of these features would necessarily assume reasonable familiarity with the memory layout, and with Z80 Assembly Language, and is therefore considered to be outside of the scope of this book. Readers interested in detailed information should consult the 'References and Further Reading' section in the appendix for relevant sources of information. A summary of the commands is given below.

Command	Purpose	Example
PEEK	Returns contents of memory location	LET A = PEEK(B)
POKE	Stores value in memory location	POKE A, O
INP	Returns value from input port	LET V = INP(P)
OUT	Sends value to output port	OUT P, V
WAIT	Waits for input status bit	WAIT P, M, X
VARADR	Returns address of variable	LET A = VARADR(U)
USR	Calls user supplied function	LET V = USR(B)
CALL	Calls user supplied subroutine	CALL "RES", V1, V2

SECTION II
Applications

To paraphrase the American
philanthropist, Carnegie, describing
and acquaintance: "[He] speaks 17
languages and has nothing to say in
any of them."
Metaphorically speaking although we
are now equipped with the alphabet
and words of BASIC, so far we have
'said' relatively little.
The best way to develop ones school-
days' French, for example, is to inflict
it on the population of France! Simi-
larily, to perfect ones BASIC language
it must be exercised on real-life programming problems. In section II you
are offered this opportunity.

Please Note:
From now on the following deviations
from the standard conventions adopted
in section I will be used when more
convenient:

?   for PRINT

:   as a separator in multi-line
       statements

C=0 for   LET C=0 i.e. assign-
       ment without LET.

CHAPTER 13

Random numbers

13.1 PROBABILITY

Born of parents who probably met through some chance event, in a locality undetermined by us, we start life on Planet Earth the product of an unpredictable grouping of genes.

Will it rain tomorrow? What is the probability that it will? In the U.K. it is certainly higher than the possibility of brilliant sunshine!!

'Beyond the certainties of death and taxes, few aspects of our lives elude the touch of chance.'† As long since noted in Ecclesiastes, 'time and chance happeneth'.

Since time began man has played at predicting the outcome of future happenings. The researches of two spare time mathematicians, Pascal and Fermat, together with a nobleman, de Mere, in the 17th century, into various gambling situations evolved into modern probability theory — the laws of chance.

Until about 70 years ago these laws were invoked almost apologetically but today scientists are making bold predictions based on the mathematics of probability.

The aspect of probability known as *the law of large numbers* accounts for much of the current practical use of probability. These laws begin to act as laws only when many instances are involved. For example, many throws of a dice.

Random Collision

Consider a jar of gas containing many millions of molecules, or a country supporting millions of motorists. Although it is possible to predict approximately how many collisions there will be between molecules in one second, or drivers in one month, it is impossible to forsee which particular molecules or motorists will collide. The overall prediction is however useful to both scientist and insurance agent!

† See References and Further Reading in the Appendix (1)

What then are *random numbers?* How do they tie in with probability?

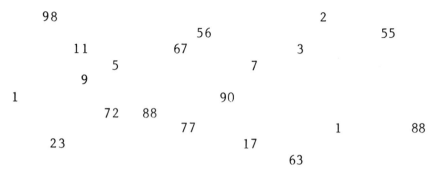

Hammerley and Handscomb have put it this way:

'*A random event* is an event which has a chance of happening, and *probability* is a numerical measure of that chance.'   †

When an event has occurred by chance, it has the same likelihood of occurring by chance again, as, for example, in the case of the tossing of a coin. In practice, however, the chance of achieving true random selection is less easy than one would imagine. Quite extensive tests are sometimes necessary to show that a certain selection is truely random.

To bypass the time consuming operation of testing, *a table of random numbers* is prepared in advance, in which every digit is intended to be chosen at random and which have been tested for randomness and found to be satisfactory in as many ways as possible. ‡ Several such tables have been produced and published. The Statistical Tables published by Fisher and Yates are but one example.

Modern practice, however, does not favour the use of these tested tables. Instead *pseudo-random numbers* are increasingly used. These are numbers generated by a mathematical operation on one or more of the preceding numbers, and not by the generation of a random process such as the flip of a coin. Few such sequences have been adequately tested for true randomness. A good attitude adopted towards computer-generated sequences of so-called pseudo-random numbers is that they are acceptable as long as nothing is known to the contrary. If one experiment showed evidence of pattern, the sequence would cease to be considered random since randomness is essentially an absence of pattern or preference. It should be noted, however, that such an experiment would need to be sufficiently exhaustive. After all the sequence 99999999999........ is as likely as any other to occur. The term random numbers is often used loosely when pseudo-random numbers is meant. *Randomness* is the set of statistical properties of such numbers as mentioned above.

‡ See References and Further Reading in the Appendix (2)
† See References and Further Reading in the Appendix (5)

Example 13.1 Program RANDOM2

```
100 REM          Program              RANDOM2
110 REM                   Elementary illustration of the generation of a
120 REM                   set of pseudorandom numbers.
130 REM                   Method:  Take  1   x    13    Store 1  and 13
140 REM                            Now   13  X    13    Scrap 100's col.
150 REM                                  69  X    13    Scrap 100's col.
160 REM                            Continue . . .       Store each result.
170 DIM D(100) :REM Stores distribution of randoms
180 PRINT TAB(1); 1;
190 LET S = 13: LET T = 1
200    FOR N = 2 TO 100
210    LET T = T + 7
220    IF T < 70 THEN 260
230    PRINT
240    LET T = 1: REM  Arranges the number of figures per line
260    PRINT TAB(T); S;
270    LET S = S * 13 - (INT((S * 13) / 100) * 100)
280    LET D(S) = D(S) + 1
290    NEXT N
300 PRINT
310 PRINT
320 PRINT "Distribution Of   R A N D O M S   Just Generated"
330 PRINT
340 LET J = 0
350    FOR I = 0 TO 100 STEP 10
360    PRINT TAB(J); I;
370    LET J = J + 5
380    NEXT I
390 PRINT
400 PRINT "-----------------------------------------------------------"
410    FOR N = 1 TO 100
420    IF D(N) = 0 THEN 440
430    PRINT TAB(N / 2); "+";
440    NEXT N
450 PRINT
460 END
RUN
1       13      69      97      61      93      9       17      21      73
49      37      81      53      89      57      41      33      29      77
1       13      69      97      61      93      9       17      21      73
49      37      81      53      89'     57      41      33      29      77
1       13      69      97      61      93      9       17      21      73
49      37      81      53      89      57      41      33      29      77
1       13      69      97      61      93      9       17      21      73
49      37      81      53      89      57      41      33      29      77
1       13      69      97      61      93      9       17      21      73
49      37      81      53      89      57      41      33      29      77

Distribution Of   R A N D O M S   Just Generated

0    10   20   30   40   50   60   70   80   90   100
-----------------------------------------------------------
+    + + + +    + + + +    + + + +    + + + +    + + +

Ready:
```

Example 13.1 illustrates the generation of a small sequence of random numbers at a very elementary level. A glance at the RUN reveals that the sequence is in fact repeated after 20 numbers. When plotted against an axis, the numbers show a rather *uniform distribution* with no obvious preference for any part of the scale. This is probably the most fundamental feature of randomness.

There are many ways of generating random numbers.

The random number generator in BASIC is an algorithm of the language processor. The RND function always returns a number between 0 and 1. Each time RND(0) is used there is equal probability that the resulting number will be $>= .5$ or $< .5$.

A list of the first 30 randoms generated by the R.M.L. BASIC random number generator is produced by the program as seen in Example 13.2.

Example 13.2 Program RND380Z

```
100 REM                Program    RND380Z
110 REM
120 PRINT "Numbers at the start of the list produced by"
130 PRINT "THE R.M.L RANDOM NUMBER GENERATOR"
140 PRINT
150    FOR N = 1 TO 30
160    PRINT RND(1),                                          †
165    IF N/5 <> INT(N/5) THEN 170
166    PRINT
170    NEXT N
180 END
RUN
Numbers at the start of the list produced by
THE R.M.L RANDOM NUMBER GENERATOR
```

.74599	.28212	.560765	.0206954	.0589514
.753802	.79155	.474534	4.04624E-03	.463917
.606188	.710012	.748825	.842713	.651384
.262305	.516361	.942173	.0382258	.159109
.948157	.72214	.53476	.491673	.622058
.560614	.977498	.274173	.397633	.90294

Ready:

Q Q Q Q Q Q Q Q Q Q Q Q Q Q Q Q Q Q Q Q Q Q Q Q Q Q Q Q Q Q Q Q Q
Q   Q
Q   In Example 13.3 these numbers are rounded, scaled, and represented   Q
Q   graphically. Compare the RUN with that of Example 13.1. Is there any   Q
Q   significant difference in distribution? Should you make bold generalisa-   Q
Q   tions and comparisons with so few numbers? Try writing a program or   Q
Q   modifying 13.3 to show the distribution of 100 or 1000 numbers. Note   Q
Q   whether or not there is a significant difference shown in the spread of   Q
Q   random numbers.   Q
Q   Q
Q Q Q Q Q Q Q Q Q Q Q Q Q Q Q Q Q Q Q Q Q Q Q Q Q Q Q Q Q Q Q Q Q

† Random Number Function (RND(X)), see Chapter 3

Example 13.3 Program RND380Z2

```
100 REM              Program        RND380Z2
130 PRINT "RND numbers scaled and rounded to 2-digit integers"
140 PRINT
150 DIM R(30),V(50)
170 LET C = 0
180   FOR N = 1 TO 30
190   LET R(N) = INT(RND(1) * 100)
200   IF C <> 15 THEN 220
210   PRINT
220   PRINT R(N);
230   LET C = C + 1
240   NEXT N
250 PRINT
290   FOR N = 1 TO 30
300   LET V(INT(R(N)/2)) = 1:REM V holds relative positions of numbers
310   NEXT N
320 PRINT
330 PRINT "Spread of the first 30 random numbers"
340 PRINT
350 LET T = 0
360   FOR J = 0 TO 100 STEP 10
370   PRINT TAB(T); J;
380   LET T = T + 5
390   NEXT J
400 PRINT
410 PRINT "----------------------------------------------------------"
430   FOR I = 1 TO 50
440   IF V(I) = 0 THEN 460
450   PRINT TAB(I); "*";
460   NEXT I
480 END
RUN
RND numbers scaled and rounded to 2-digit integers

 74  28  56   2   5  75  79  47   0  46  60  71  74  84  65
 26  51  94   3  15  94  72  53  49  62  56  97  27  39  90

Spread of the first 30 random numbers

 0    10   20   30   40   50   60   70   80   90   100
-----------------------------------------------------------
**   *    **   *    **** * ***  *** *   *   * **

Ready:
```

```
Q Q Q Q Q Q Q Q Q Q Q Q Q Q Q Q Q Q Q Q Q Q Q Q Q Q Q Q Q Q Q Q Q Q
Q                                                                    Q
Q   Have you observed . . . . . . . . ?                              Q
Q                                                                    Q
Q   In example 12.3 the position of 30 numbers are to be represented Q
Q   graphically, yet only 25 *'s appear in the output.               Q
Q                                                                    Q
Q   Can you explain why there is an apparent discrepancy?            Q
Q                                                                    Q
Q Q Q Q Q Q Q Q Q Q Q Q Q Q Q Q Q Q Q Q Q Q Q Q Q Q Q Q Q Q Q Q Q Q
```

13.2 USING RANDOM NUMBERS

The random number may be used as the basis of, or controlling element in, a wide variety of computer programs.   †

Where a predictable sequence is needed each RUN use RND(1). When an unpredictable sequence is required, for example in games programs, use RANDOMIZE, to set the sequence to a random point each RUN.

From this point on, the words 'random number' will be taken to mean a computer generated pseudo-random number. Streams of such numbers have specific characteristics some of which are described below.

13.2.1 Characteristics of Random Numbers

Range A random number generator usually delivers positive fractional values which may include zero.

Resolution Full machine accuracy is used by a good random number generator (RNG). If, as is common, random integers of say 2, 4 or 6 decimal digits are generated the range and resolution are directly related to the number of digits generated.

Stream length Normally a RNG repeats its sequence of randoms after some large quantity of numbers, say one million, has been generated.

Repeatability It is desirable to be able to repeat a particular short series during a program run. This may mean using the same sequence of random numbers, as generated by RND(1). (Ref. page 56).

Initialisation The initialisation of the RNG is usually controllable. Common facilities include a standard start, an optional start or one set up by the time-of-day. RML 380Z and other BASICs offer the RANDOMIZE command which sets the sequence to a random point.

Distribution Most RNGs deliver random values which have an equi-probable distribution over the stated range.

† See References and Further Reading in the Appendix (6)

When simulating a process it is usual to have in mind a probable distribution that the model will follow. In order to make predictions it is necessary to generate random numbers that will follow that distribution.

In generating a stream of random numbers the value of the generated number will alter at each call of the function. Since the name of a function carries its value it is called a variable. For a given random number generator the variable has an 'expectation' shown by the distribution diagrams below, for example.

13.2.2 Distributions Functions of Random Variable (R)

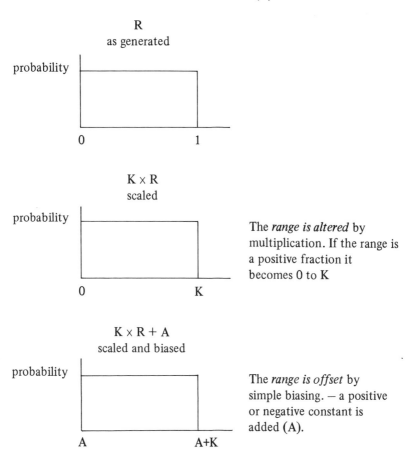

R
as generated

probability

0   1

K × R
scaled

probability

0   K

The *range is altered* by multiplication. If the range is a positive fraction it becomes 0 to K

K × R + A
scaled and biased

probability

A   A+K

The *range is offset* by simple biasing. — a positive or negative constant is added (A).

Note The probability distribution profile is unaltered by any of the above operations. Such rectangular distributions are called uniform distributions.

13.2.3 Distribution Modifications from the Equiprobable

Most random number generators are designed to provide and equal expectation for any value within a given range. This equi-probable distribution may be altered in a variety of ways. The simple modifications illustrated below assume the range to be positive fractions.

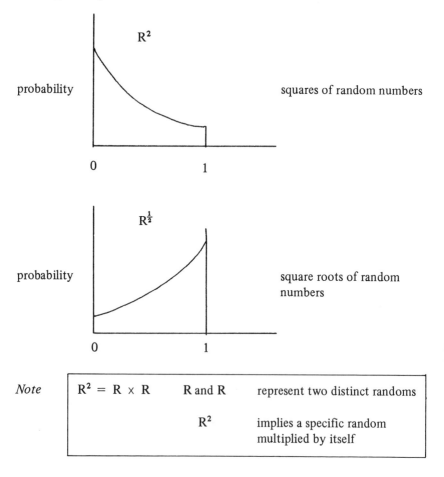

R^2

probability   squares of random numbers

0   1

$R^{\frac{1}{2}}$

probability   square roots of random numbers

0   1

Note $R^2 = R \times R$ R and R   represent two distinct randoms

R^2 implies a specific random multiplied by itself

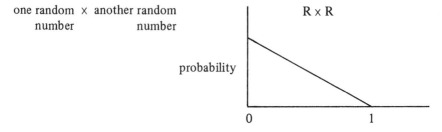

one random × another random
  number   number

$R \times R$

probability

0   1

absolute value of a random
number — a random number

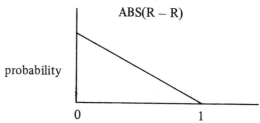

ABS(R − R)

probability

0   1

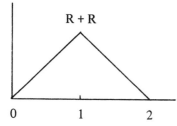

R + R

probability   sums of two random numbers

0   1   2

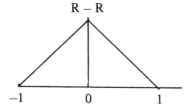

R − R

probability   differences between two
                                                   random numbers

−1   0   1

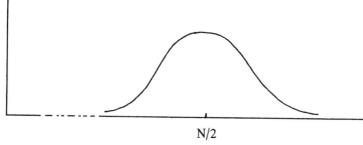

probability

N/2

Sets of sums of N random numbers gives an approximation to a Normal Curve
which improves as N increases.

Mean   N/2
Variance   N/12

The method used above to arrive at the Normal Curve was chosen for its simplicity. However it is uneconomical and more complex methods involving transformations according to probability distributions are more often used in practice.

The Normal Curve is applied in practice to processes which result from large numbers of random events working together. A simple example is that of heights and weights.

Restricting the resolution of a random variable is sometimes desirable. For example a random fraction may be multiplied by some power of ten and then truncated by one of the integer functions available in the system, as illustrated below:

In BASIC $Y = \text{INT(RND(1)} * 100)$

13.3 RANDOM (STOCHASTIC) CONTROL OF A PROGRAM

How much easier it is to adjust a 'toy' road system in a computed simulation, than to rebuild a complex junction on one of Britain's major motor routes, and all because of a planning miscalculation.

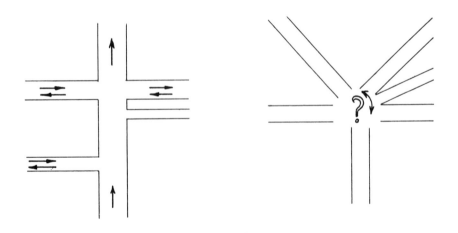

It is extremely useful, in the planning stages of road-making, to include such simulations as traffic flow at junctions. For this, the volume, and possibly the type, of traffic at each junction entry-point needs to be known, or 'created', throughout the day and seven days a week. A program segment testing traffic flow on a road could be:

```
500   IF  X < RND( 1)   THEN  999
      .
      .
      .
999   REM   VEHICLES ENTERING JUNCTION FROM NORTH
```

Where X is a value representing a vehicle. When X is less than the value of some random number the program flow is adjusted accordingly and vehicle X is recognised as coming in from the north.

When the spread of required values is known the stream of numbers from the random number generator can be adjusted accordingly to give the required distribution.

Another possible program segment in this simulation is one which scales an incoming random number to the range 1 to 10 and uses this scaled value as a pointer to the program modules representing different entry points as indicated below:

```
110   GO TO RND(1) * 10 + 1   OF   250,350,450,550,....

250   REM JUNCTION 1
```

An incomplete and brief introduction to random numbers has been presented in these pages. A few of their uses have been indicated. Those interested in further reading should consult the references in the appendix.

Examples in this book which use random numbers are to be found in chapter 15 on sorting, and chapter 16 on simulation. In the latter the random number function is used in simulating the throw of a dice.

13.4

Q Q Q Q Q Q Q Q Q Q Q Q Q Q Q Q Q Q Q Q Q Q Q Q Q Q Q Q Q Q Q
Q						Q
Q				PROBLEMS			Q
Q 1(a)	Write a program to generate a set of sums of random numbers.	Q
Q		Represent these graphically. What is the range covered?	Q
Q (b)	Alter your program so that Y is obtained thus:		Q
Q							Q
Q		$Y = RND(1) - RND(1) + RND(1) - RND(1)$		Q
Q							Q
Q		What differences do you detect between the two graphs?	Q
Q 2. Simulate the tossing of a coin and the resulting count of heads and	Q
Q	tails. Initially your program should provide for 100 throws. Modify	Q
Q	it for 200 and then 500 throws. Finally make it more flexible by	Q
Q	allowing a user of the program to determine how many tosses he	Q
Q	wants.						Q
Q 3. Find the probability that a random number RND(1) will be less than	Q
Q	a chosen number P. $(0 < P < 1)$			Q
Q 4. Use random numbers as pointers to an array of 10 items which you	Q
Q	want placed in random order.				Q
Q 5. Select 10 items at random from a list of 100.			Q
Q 6. Graph the expectation of likelihood for:			Q
Q	(a) RND					Q
Q	(b) RND + RND					Q
Q	(c) RND − RND					Q
Q							Q
Q Q Q Q Q Q Q Q Q Q Q Q Q Q Q Q Q Q Q Q Q Q Q Q Q Q Q Q Q Q Q

CHAPTER 14

Design of programs

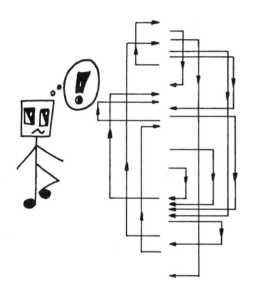

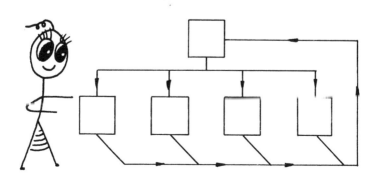

14.1 INTRODUCTION

A mere five years or so after completion, hundreds of houses in Britain have been rendered uninhabitable due to condensation problems. Somewhere the designers didn't do their homework thoroughly! Or can we perchance blame it on the modern design-aid they surely used — the computer?

No! This would be unfair, for behind every bit of computer hardware, and every line of program (the software), is at least one human being!

Now, none of us enjoys being wrong, especially not when the wrong affects and disrupts the lives of hundreds of people as in the case just cited. It is of vital importance that program designs are as near to perfect as is humanly possible. By the laws of probability and chance there will be some reading this book whose future work using computers will significantly affect the lives of hundreds, if not thousands, of people. Could it be you? Even if you are not in this category, remember, there is satisfaction in any job well done! To end right why not begin right?

If you have worked your way through earlier chapters you will have already met some of the guides to good programming practice! These are amplified (and summarised!) below. For a more thorough look at these principles consult: *Guide To Good Programming Practice* edited by Brian Meek and Patricia Heath. (Ellis Horwood, 1980)

14.2 TWELVE GOLDEN RULES FOR GOOD PROGRAM DESIGN
(not necessarily in order of importance)

Rule No. 1 Make sure you **understand the problem** fully before attempting to write a program. (Too obvious? Too frequently side-stepped.) Whatever the size of the project you're programming for, first **take a complete look at the project as a whole**. This is an essential step for realistic program writing.

Rule No. 2 **Analyse the requirements of the problem.** It may be appropriate to use a language other than BASIC, for example an ALGOL, FORTRAN or PASCAL.

Rule No. 3
Stop and **THINK**
and **THINK** again!

This is the most golden rule!

Rule No. 4 Use **available literature** for background reading to the problem.

Rule No. 5 **Find out whether or not known methods exist** for solving your problem or whether in fact a suitable program exists. There could be a **package** that will do most, if not all, you want done, or a **process** that can be slotted into your program. On the other hand, you may have to **start writing from scratch**. There is, to borrow from current jargon, 'not much point in re-inventing the wheel!'

Rule No. 6 **Develop a step-by-step set of instructions** to describe how tasks may be performed. (The jargon-word for this is algorithm.)

Rule No. 7 **Don't try and be clever!** A simple method where it will do is far superior to a complicated one!

Rule No. 8 **Avoid**, as far as possible, **spaghetti-junction-type programs** by using as few 'jumps' as you can get away with, simple loops, segmentation, e.g. program processes, and recursuion (see chapter 15, Sorting) where appropriate.

Rule No. 9 Use **meaningful variable names** (identifiers).

Rule No. 10 Use **REMarks** whenever relevant.

Rule No. 11 **A program must be totally reliable in use.** This implies that every part of the program must do just what is claimed for it. Further, all results must be valid. This does not necessarily mean numerically exact, but numerically valid, that is of sufficient accuracy to satisfy the requirements.

Rule No. 12 **The complete program,** as well as the supporting documentation or other audio-visual aids **must be designed from the point of view of the user**, not from that of the designer.

You may not need to apply all rules rigidly for every program you write. That will depend on the nature and size of the problem. However, establish good habits from the start and you'll never regret it!

As an example of good program design we will now examine program FRAMEMOD of Example 14.1. It is a modified and slightly trimmed down version of a program called FRAME, developed by Frank Pettit of Oxford University Computing Teaching Centre. It has been successfully adapted to run on many different computers in BASIC, FORTRAN IV, ALGOL 60 and PASCAL.

The program is in effect a design strategy for large complex interactive programs. In fact it is useful as an aid to the development of any program involving several distinct processes. It provides, at the very least, a reliable structure.

First here are a few 'jargon words' used in the program.

MACRO – a sequence of commands. In example 14.1 a MACRO may be input while the program is running. The commands contained in the MACRO will then be obeyed by the computer in sequence without further intervention from the keyboard.

PROGRAM PROCESS – a segment of program. Often a process is, in effect, a stand-alone program. As such it can be thoroughly tested in its own right before being included as a process in a larger program.

Figure 14.1 FRAMEMOD LINKAGE DIAGRAM

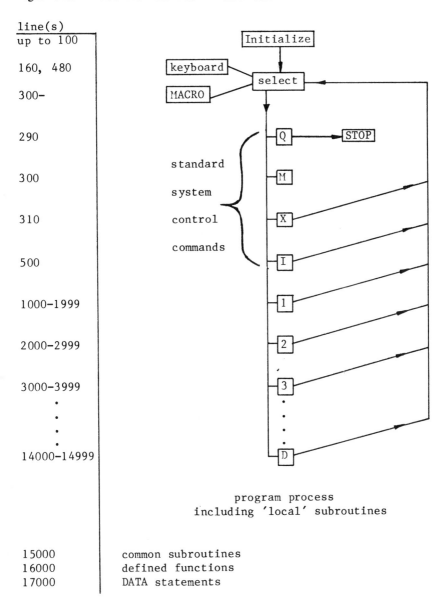

line(s)	
up to 100	
160, 480	
300-	
290	
300	
310	
500	
1000-1999	
2000-2999	
3000-3999	
14000-14999	

program process
including 'local' subroutines

15000	common subroutines
16000	defined functions
17000	DATA statements

Example 14.1 Program FRAMEMOD

```
1 PUT 12                                    :REM clears screen; cursor bottom LH
2 ?"This is ";
4 ?"program  FRAMEMOD"                       :REM change name to suit program
5 ?"Type  I  for instructions"
8 CLEAR 200
100 REM   FRAME body from here to 500 ........................................
110 L$="QMXI1234567890ABCD"                  :REM Command letters  -  use CAPITALS
120 M$="I1234567890ABCD"                     :REM initial (default) macro
130 M8=1:M9=0                                :REM M9 pointer to macro-process
160 ?"What next ";                           :REM letter of NEXT instruction
170 ON M8 GOTO 480,320                       :REM M8=1 process selected fr. keybd.
175 REM                                           M8=2 process selected fr. MACRO
180    FOR N9=1 TO LEN(L$)
190      IF LEFT$(K$,1)=MID$(L$,N9,1) THEN GOTO 210 :REM next process identified
200    NEXT N9
210 REM
250 ON N9 GOTO 290,300,310,500               :REM Next process selected
260 ON N9-4 GOTO 1000,2000,3000,4000,5000,6000,7000
270 ON N9-11 GOTO 8000,9000,10000,11000,12000,13000,14000
280 GOTO 160
290 STOP                                     :REM Quit
300 ?"Your MACRO please";:INPUT M$:M9=0      :REM sequence for your processes   ***
310 M8=2
320 M9=M9+1                                   :REM M9 counts macro commands executed
330 IF M9>LEN(M$) THEN M9=0:M8=1:GOTO170      :REM switch to keyboard as macro ends
340 K$=MID$(M$,M9,1)
350 ?TAB(10);M$                               :REM M$ the 'newly' defined macro
360 ?TAB(M9+9);"^"                            :REM "^" indicates currrent command
470 GOTO 180                                  :REM                              ***
480 INPUT K$                                  :REM single instruction
490 GOTO 180
500 ?CHR$(12):?"USE :-"  :REM ............................................
910 ?"  I  for Instructions"
920 ?"  M  to define a new MACRO"
930 ?"  X  to eXecute current Macro"
940 ?"  Q  to Quit (terminate)"
989 REM                          Insert your own 'processes' from here on
990 GOTO160
1000 ?"PROCESS 1"
1900 GOTO160
2000 ?"PROCESS 2"
2900 GOTO160
3000 ?"PROCESS 3"
3900 GOTO160
4000 ?"PROCESS 4"
4900 GOTO160
5000 ?"PROCESS 5"
5900 GOTO160
6000 ?"PROCESS 6"
6900 GOTO160
7000 ?"PROCESS 7"
7900 GOTO160
8000 ?"PROCESS 8"
8900 GOTO160
9000 ?"PROCESS 9"
9900 GOTO160
10000 ?"PROCESS 0"
10900 GOTO160
11000 ?"PROCESS A"
11900 GOTO160
12000 ?"PROCESS B"
12900 GOTO160
13000 ?"PROCESS C"
13900 GOTO160
14000 ?"PROCESS D"
14900 GOTO160
15000 REM   SET COMMON SUBROUTINES HERE
16000 REM   SET DEFINED FUNCTIONS HERE
17000 REM   DATA STATEMENTS HERE
20000 END
```

```
RUN

This is program  FRAMEMOD
Type  I  for instructions
What next ? I

USE  :-
  I   for Instructions
  M   to define a new MACRO
  X   to eXecute current Macro
  Q   to Quit (terminate)
What next ? m
What next ? i
What next ? m
What next ? M
Your MACRO please? 1234Q
          1234Q
              ^

PROCESS 1
What next 1234Q
              ^

PROCESS 2
What next 1234Q
              ^

PROCESS 3
What next 1234Q
              ^

PROCESS 4
What next 1234Q
              ^


Interrupted at line 290
Ready:
```

Note

In the MACRO and COMMAND lists capital letters were used. The computer therefore 'ignores' such 'non-instructions' as the m and i given here.
Got it ?

Isn't it clever?

It works its way through a sequence without any human assistance!

A conclusion: Upper and lowercase characters ARE distinct to the computer!

The following table is helpful when planning the insertion of program processes. The 'process-identifiers' (1, 2, 3, . . . D) are the same symbols used to activate the commands when using the program of Example 14.1. The processes named below are those inserted into program TRIVIA, Example 14.2.

Figure 14.2 Planning table

Process	Purpose	New name
1	Read in data	R
2	Graph the 'RAW' data	G
3		
4		
5		
6		
7		
8		
9		
A		
B		
C		
D		

Note: The command letters Q M X I are reserved as standard system control commands.

It is advisable to set up table such as the one above from the start. Keep a list of the variable names together with a full description of their function. This can prevent considerable confusion later on.

We will now insert two trivial processes to demonstrate just how easy it is to use this framework.

The Purpose of the new program called TRIVIA is:
1. to READ up to 100 numbers into array D. Include RESTORE to allow the DATA to be read as often as the process is entered.
2. to give a rough histogram-type picture of the 'raw' data.

The steps below outline a method of approach to the modification.

Step	Line number	Action
1	1000–1899	The READ–DATA process R inserted
2	2000–2899	The GRAPH process G inserted
3	510, 520	Update instruction list
4	110, 120	Update command letters and MACRO
5	20	Initialise the DATA array
6	4	Change program name

Follow these steps through in Example 14.2.

Example 14.2 Program TRIVIA

```
1 PUT 12                                :REM clears screen; cursor bottom LH
2 ?"This is ";
4 ?"program  TRIVIA"
5 ?"Type  I  for instructions"
8 CLEAR 200
20 DIM D(100)                           :REM Data-array
100 REM   FRAME body from here to 500 ........................................
110 L$="QMXIRG34567890ABCD"             :REM Command letters  -  use CAPITALS
120 M$="IRG34567890ABCD"                :REM initial (default) macro
130 M8=1:M9=0                           :REM M9 pointer to macro-process
160 ?"What next ";                      :REM letter of NEXT instruction
170 ON M8 GOTO 480,320                  :REM M8=1 process selected fr. keybd.
175 REM                                      M8=2 process selected fr. MACRO
180   FOR N9=1 TO LEN(L$)
190   IF LEFT$(K$,1)=MID$(L$,N9,1) THEN GOTO 210 :REM next process identified
200   NEXT N9
210 REM
250 ON N9 GOTO 290,300,310,500          :REM Next process selected
260 ON N9-4 GOTO 1000,2000,3000,4000,5000,6000,7000
270 ON N9-11 GOTO 8000,9000,10000,11000,12000,13000,14000
280 GOTO 160
290 STOP                                :REM Quit
300 ?"Your MACRO please";:INPUT M$:M9=0 :REM sequence for your processes  ***
310 M8=2
320 M9=M9+1                             :REM M9 counts macro commands executed
330 IF M9>LEN(M$) THEN M9=0:M8=1:GOTO170 :REM switch to keyboard as macro ends
340 K$=MID$(M$,M9,1)
350 ?TAB(10);M$                         :REM M$ the 'newly' defined macro
360 ?TAB(M9+9);"^"                      :REM "^" indicates currrent command
470 GOTO 180                            :REM                              ***
480 INPUT K$                            :REM single instruction
490 GOTO 180
500 ?CHR$(12):?"USE :-"  :REM ........................................
510 ?"  R  to Read numbers"
520 ?"  G  to Graph data"
910 ?"  I  for Instructions"
920 ?"  M  to define a new MACRO"
930 ?"  X  to eXecute current Macro"
940 ?"  Q  to Quit (terminate)
```

```
989 REM                                 Insert your own 'processes' from here on
990 GOTO160
1000 ?"Read in data  "                  :REM (PROCESS R)
1001 ?"------------"
1005 RESTORE 17010                      :REM This ensures "sufficient" data
1020   FOR N = 1 TO 100
1030   READ D(N)
1040   IF D(N) < 0 THEN 1055
1050   NEXT N
1055 T1 = N - 1
1060 ?T1;" numbers are now in array D"
1070 ?"..............................."
1900 GOTO160
```

```
2000 ?"Graphical Rep. of 'RAW' data"        :REM (PROCESS G)
2009 ?"--------------------------------"
2010    FOR N = 1 TO T1
2015    ?D(N);TAB(7);
2020       FOR J = 1 TO D(N)
2030         ?"=";
2040       NEXT J
2050    ?
2060    NEXT N
2070 ?"--------------------------------"
2900 GOTO160
3000 ?"PROCESS 3"
3900 GOTO160
- - - -
= = = =
17000 REM   DATA STATEMENTS HERE
17010 DATA  4, 5, 16, 2, 7, 10, 9, 8
17020 DATA -1
20000 END
```

Note: The unused processes, omitted in this listing, are as those in example 14.1.
The **underlined** statements are those which have been inserted or altered.

```
RUN
This is program  TRIVIA
Type   I  for instructions
What next ? I

USE :-
   R  to Read numbers
   G  to Graph data
   I  for Instructions
   M  to define a new MACRO
   X  to eXecute current Macro
   Q  to Quit (terminate)
What next ? 123
What next ? M
Your MACRO please? 4RGQ
           4RGQ
           ^
PROCESS 4
What next 4RGQ
          ^
Read in data
------------
   8  numbers are now in array D
..............................
What next 4RGQ
          ^
Graphical Rep. of 'RAW' data
--------------------------------
   4    ====
   5    =====
  16    ================
   2    ==
   7    =======
  10    ==========
   9    =========
   8    ========
--------------------------------
What next 4RGQ
          ^

Interrupted at line 290
Ready:
```

Only the first character
following the 'What next'
is checked by the program.
This is because it is a
single command.

However '1' is not a
recognised process name
and therefore is ignored.
Once again the prompt:

'What next ?'

is displayed.

The following are the records as kept in 'developing' TRIVIA.

14.3 DATA ORGANISATION

Arrays

Name	Size	Purpose	Referenced by Process
D	100	to store 'RAW' data	D (data read in)

Variables

Name	Initial value	Purpose	Used in process
N	1	loop-control for reading in data	D
T1	N-1	number of values in array D	D, G

14.3.1 Use LVAR in command mode to find values of variables at the end of a RUN.
LVAR typed in command mode gives the current value of variables at the end of any RUN. The example of this command below was given after RUNning TRIVIA.

```
RUN
This is program   TRIVIA
Type  I  for instructions
What  next ? M
Your  MACRO please? 9DG
              9DG
              ^
PROCESS 9
What next 9DG
          ^
PROCESS D
What next 9DG
          ^
Graphical Rep. of 'RAW' data
-------------------------------
  0     =
-------------------------------
What next ? Q

Interrupted at line 290
Ready:
LVAR
L$="QMXIRG34567890ABCD"
M$="9DG"
M8= 1
M9= 0
K$="Q"
N9= 1
N= 2
J= 2

Ready:
```

Another example based on **FRAMEMOD** is Example 18.1, the INDEX program.

14.4

Q Q Q Q Q Q Q Q Q Q Q Q Q Q Q Q Q Q Q Q Q Q Q Q Q Q Q Q Q Q Q Q

Q   PROBLEMS   Q

Q

Q 1. Include other processes in Example 14.2. For example

Q   (a) Scan the data for bad values, e.g. any item outside of 3 standard

Q   deviations of the set.

Q   (b) Correct the bad data.

Q   (c) Search for the largest and smallest numbers in the data.

Q   (d) Calculate a scaling factor.

Q   (e) Scale and graph the data.

Q 2. Use FRAMEMOD for a problem of your own.

Q   Edit out all irrelevant REMarks.

Q Q Q Q Q Q Q Q Q Q Q Q Q Q Q Q Q Q Q Q Q Q Q Q Q Q Q Q Q Q Q Q

CHAPTER 15
Sorting

15.1 INTRODUCTION

Sorting is the process of comparing and rearranging records in a file. It is one of the most frequently performed tasks in the business world. For example, surnames of customers are arranged in alphabetical order, lists are prepared based on account numbers, and some firms distribute product lists ordered according to consumer prices.

Sorting is used to arrange items into ascending or descending order, or the non-numeric equivalent. Numerical sorts are frequently used in, for example, the world of science and sociology. Word sorts, essential in the making and updating of an index, catalogue, or dictionary, are vital tools in libraries and hospitals, to mention only two of the many applications.

The aim of this chapter is to introduce some of the sorting techniques in use today. Much has been written on the subject. Those who require further information should consult the references for this chapter in the Appendix.

Sorting methods are varied in complexity and efficiency. When choosing a sort care should be taken to weigh up factors such as the effectiveness of the algorithm with relation to the length and state of the list.

The fundamental components of any sort are:

(a) The selection of items for comparison
(b) The comparison of these items
(c) The change of 'misplaced' items.

Differences between sorting methods are a result of variations in the combination of these components.

Two categories of sorting techniques are presented in this chapter as indicated below:

(a) **Numeric Lists**
    1. Double list sort.
    2. Bubble (or Ripple) Sort.
    3. Exchange Sort.
    4. Shuttle Sort.
    5. Shell Sort.
    6. Quicksort.

(b) **Numeric Tables and Alphanumeric Lists**
    7. Vector Sort.
    8. Ranking.
    9. Derandomizer.
    10. Word-list (Index) Sort.

15.2 NUMERIC LISTS

15.2.1 Double-list Sort

Method: (On sorting into ascending order)   N   S

(i)   (ii)

(i) Store numbers to be sorted into array N.

(ii) Set up a second array, S, the same size as N.

(iii) Search for the lowest, (or "next lowest"),   S
number in N and enter it into the "next"
position in S.

(iii)

(iv) **A problem** arises when N contains two or more   N
numbers of equal value.
A solution lies in replacing each next-lowest value
in N by a number the program recognises as
irrelevant. In this case 999 would do.

(after 'round-1')

Comment

This sort is seldom used because of the double amount of storage capacity
required. It can also be very costly on time. See example 15.1.

Example 15.1 Program NUMSORT

```
100 REM                    program NUMSORT
110 REM
120 REM    D O U B L E - L I S T   S O R T
130 REM
140 REM    Original list is read into   N
150 REM    Sorted list is arranged in   S
160 REM
170 DIM N(10), S(10)
175   FOR I = 1 TO 10
180   READ N(I)
185   NEXT I
190   FOR I = 1 TO 10
200   LET L = 999
210     FOR V = 1 TO 10
215     IF L < N(V) THEN 230
220     L = N(V)
230     NEXT V
240   LET S(I) = L
250     FOR P = 1 TO 10
260     IF N(P) = L THEN 280
270     NEXT P
280   LET N(P) = 999
290   NEXT I
300 PRINT " N", " S"
310 PRINT
320   FOR Q = 1 TO 10
330   PRINT N(Q), S(Q)
340   NEXT Q
350 DATA 2, 3, 4, 5, 7, 2, 9, 4, 4, 1
360 END
RUN
```

N	S
999	1
999	2
999	2
999	3
999	4
999	4
999	4
999	5
999	7
999	9

Ready:

15.2.2 Bubble (or Ripple) Sort

Method: (Arranging a list into descending order)

N

5
-1
7
-3
7
1
0

(i) Store the numbers to be sorted in N.

(ii) Compare adjacent elements and exchange if
necessary. After a single scan of the list a partial
sort has been achieved. The lowest number is in
the correct position.

N

5
7
-1
7
1
0
-3

(iii) The next scan can be shortened by omitting the
final, correctly positioned, item. Each successive
scan of the list is one shorter than the previous scan.
The length of a scan is controlled by an end-pointer.

N

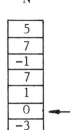

5
7
-1
7
1
0
-3

scan-2 stops
at indicated
pointer level.

(iv) The program should cater for extremes. The list
could, for example, be in the best or the worst
possible order. It would be advantageous to leave
the sort as soon as it has been completed. To do
this a 'flag', (any variable), is set at the start of
each scan, in this case to 0 (zero). When an
exchange is made, the flag is set to 1. If no
exchanges are made in a complete scan the
flag remains at 0.

At the end of each complete   N
scan there is a test for:

$$\boxed{\quad 0 \quad}$$

'flag $= 0$'

If 'flag $= 1$' the sort is repeated.
If 'flag $= 0$' the task has been completed.

N
5
−1
7
−3
7
1
0

F

$$\boxed{\quad 1 \quad}$$

Comment
This sort is very commonly used. On reasonably small sets, (up to about 200
numbers), it is good.
   A Bubble Sort is used in Chapter 8.

15.2.3 Exchange Sort

Method (for ascending order)

(i) Scan list E for the lowest number and exchange   E
   it with the first.

8
9
1
2
7

(ii) Shorten the list by one each time as indicated.

1 ←		1		1		1
9		2 ←		2		2
8		8		7 ←		7
2		9		9		8 ←
7		7		8		9

(iii) Repeat until completely sorted.

Comment
The description above fits one of several exchange sorts.

Problem: Write an exchange sort program.

15.2.4 Shuttle Sort – (Modifications on a Bubble Sort)

Method (for ascending order)

(i) Add to the bubble sort by stepping the pointer back after an exchange. Make an exchange if necessary and keep stepping back until no exchange is made but don't drop off the bottom of the list. At this point the 'forward-ripple' starts again. The sort ends naturally when the list is in order.

First list		sorting process						Final list

Comment

The sort terminates naturally without the use of flags. Sometimes the performance is superior to the Bubble sort depending on the state of the list and the algorithm used.

Problem: Write a Shuttle Sort program.

15.2.5 Shell Sorts

Method (for ascending order)

(i) Segment the large list (L) into 'sub-lists'.

L

8
3
1
7
2
5
4
1

(ii) Sort each sub-lists.

3		1		2		1
8		7		5		4

(iii) Merge the sorted sub-lists.

L

1
1
2
3
4
5
7
8

Comment

There are dozens of algorithms for Shell sorts. Some require there to be 2^n elements in the list. A list can be 'padded' out to the required size. The reason for segmenting the list is to reduce the time taken to complete the sort. Shell sorts are amongst the most efficient and are widely used, particularly on large data sets.

Example 15.2 illustrated the type of Shell Sort which does not require 2^n elements in a list. The number of elements to be sorted is read (line 120), and currently is 10, (line 500). To facilitate an understanding of the process involved, a trace of the sort is embodied in the program.

Example 15.2 Program CSHELLS (ascending order)

```
100 REM              program    CSHELLS   (ascending order)
110 DIM V(500)
120 READ Q  :PRINT Q; "number to be sorted:  ";
160    FOR I = 1 TO Q
170    READ V(I): PRINT V(I);
180    NEXT I
190 PRINT
200 PRINT
210 PRINT TAB(19);"*** TRACE OF SORT   ***"
230 PRINT " Q"; TAB(11); "G"; TAB(21); "I"; TAB(31); "J";
240 PRINT TAB(41);' "K"; TAB(51); "V(J)"; TAB(61); "V(K)"
250 PRINT "--------------------------------------------------------------"
260 PRINT Q; TAB(10);                            :REM Trace
265 REM             THE  S H E L L S O R T
270 LET G = Q
280 LET G = INT(G / 2)                           :REM Divide list into 2
290 PRINT TAB(10); G;                            :REM Trace
300 IF G = 0 THEN 440                            :REM Test for sorted list
310    FOR I = G + 1 TO Q
320       FOR J = I - G TO 1 STEP -G             :REM I and J select
330       LET K = J + G                          :REM items for comparison
340       PRINT TAB(20); I; TAB(30); J; TAB(40); K;   :REM Trace
350       PRINT TAB(50); V(J); TAB(60); V(K)     :REM Trace
360       IF V(J) <= V(K) THEN 420
370       LET T = V(J)
380       LET V(J) = V(K)
390       LET V(K) = T
400       PRINT TAB(53); "EXCHANGE"              :REM Trace
410       NEXT J
420    NEXT I
430 GOTO  280                                    :REM To sort shell
440 PRINT
450 PRINT "List after SHELL Sort  ";
470    FOR K = 1 TO Q
480    PRINT V(K);
490    NEXT K
500 DATA 10
510 DATA 2, 0, 3, 5, 1, 4, 7, 8, 9, 6
580 END
```

```
RUN
10 number to be sorted:     2   0   3   5   1   4   7   8   9   6
```

```
                        ***  TRACE OF SORT  ***
```

Q	G	I	J	K	V(J)	V(K)
10	5	6	1	6	2	4
		7	2	7	0	7
		8	3	8	3	8
		9	4	9	5	9
		10	5	10	1	6
	2	3	1	3	2	3
		4	2	4	0	5
		5	3	5	3	1
					EXCHANGE	
		5	1	3	2	1
					EXCHANGE	
		6	4	6	5	4
					EXCHANGE	
		6	2	4	0	4
		7	5	7	3	7
		8	6	8	5	8
		9	7	9	7	9
		10	8	10	8	6
					EXCHANGE	
		10	6	8	5	6
	1	2	1	2	1	0
					EXCHANGE	
		3	2	3	1	2
		4	3	4	2	4
		5	4	5	4	3
					EXCHANGE	
		5	3	4	2	3
		6	5	6	4	5
		7	6	7	5	7
		8	7	8	7	6
					EXCHANGE	
		8	6	7	5	6
		9	8	9	7	9
		10	9	10	9	8
					EXCHANGE	
		10	8	9	7	8
	0					

```
List after SHELL Sort    0  1  2  3  4  5  6  7  8  9
Ready:
```

15.2.6 Quicksort

Method (for ascending order) see example 15.3.

(i) Generate (or read into array K)   N numbers.

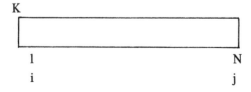

(ii) Set up two pointers i and j such that i=1 and j=N initially.

(iii) Compare K_i and K_j

    If no exchange is necessary j=j−1

        Repeat the process until an exchange occurs.

    At this point i=i+1

        Continue comparing and increasing i until an exchange occurs.

    j is again decreased at this point, and continues, as before, to decrease as long as no exchanges are made.

    Repeat the process until i=j. (This point is sometimes referred to as the pivot point (P).)

    The original list has thus been partitioned so that all numbers less than Kp lie to it's 'left' and those greater than Kp to it's 'right'.

    This partitioning of the list results in two smaller sublists which can be sorted in a similar way.

(iv) Apply the same technique to each sublist.

    At the end of each stage put the latest 'pivot-pointer' (P_L) on the stack.

    (**Stack**: A stack is a list of elements with access at only one end — the top. A stack is sometimes called a LIFO, a Last In First Out list).

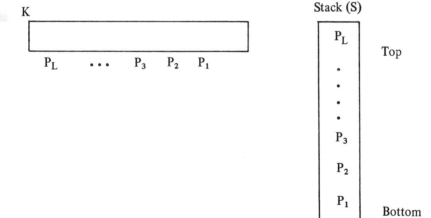

Comment

The Quicksort algorithm, originally developed by Professor C. A. R. Hoare, is based on a strategy different from those used in the sort-programs thus far examined. The results of each comparison are used to determine which items are to be compared next.

At a given stage, all comparisons are made against a specified, (determined) pivot. At the end of each stage the 'pivot' is either stored in the stack and a new pivot found, or the next pivot to be used is fetched off the stack.

Quicksort is particularly efficient on large sets of data. Many variations on the original algorithm currently exist.

In Example 15.3 the process sort may be defined as 'determine a pivot point and sort'.

This can be expressed directly in a recursive language such as Algol. In BASIC it is necessary to build your own stack.

Using this method the stack can never contain more than about $\log_2 N$ entries.

Example 15.3 Program TOOQUICK (QUICKSORT)

```
100 REM            PROGRAM    T O O Q U I C K      (QUICKSORT)
110 DIM K(100), S(50)
115   FOR I = 1 TO 50:  LET S(I) = 0: NEXT I
140 PRINT "INITIAL SEQUENCE:"
150 LET N = 17        : REM   N   Quantity of numbers
160   FOR P = 1 TO N
170   LET K(P) = INT(RND(1) * 100) : PRINT K(P);
190   NEXT P
200 PRINT
280 J = N             : REM   J   POINTER to second item in a comparison
285 S(1) = N          : REM   S   THE STACK
290 LET Z = 2         : REM   Z   STACK POINTER
300 LET I =  1        : REM   I   Pointer to first item in a comparison
310 LET F = I         : REM   F   Holds the First item in a sort sequence
320 LET G = 1         : REM   G   A GATE
330 IF I = J THEN 460
340 IF K(I) <= K(J) THEN 400
360 LET T = K(I) : LET K(I) = K(J) : LET K(J) = T  :  REM  The exchange
390 LET G = -G             : REM   Gate change after exchange
400 IF G > 0 THEN 430
410 LET I = I + 1
420 GOTO  440
430 LET J = J - 1
440 IF I <> J THEN 340
450 LET I = F
460 REM            PUSH SEQUENCE
470 LET S(Z) = J : LET Z = Z + 1
490 IF J <> F THEN 310
500 REM            POP SEQUENCE
510 LET Z = Z - 1
520 LET I = S(Z) + 1 : LET F = S(Z) + 1 : LET J = S(Z - 1)
535 REM ----------: TEST FOR COMPLETION  :------------------
540 IF I = N THEN 570
550 IF I = J THEN 500
560 GOTO  320
570 PRINT "SORTED SEQUENCE:"
580   FOR L = 0 TO N : PRINT K(L); : NEXT L
610 END
```

```
RUN

INITIAL SEQUENCE:
 74  28  56   2   5  75  79  47   0  46  60  71  74  84  65  26  51
SORTED SEQUENCE:
  0   0   2   5  26  28  46  47  51  56  60  65  71  74  74  75  79  84
Ready:
```

15.2.6.1 To Use or to Modify Program TOOQUICK

1. Type TOOQUICK into your computer.
2. 150   insert your own value for N. If you want more than 100 numbers, modify

   110   so that K( ) indicates the maximum number you require.
          RUN the program.
3. If you want to sort your own data change 170 to READ K(P). Insert your data lines from say, 590.
   RUN the program.
4. To investigate the movement of numbers as the sort proceeds include relevant trace-statements. For example:

   335 PRINT I, J, K(I), K(J)

   or insert the words "PUSH" and "POP" to indicate to the user when the stack is activated.

15.3 NUMERIC TABLES and ALPHANUMERIC LISTS

The Sorting Methods outlined so far can be extended to act on more than one list. Sorting may be performed on several lists or tables, or on combinations of strings and numbers.

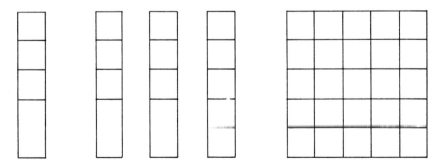

A new approach to sorting is necessary.

15.3.1 Vector Sort (Line number references are to example 15.4)
The Vector Sort provides a valid and suitable method for sorting on multiple lists or tables.

Method

(i) Set up a 'new' vector V, of the same length, L, as that of the lists, (A, B and C).

A	B	C	V
7	2	9	
9	9	1	
1	7	3	
5	4	4	
8	9	1	
3	5	2	

(ii) Fill V sequentially with integers 1 to L to be used as pointers to the rows (row reference numbers).

V

V
1
2
3
·4
5
6

(iii) Choose a list, say A, and sort it (a Bubble Sort is used in the example), into ascending order. Instead of rearranging the items in A when their order needs changing, rearrange the row reference numbers in V. (See lines 320-350)

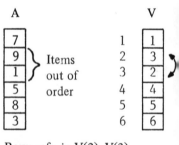

Rows refs. in V(2), V(3) are exchanged.

Note: A is always referred to via V.

(iv) Continue until V holds in sequence the row numbers of the sorted list.

(v) The list A is ordered via reference to the sorted vector (V) and B and C may be ordered on the basis of A's order.

Comment

It is relatively simple to exchange items in the integer vector. On the other hand exchanging the data items would be complex and costly, particularly in the case of large tables. When all items in a row would have to be changed on the bases of 'ordering' one column. In a vector sort the data is never reordered. An ordered list is produced via the pointer vector. Thus the Vector Sort is very efficient.

Example 15.4 Program CVECTOR

```
100 REM                         PROGRAM      C V E C T O R
120 DIM A(10), B(10), C(10), V(10)
125   FOR I = 1 TO 10
130   READ A(I),B(I),C(I)
135   NEXT I
160 PRINT "BUBBLE / VECTOR  S O R T  ON   A   (ASCENDING ORDER)"
170 PRINT "--------------------------------" : PRINT
190 PRINT "ORIGINAL POINTERS IN  V"; TAB(32);
200   FOR N = 1 TO 10
210   LET V(N) = N
220   PRINT V(N);
230   NEXT N
240 PRINT : PRINT
260 PRINT "TRACING THE MOVEMENT OF POINTERS:  "
290 LET F = 0 :REM-----------START OF SORT-----------
300 LET X = 9
310   FOR N = 1 TO X
320   IF A(V(N)) <= A(V(N + 1)) THEN 370
330   LET T = V(N)
340   LET V(N) = V(N + 1)
350   LET V(N + 1) = T
360   LET F = 1
370   NEXT N
380 PRINT TAB(32);
390   FOR I = 1 TO 10 : PRINT V(I); : NEXT I
420 PRINT
430 LET X = X - 1
440 IF F = 1 THEN 290
450 PRINT
460 PRINT "ORIGINAL A" , "SORTED A"
470 PRINT
480   FOR J = 1 TO 10 : PRINT A(J), A(V(J)) : NEXT J
510 PRINT
530 PRINT TAB(21); "ORIGINAL DATA TABLE"; "          REARRANGED TABLE"
540 PRINT
550   FOR N = 1 TO 10
560   PRINT TAB(32);
570   PRINT A(N); B(N); C(N);"          "; A(V(N)); B(V(N)); C(V(N))
580   NEXT N
590 DATA 2, 8, 3, 9, 5, 8, 4, 3, 5, 6, 1, 2, 9, 2, 6
600 DATA 6, 6, 3, 8, 1, 9, 1, 3, 1, 5, 6, 4, 3, 7, 2
610 END
```

RUN
BUBBLE / VECTOR S O R T ON A   (ASCENDING ORDER)

ORIGINAL POINTERS IN V   1 2 3 4 5 6 7 8 9 10

TRACING THE MOVEMENT OF POINTERS:

1	3	4	2	6	7	8	9	10	5
1	3	4	6	7	8	9	10	2	5
1	3	4	6	8	9	10	7	2	5
1	3	4	8	9	10	6	7	2	5
1	3	8	9	10	4	6	7	2	5
1	8	3	10	9	4	6	7	2	5
8	1	10	3	9	4	6	7	2	5
8	1	10	3	9	4	6	7	2	5

ORIGINAL A   SORTED A

ORIGINAL A	SORTED A
2	1
9	2
4	3
6	4
9	5
6	6
8	6
1	8
5	9
3	9

ORIGINAL DATA TABLE   REARRANGED TABLE

ORIGINAL DATA TABLE			REARRANGED TABLE		
2	8	3	1	3	1
9	5	8	2	8	3
4	3	5	3	7	2
6	1	2	4	3	5
9	2	6	5	6	4
6	6	3	6	1	2
8	1	9	6	6	3
1	3	1	8	1	9
5	6	4	9	5	8
3	7	2	9	2	6

Ready:

15.3.2 Ranking
(References are to Example 15.5)
Ranking is the assigning of symbols or 'position-indicators' to each item in an ordered list.

Method

	A		R
(i) A contains X ordered numbers. Fill Rank Vector R with integers 1 to X.	3	1	1
	3	2	2
	4	.	3
	7	.	4
	7		5
	7		6
	.		.
		.	
	9	X	X

	A	R
(ii) Search A for identical items, (line 290). Record the 'average position' of all such groups of items, in relevant positions in R, (lines 260–400).	3	1.5
	3	1.5
	4	3
	7	5
	7	5
	7	5
	.	.
	.	.
	9	X

Comment
Ranking may follow any sort. It is frequently used in conjunction with a vector sort. The numbers in R can easily be converted to symbols, or to integers, as required.

Ranking may also be done in terms of number groupings, rather than on actual values. For example: $N < 30$, $31 < N < 50$ and $N > 51$.

A typical use for ranking is in class scores.

Example 15.5 Program CRANKY

```
100 REM                              program     C R A N K Y
120 REM    12 ordered numbers are read into A.    Rank Order  is
130 REM    found and recorded in R.- - - - - - - - - - - - - - -
150 DIM A(12), R(12)
155   FOR I = 1 TO 12 : READ A (I) : NEXT I
170   FOR I = 1 TO 12 : LET R(I) = I : NEXT I
260 LET K = 1                :REM  K - A count of equal items
270   FOR N = 1 TO 11        :REM  N - Pointer to items in A
280   LET F = N              :REM  F - Position in A of first of equal items
285   LET T = N              :REM  T - Sum of reference numbers of equal items
290   IF A(N) <> A(N + 1) THEN 370
300   LET K = K + 1
310   LET T = T + (N + 1)
320   LET N = N + 1
330   IF N > 11 THEN 370
340   GOTO   290
370   LET P = T / K          :REM  P - Average position of equal items - the ra
380     FOR X = F TO N
390     LET R(X) = P
400     NEXT X
410   LET K = 1
420   NEXT N
440 PRINT " A", "RANK"
460   FOR N = 1 TO 12 : PRINT A(N), R(N) : NEXT N
490 DATA 2, 3, 3, 4, 5, 6, 7, 7, 7, 7, 8, 9
500 END
RUN
```

A	RANK
2	1
3	2.5
3	2.5
4	4
5	5
6	6
7	8.5
7	8.5
7	8.5
7	8.5
8	11
9	12

Ready:

15.3.3 Derandomizer

The relative efficiency and behaviour of the sorts so far considered are well known.

The 'cost' of a sort partly depends on the number of comparisons and exchanges which have to be made in order to complete the task.

The number of exchanges made is dependent on the sorting algorithm and on the state of the list. Efficiency is maximised by exchanging items furthest apart. A method offered by Frank Pettit of Oxford University uses a Random sort until a specified measure of 'order' is indicated, at which point a conventional sort is used to complete the process.

Note on a Random Walk: Two random numbers are used to point to the positions of two items in a list. The selected items are compared and exchanged if necessary. A third (and successive) random 'pointer' is used together with the last of the previous pair to select two items for comparison, etc.

The Derandomiser method: (references are to Example 15.6). A Random Walk Sort is used to select elements, at random, for comparison and if necessary exchange, in a given list. (Refer to lines 150-330 and the program RUN)

$$9 \quad 2 \quad 5 \quad \boxed{8} \quad 1 \quad 6 \quad 2 \quad 4 \quad 4 \quad 6 \quad 5 \quad 7 \quad 0$$

$$1 \quad 1 \quad 1 \quad 4 \quad 3 \quad 8 \quad \boxed{7} \quad 6 \quad 7 \quad 7 \quad 9 \quad 4 \quad 5$$

Determine the level of 'order' in the list, after each complete scan through it. This may be done for example, by calculating the ratio, R, of the number of exchanges to the number of tests per scan. A fully sorted list will always give R = 0. This does not necessarily indicate a fully sorted list, but one scan of the list in which no exchanges have been made.

When the level of 'order' reaches a predetermined point, say .2, the program takes up some other sort to complete the process. (lines 600-720)

Example 15.6 Program CRNDSHUT

```
1 REM   Random walk sort (descending order)   program    C R N D S H U T
50 DIM A(30)            : REM  Fill A with random numbers
60    FOR N = 1 TO 30 : LET A(N) = INT(RND(1)* 100) : NEXT N
70 LET F = 0
110 PRINT "Items in  A  in Original Order"
125    FOR P = 1 TO 30
126    PRINT A(P);
127    IF (P + 10) / 10 <> INT((P + 10) / 10) THEN 130 ELSE  PRINT
130    NEXT P
180 REM   N O T E      Exchange items when that in
210 REM                the lower position is the smaller
216 LET Q = 0
220    FOR M = 1 TO 10
230    LET L = 1
240      FOR H = 1 TO 30
250      LET J = INT(RND(1) * 30 + 1)
252      IF J < L THEN 260
255      IF A(J) <= A(L) THEN 310
257      GOTO 280
260      IF A(L) <= A(J) THEN 310
280      LET W = A(J)
290      LET A(J) = A(L)
300      LET A(L) = W
305      LET Q = Q + 1
310      LET L = J
320      NEXT H
330    NEXT M
340 PRINT
350 PRINT "----Items in  A  after Partial Sorting----"
370    FOR Z = 0 TO 2
380      FOR Y = 1 TO 10 : PRINT A(Y + (10 * Z)); : NEXT Y : PRINT
420    NEXT Z
430 PRINT
432 PRINT Q; "  Exchanges made in  10  scans" : PRINT : PRINT
445 GOSUB   600
447 PRINT : PRINT :IF F = 1 THEN 800
450 PRINT "--O---  A-items in Worst Order   ---O--"
480    FOR C = 1 TO 30 : LET A(C) = C : NEXT C
510 LET F = 1
520 GOTO   125
599 STOP
600 REM                       Subroutine Shuttle Sort
601 LET Q1 = 0
610    FOR L = 2 TO 30
620    IF A(L) <= A(L - 1) THEN 700
640    LET W = A(L) : LET A(L) = A(L - 1) : LET A(L - 1) = W : REM Exchange
675    IF L - 2 < 2 THEN L=2                       : REM Now shuttle
680    IF L -2  > 30 THEN L = 30
685    IF L-2 ? 30 THEN L = L-2
690    LET Q1 = Q1 + 1
700    NEXT L
710 PRINT "Shuttle completes sort in "; Q1; "exchanges"
720 RETURN
800 END
```

```
          Bubble Sort
230    FOR L = 2 TO 30
240    IF A(L) < = A(L-1) THEN 310
250    REM                 Exchange
252    IF J < L THEN 260
255    IF A(J) <= A(L) THEN 310
257    GOTO 280
260    LET W = A(L)
270    LET A(L) = A(L-1)
280    LET A(L-1) = W
290    LET Q = Q + 1
300    LET A(L) = W
305    LET Q = Q + 1
310    NEXT L
```

```
RUN
Items in  A  in Original Order
74  28  56   2   5  75  79  47   0  46
60  71  74  84  65  26  51  94   3  15
94  72  53  49  62  56  97  27  39  90

----Items in  A  after Partial Sorting----
94  90  97  84  74  79  75  74  72  94
60  51  65  53  71  56  28  56  62  49
47  27  15   0  26  39  46   5   2   3

62   Exchanges made in  10  scans


Shuttle completes sort in  77 exchanges


--0---  A-items in Worst Order  ---0--
 1   2   3   4   5   6   7   8   9  10
11  12  13  14  15  16  17  18  19  20
21  22  23  24  25  26  27  28  29  30

----Items in  A  after Partial Sorting----
27  30  29  28  24  21  25  26  23  20
13  17  22  19  16  18  15   7  12  11
 6   8  14   9   5   2   4  10   1   3

67   Exchanges made in  10  scans


Shuttle completes sort in  44 exchanges


Ready:
```

```
RUN
Exchanges made in bubble sort on A
Items in  A  in Original Order
74  28  56   2   5  75  79  47   0  46
60  71  74  84  65  26  51  94   3  15
94  72  53  49  62  56  97  27  39  90

----Items in  A  after Partial Sorting----
79  75  74  84  74  71  65  94  60  56
94  72  53  51  62  56  97  49  47  90
46  39  28  27  26  15   5   3   2   0

362   Exchanges made in  10  scans


Shuttle completes sort in  90 exchanges


--0--   A-items in Worst Order   ---0--
 1   2   3   4   5   6   7   8   9  10
11  12  13  14  15  16  17  18  19  20
21  22  23  24  25  26  27  28  29  30

----Items in  A  after Partial Sorting----
11  12  13  14  15  16  17  18  19  20
21  22  23  24  25  26  27  28  29  30
10   9   8   7   6   5   4   3   2   1

490   Exchanges made in  10  scans


Shuttle completes sort in  190 exchanges


Ready:
```

Comment

It is difficult to make generalisations when comparing the efficiency of different sorts. There are many contributory factors. In particular, variations in the length of a list, and the relative order of its elements, cause changes in the efficiency of a sort.

In Example 15.6, it is impossible to make any meaningful deductions from a comparison of the results in the RUNs. The 30 item sample is very small, and the number of test runs too few. Other tests have shown the Random Walk Sort to be most efficient on large sets of 'highly disordered' items. It is for this reason that a second sort is used after a certain measure of order has been reached.

15.3.4 Word-List Sorts

Word lists are sorted using the same methods as for numeric sorts. On large amounts of string data it is advisable to use a vector sort. This is because it takes the computer less time to exchange numbers.

An example of a word sort is to be found in the INDEX, Program BOOKINDX, Example 18.1.

15.4

Q Q Q Q Q Q Q Q Q Q Q Q Q Q Q Q Q Q Q Q Q Q Q Q Q Q Q Q Q Q Q
Q PROBLEMS Q
Q Q
Q 1. Generate 50 random numbers in the range 100 to 500 inclusive. Q
Q Store these numbers in array R. PRINT the numbers generated. Q
Q 2. SORT the numbers in R in two stages: (Ascending order) Q
Q (a) **Use a Random Sort** Q
Q *At each stage of the sort use two new randoms as pointers to Q
Q values in R. Exchange if necessary. Q
Q *Continue the sort in this manner until 10 successive comparisons Q
Q fail to result in an exchange. Q
Q *PRINT this partly sorted list. Q
Q *PRINT the number of comparisons which have been made. Q
Q *Examine the two lists and determine how many numbers have Q
Q changed place. Can you account for these exchanges? Q
Q (b) Complete the Sort by another method; for example, use a *ripple* Q
Q *sort.* Q
Q Q
Q *PRINT the sorted numbers. Q
Q Q
Q *Note:* Q
Q The Random Sort suggested above is called a RANDOM LEAP ABOUT. Q
Q Instead, a RANDOM WALK could have been used. Explain the differ- Q
Q ence between these two methods. Q
Q Q Q Q Q Q Q Q Q Q Q Q Q Q Q Q Q Q Q Q Q Q Q Q Q Q Q Q Q Q Q Q

CHAPTER 16

Simulation
and Modelling

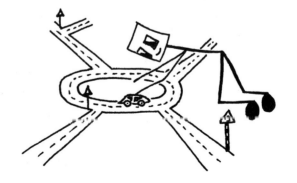

16.1 SIMULATION

It is sometimes desirable to simulate or imitate processes from real life. For example, when designing business systems the program should simulate the business activities.

Simulation always involves using a model or models, and data, plus control in time. Models are many and varied. They are used, for example, in the training of pilots, (flight simulation), and medical students, (diagnosis and prognosis). Models are also used by environmentalists (pollution control, erosion investigations etc., where the compression of time is involved), and in a growing number of other fields.

Processes are dependent on the outcome of chance events. Thus in BASIC we use RND, the random number function, as a tool in simulation.

Another vital tool is that of transformation. This involves rethinking and reframing a problem from a human way of thinking, into one that is economical and convenient for a computer to work on. In the pages that follow an aspect of transformation is used in the simulation of a game of Snakes and Ladders.

The game, though not the most stimulating of computer games, has never the less been chosen because of its simplicity in providing a clear example of transformation.

16.2 SIMULATING a game of SNAKES and LADDERS

Figure 16.1

25	24	23	22	21
16	17	18	19	20
15	14	13	12	11
6	7	8	9	10
5	4	3	2	1

6.2.1 Definition and Rules

1. This game is played on a 5 by 5 board numbered as shown.
2. Two snakes and two ladders are to be placed on the board.
3. One or more players may play.
4. **Start** is off the board.
5. Players take it in turns to throw a dice and move the number of squares indicated.
6. A throw of 6 gives the player a free throw.
7. A player who lands on a snake's mouth slides down to it's tail.
8. Landing at the foot of a ladder lifts a player to it's top.
9. **Finish** is reached only when a player's dice-throw causes him to land on the winning square. If the winning-post is overshot he remains where he is and waits for his next turn.
10. The first player to reach square 25 is **the winner**.

16.2.2 Approaching the Problem

Obviously the simulation must match the definitions and rules of the game. Each facet of the game can be represented by a program process or module as illustrated in the table below.

Step	Human Process	Program Processor Module	Result
Throw dice	Dice thrown	Simulation of a throw using RND function	A number, N value 1 to 6
Move N squares on board	Move is made	Position of new square calculated	Player moves N positions
Check square	State of square is checked	State of square is checked	Ladder found
Move	Move up ladder	New position at ladder top adopted	Player at top of ladder

etc.

There is great advantage in programming each facet of the game as a separate module (or 'self-contained' segment of a program). These can then be linked together to form an easily modifiable whole. This method ensures that each module is easily understood, easily checkable, and far more likely to be error-free.

A Suggestion

With this approach in mind try formulating your own ideas on simulating the game. Write a program and test it for reliability under a wide set of conditions. Compare your program with that set out on the pages which follow. Start by writing a program to cater for the requirements of **stage 1** as described next.

The simulation of a game of snakes and ladders as set out below has been developed in two stages.

Stage 1   * Game for one player
             * No free throw for a six offered
             * Player may elect to play another game

Stage 2   * Game for up to ten players
             * A free throw given for each six thrown
             * The 'board' is displayed at the beginning of a RUN

Suitable prompts and messages should be built in for all aspects of play. In programming **stage 1** care should be taken to ensure that the program can be easily modified to suit the conditions for **stage 2**.

16.2.3 Stage 1 Possible program modules are:

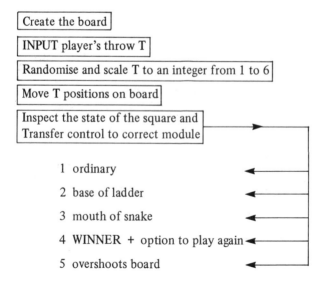

| Create the board |

| INPUT player's throw T |

| Randomise and scale T to an integer from 1 to 6 |

| Move T positions on board |

| Inspect the state of the square and Transfer control to correct module |

1 ordinary

2 base of ladder

3 mouth of snake

4 WINNER + option to play again

5 overshoots board

16.2.4 Transforming the Problem

Before a problem is transformed it must be clearly defined and understood in it's existing form. The first task in this case is to complete the board design, i.e. position the two snakes and two ladders.

Figure 16.2

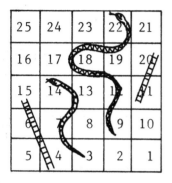

The next step is to trace the route through the board. It's threadlike nature is soon obvious. (Fig. 16.3)

If this is compared with a 5 by 5 array (Fig. 16.4), which is not sequential, the difficulties of mapping, one to one, board to an array in the program, become apparent.

Is there an obvious transformation?

Figure 16.3

25	24	23	22	21
16	17	18	18	20
15	14	13	12	11
6	7	8	9	10
5	4	3	2	1

Why? Yes there is! If the 'thread' is held at either end and 'pulled', the route through the board becomes a straight line.

Hence an apparent solution is to transform the board into a linear board, and in the program It will be mapped onto a linear vector.

Figure 16.4

A	1	2	3	4	5
1	1, 1	1, 2	1, 3	1, 4	1, 5
2	2, 1	2, 2	2, 3	2, 4	2, 5
3	3, 1	3, 2	3, 3	3, 4	3, 5
4	4, 1	4, 2	4, 3	4, 4	4, 5
5	5, 1	5, 2	5, 3	5, 4	5, 5

The Linear Board

| 1 | 2 | 3 | 4 | 5 | | 25 |

The board shown above allows for a one to one mapping of the squares on the square board to the squares on the linear board. To deal with the 'overshoot' conditions in the end game, however, the board needs to be extended by 5 squares. (See page 243 for a description of the program modules).

The Extended Board

| 1 | 2 | 3 | 4 | 5 | | 25 | 26 | 30 |

The state of each square is defined according to:

    1 ordinary   2 ladder   3 snake   4 winner   5 overshoot

In the program this information is stored in array A.

A 1 2 3 4 5   11   14   22   25 26   30

| 1 | 1 | 1 | 2 | 1 | | 2 | | 3 | | | 3 | 1 | | 4 | 5 | 5 | | 5 |

Another array, B, is used to store the end points of the Snakes and Ladders; All squares not corresponding to a snake or ladder have the value 0.

B 1 2 3 4 5   11   14   22   25 26   30

| 0 | 0 | 0 | 15 | 0 | | 20 | | 2 | | | 9 | | 0 | 0 | 0 | | 0 |

The program tool used in processing this information is the computed GOTO. It is in fact the *pivot* line of the program as can be seen in line 430 of Program LADSNAKE.

Example 16.1 Program LADSNAKE

```
100 REM           Program       LADSNAKE
110 PRINT"Play a game of Snakes and Ladders"
120 PRINT"          -------S-------"
130 PRINT "Enter any number for your 'dice throw'"
140 PRINT "which randomised gives a number in the range 1 to 6"
150 DIM A(30),B(30)
160   FOR I =  1 TO 30
170   A(I) = 1  :LET B(I) = 0
180   NEXT I
200 LET A(14) = 3  :LET A(22) = 3 : REM      Snakes
210 LET B(14) = 2  :LET B(22) = 9
230 LET A(4) = 2  :LET A(11) = 2  : REM      Ladders
240 LET B(4) = 15  :LET B(11) = 20
255 LET P = 0  :LET C = 0            : REM      Past-post numbers
260   FOR N = 26 TO 30 : LET A(N) = 5 : NEXT N
300 LET A(25) = 4               : REM      Winning Square
310 LET P = 0  :LET C = 0
330   INPUT "    T H R O W";T
350   FOR K = 1 TO T             : REM      Randomize throw
360   LET Y = RND(1)
370   NEXT K
380 LET R = INT(6*RND(1)+1)
390 PRINT "Your throw of ";R;
410 LET C = C + 1  :LET P = P + R : REM      Throw counter
430 ON A(P) GOTO 440,460,490,520,590
440 PRINT "    Lands you on square ";P
450 GOTO 330
460 LET P = B(P)
470 PRINT "Sends you up the ladder to square ";P
480 GOTO 330
490 LET P = B(P)
500 PRINT "  Slides you down the snake to ";P
510 GOTO 330
520 PRINT "And you're the WINNER !!!"
530 PRINT "in ";C;" moves"
540 PRINT
550 INPUT "To play again type    1";Y
570 IF Y <> 1 THEN 640
580 GOTO 310
590 PRINT "Makes you overshoot the winning post !"
600 PRINT "try again !! "
610 LET P = P-R
620 GOTO 330
630 PRINT
640 PRINT "Good Day !!"
650 END
```

Creating
the
board

Determing
the next
move

PIVOT Line

The
PROCESSORS

```
RUN
Play a game of Snakes and Ladders
        -------S-------
Enter any number for your 'dice throw'
which randomised gives a number in the range 1 to 6
    T H R O W? 1
Your throw of  2      Lands you on square  2
    T H R O W? 7
Your throw of  3      Lands you on square  5
    T H R O W? 5
Your throw of  2      Lands you on square  7
    T H R O W? 6
Your throw of  4 Sends you up the ladder to square  20
    T H R O W? 90
Your throw of  3      Lands you on square  23
    T H R O W? 2
Your throw of  6 Makes you overshoot the winning post !
try again !!
    T H R O W? 4
Your throw of  2 And you're the WINNER ! ! !
in  7  moves

To play again type     1? 2
Good Day ! !

Ready:
```

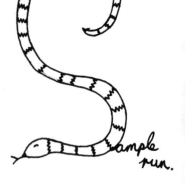

Note:

The number INPUT by the player appears on the VDU screen but not on this printed page. This is due to the design of the software. It is inconsequential for the game.

   LADSNAKE is just one of many ways of writing a program to simulate a game of Snakes and Ladders. The two diagrams which follow show the flow of program control at the 'pivot' point, or at the main decision point where the state of a square is discovered. Figure 16.5 illustrates LADSNAKE line 480 and following.

Figure 16.5 Program Modules

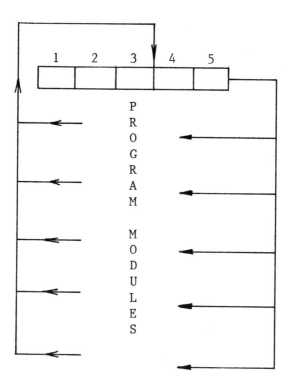

The state of a square immediately determines which program module is to be entered. One decision only is to be made. At the end of a module control is redirected to the relevant line of the program. This method, using the computed GOTO, has much to commend it. It is neat and efficient and makes for easily understandable programs.

In contrast, the flowchart illustrates the awkwardness of the method of using multiple IF-THEN statements. (Fig. 16.6)

Instead of the state of a square being determined by a single statement, the multiple IF-THEN method may result in up to four tests being made for any one square. Also, such a program is not easily modifiable. Try to modify it to meet the requirements of **stage 2** and compare its flexibility with that of the computed GO TO program.

Figure 16.6 An Illustration of Awkwardness

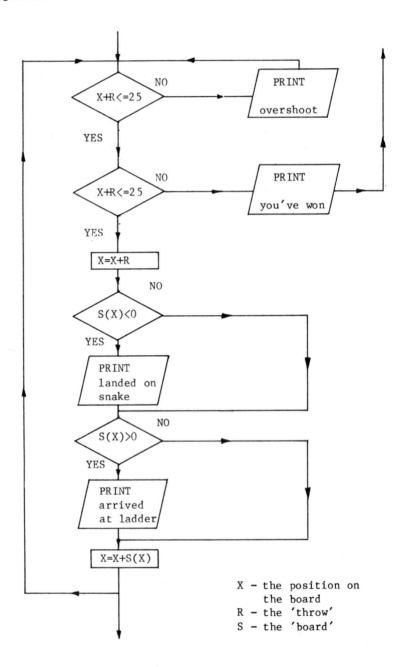

X – the position on
    the board
R – the 'throw'
S – the 'board'

16.2.5 Stage 2 Modifications to Stage 1

Of the three modifications to the game suggested for stage 2,

1. Display the board
2. A free throw for each six
3. Up to ten players may play together

only the third requires a little more than superficial thought.

1. The board can be programmed as a free-standing module. (LADSNAWB lines 180-400)
2. The free throw (LADSNAWB line 730) is given if the test for 'throw' = 6 is true. (line 980). The test is made at the end of the group of program processors.
3. For ten or less players a change must be made to the simple variables:

> P players
> C throw counter

These must become P(10) C(10) (line 140)

The section from LADSNAKE (130-620), throw of dice to arriving on the new square, must be repeated as many times as there are players. In LADSNAWB this is achieved by the inclusion of a FOR-NEXT loop, (lines 690-990).

The extended program is now complete.

Example 16.2 Program LADSNAWB

```
100 REM       Program       LADSNAWB
110 REM
120 PRINT" Play a game of Snakes and Ladders for many players"
130 DIM R$(31)
140 DIM A(30),B(30),P(10),C(10)
150   FOR N = 1 TO 16
160   READ R$  :PRINT R$
170   NEXT N
180 PRINT
190 PRINT "Snakes ($) and Ladders (= OR /-/)"
200 PRINT "Board appears once only. Type  R  when ready to play."
210 INPUT R$
220 IF R$ <> "R" THEN 200
230 DATA "-------------------------------"
240 DATA "! 25  ! 24  ! 23  ! 22 $! 21  !"
250 DATA "!     !     !     !    $ !     !"
260 DATA "!-------------------$-----------!"
270 DATA "! 16  ! 17  ! 18  ! $9  ! 20/-!"
280 DATA "!     !     !     !  $  ! /-/!"
290 DATA "!-------------------$---/-/-!"
300 DATA "! 15 =! 14  ! 13  ! 12$ !/-/  !"
310 DATA "!   = $ !     !    $ !-/   !"
320 DATA "!------=--$-!------------$-----!"
330 DATA "! 6   ! =  $ 8  ! 9 $! 10  !"
340 DATA "!     ! = $    !   $ !     !"
350 DATA "!----------=--$----------------!"
360 DATA "! 5   ! 4  =! $   ! 2   ! 1   !"
370 DATA "!     !     !  $ !    !     !"
380 DATA "-------------------------------"
410 PRINT "Maximum number of players is   10"
420 PRINT "A 'throw ' is any number (N)  of player's choice"
430 PRINT "N is randomised and scaled to a value from 1 to  6"
440   FOR I = 1 TO 30
450   B(I) = 0
460   NEXT I
480 LET A(22) = 3  :LET A(14) = A(22)  : REM       Snakes
490 LET B(14) = 2  :LET B(22) = 9
510 LET A(11) = 2  :LET A(4) = A(11)  : REM       Ladders
520 LET B(4) = 15  :LET B(11) = 20
530 REM                              Past-post numbers
540   FOR N = 26 TO 30 : LET A(N) = 5 : NEXT N
```

```
580 LET A(25) = 4                          : REM        Winner
590    FOR N = 1 TO 10
600    LET P(N) = 0  :LET C(N) = 0
610    NEXT N
620 INPUT "How many will play this game";H
630 IF H <= 10 THEN 660
640 PRINT " Instructions say    max 10 players "
650 GOTO   620
660 PRINT
670 PRINT "  Game for "; H; " players"
680 REM        *************************************************
690    FOR X = 1 TO H
700    PRINT
710    PRINT " Player "; X; ", on square"; P(X); ", throw please";
720    GOTO  740
730    PRINT"         A free throw for player";X;
740    INPUT T
760      FOR K = 1 TO T                    : REM    Randomise throw
770      LET Y = RND(1)
780      NEXT K
790    LET R = INT(6 * RND(1) + 1)
800    PRINT "            Your throw of "; R;
820    LET C(X) = C(X) + 1  :LET P(X) = P(X) + R  : REM  C - Throw counter
830    ON A(P(X)) GOTO 840, 860, 890, 920, 960
840    PRINT " lands you on "; P(X)
850    GOTO   980
860    LET P(X) = B(P(X))
870    PRINT " sends you up a ladder to  "; P(X)
880    GOTO   980
890    LET P(X) = B(P(X))
900    PRINT " slides you down  snake to "; P(X)
910    GOTO   980
920    PRINT "  and you've won in  "; C(X); "moves"
930    PRINT
940    PRINT " To play again    type    1    ";
950    GOTO  1020
960    PRINT "overshoots  -  try next round"
970    LET P(X) = P(X) - R
980    IF R = 6 THEN 730
990 NEXT X
1000 REM        *************************************************
1010 GOTO   690
1020 INPUT Y                              :REM  To play or not to play again
1040 PRINT
1050 IF Y <> 1 THEN 1080
1060 GOTO   590
1080 PRINT "    Good Day !"
1090 END
```

```
RUN
Play a game of Snakes and Ladders for many players
--------------------------------
! 25  ! 24  ! 23  ! 22 $! 21   !
!     !     !     !    $ !      !
!-------------------$----------!
! 16  ! 17  ! 18  ! $9  ! 20/-!
!     !     !     !  $  ! /-/!
!--------------------$---/-/-!
! 15 =! 14  ! 13  ! 12$ !/-/  !
!    = $ !     !    $ !-/   !
!------=-$-!-----------$-----!
! 6   ! =  $ 8  ! 9  $! 10   !
!     !  = $    !    $ !      !
!---------=--$--------------!
! 5   ! 4  =! $    ! 2   ! 1    !
!     !    !  $ !     !      !
--------------------------------
```

Snakes ($) and Ladders (= OR /-/)
Board appears once only. Type R when ready to play.
? R
Maximum number of players is   10
A 'throw' is any number (N) of player's choice
N is randomised and scaled to a value from 1 to 6
How many will play this game? 2

    Game for 2 players

    Player 1 , on square 0 , throw please? 5
                Your throw of 5 lands you on 5

    Player 2 , on square 0 , throw please? 4
                Your throw of 4 sends you up a ladder to   15

    Player 1 , on square 5 , throw please? 6
                Your throw of 6 sends you up a ladder to   20
            A free throw for player 1 ? 6
                Your throw of 4 lands you on 24

    Player 2 , on square 15 , throw please? 5
                Your throw of 3 lands you on 18

    Player 1 , on square 24 , throw please? 8
                Your throw of 1 and you've won in   4 moves

To play again   type   1   ? 9

    Good Day !

Ready:
```
```

16.3

QQQQQQQQQQQQQQQQQQQQQQQQQQQQQQQQQQQ

Other MODIFICATIONS to Make

1. Alter the program to calculate the mean number of 'throws'-to-win per 100 games.
2. If you have RANDOMIZE in your BASIC use this to simplify the dice throw section of the program.
3. Make it possible within the program to randomly alter the positions of the snakes and ladders on the board.
4. Design an optimum board. For example the average game should not be over too quickly whilst not being boringly slow.
5. Make the necessary changes to the program to enable a player to see the board virtually on request.
6. Why not reprogram this game using High Resolution Graphics to display the board?

You may make your fortune yet on selling your sets of:

Computed Snakes and Ladders ! ! !

Be that as it may, do you see that simulation is a very useful tool in design? The planning of new roads in England is being done with the aid of simulation models. Wallpaper and fabric design are also simulated before production begins. Do you know how the models are designed and used in these cases?

A few suggestions for further simulations:

GAMES: *Mastermind
           *Three-dimensional noughts & crosses
           *Tennis

Simulate playing a set of tennis. Let P be the probability of player number one winning a point. P should be entered as DATA. Over 100 sets determine how the probability of winning a set depends on the probability of winning a point. Repeat for other values of P.

QQQQQQQQQQQQQQQQQQQQQQQQQQQQQQQQQQQ

CHAPTER 17
The computer in statistics

17.1 INTRODUCTION: WARNING AGAINST RASH INTERPRETATIONS OF COMPUTER RESULTS

Why have you turned to this chapter? Is it perchance because you share a common belief that using a computer is the key to all your statistical problems?

The computer **is** frequently an invaluable aid in this realm, but, be warned, the results of statistical computations are not always right. Why is this so? In some cases it is because results are strongly influenced by errors generated resulting from rounding of numbers by the computer.

If you need to analyse data statistically it may be worth your while to first find out whether or not a known and tried program or package exists that will do the job for you. One such package which offers a wide choice of statistical analysis is SPSS (Statistical Package for the Social Sciences). It is not necessary to be conversant with a programming language in order to use this package. In any event it might be well worth your while to consult a statistician before embarking on any major analysis even before collecting the data. It could save you hours!

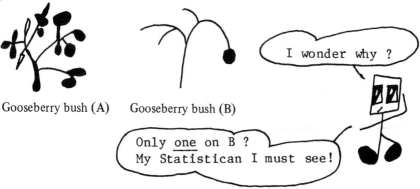

Gooseberry bush (A)   Gooseberry bush (B)

I wonder why ?

Only one on B ?
My Statistican I must see!

If you are using a micro computer as an aid to your statistical analysis you may well come across limitations when handling large amounts of data. This is a good case for using a suitable package if one is available to you.

This chapter is not a comprehensive guide to computing in statistics. Neither does it aim to teach statistics in one easy lesson. Courses and books abound on the subject, and those interested in improving their expertise are encouraged to consult these. Some references are given in the appendix.

The aim of this chapter is rather to warn against rash interpretations of computer results for two main reasons. First, under certain conditions, the computer generates arithmetical errors. Program BEWARE, Example 17.1 demonstrates a 'classic error' resulting from the rounding of numbers by the computer. It also points to some ways in which the computer is useful in statistical analysis of data.

Example 17.1 Program BEWARE

```
100 REM                    program BEWARE
110 DIM A(500)   :REM Modified version of $BEWARE by Frank Pettit
120 ?"  A DEMONSTRATION OF ARITHMETICAL ERRORS"
130 ?"IN THE CALCULATION OF MEAN AND STANDARD DEVIATION"
140 ?"Two methods are used:-"
150 ?"1. based on   mean of sqs - sq of means"
160 ?"2. based on   sq of diffs from mean"
170 ?"-----------------------------------------"
180 INPUT "Pick a centre value ";C
190 INPUT "and a quantity";K
200 IF K < 1 THEN K = 1            :REM Quantities outside range 1-500
210 IF K > 500 THEN K = 500        :REM   are included on the boundary
220   FOR N = 1 TO K               :REM Values in A generated by RND
230   LET A(N) = C + RND(1) - RND(1)  :REM   around the centre value C.
240   NEXT N                       :REM Consult chap.13 on random nos.
250 REM ..................... METHOD 1 ............................
260 T = 0   :T2 = 0
270   FOR N = 1 TO K
280   T = T + A(N)                 :REM T - sum of the numbers
290   T2 = T2 + A(N)^2             :REM T2 - sum of nos. squared
300   NEXT N
310 M = T/K                        :REM M - mean of the numbers
320 VAR = T2/K - M*M               :REM VARiance-mean of SQS-SQ of means
330 IF VAR > 0 THEN 360
340 ?"Using Method 1. variance is negative. Method 2. gives:- "
350 GOTO 390
360 S1 = SQR(VAR)
370 ?"MEAN is ";M;TAB(20); "STD DVN is";S1
380 REM .....................METHOD 2 ............................
390 T3 = 0                         :REM T3 - sum of sqs of diffs fr.mean
400 REM T - sum           and         M - mean are as for method 1
410   FOR N = 1 TO K
420   T3 = T3 + (A(N) - M)^2
430   NEXT N
440 M2 = T3/K                      :REM M2 - mean of (diffs fr M)↑2
450 S2 = SQR(M2)
460 ?"MEAN is ";M;TAB(20); "STD DVN is";S2
470 ?"-----------------------------------------"
480 INPUT "Will you try another case? -- Y/N --";A$
490 IF LEFT$(A$,1)="Y" OR LEFT$(A$,1)="y" THEN 180
500 ?"-----------------------------------------"
510 ?"      W A R N I N G    !!!"
515 ?"      ------------------"
520 ?"      Do not use either of these methods with high valued numbers"
530 ?"      or numbers of accuracy of more than about 4 decimal digits."
540 ?"      For such data rather use a method of FALSE MEANS.   Consult"
550 ?"      one of the references in the appendix or another book.
560 END
```

```
RUN
    A DEMONSTRATION OF ARITHMETICAL ERRORS
IN THE CALCULATION OF MEAN AND STANDARD DEVIATION
Two methods are used:-
1. based on    mean of sqs - sq of means
2. based on    sq of diffs from mean
----------------------------------------
Pick a centre value ? -99
and a quantity? 100
MEAN is -99.0348    STD DVN is .398973
MEAN is -99.0348    STD DVN is .391007
----------------------------------------
Will you try another case? -- Y/N --? y
Pick a centre value ? 1000
and a quantity? 200
MEAN is  1000.03    STD DVN is .661438
MEAN is  1000.03    STD DVN is .405328
----------------------------------------
Will you try another case? -- Y/N --? y
Pick a centre value ? 10000000
and a quantity? 200
Using Method 1. variance is negative. Method 2. gives:-
MEAN is  1E+07      STD DVN is .685566
----------------------------------------
Will you try another case? -- Y/N --? y
Pick a centre value ? .0000009
and a quantity? 200
MEAN is  2.89124E-03 STD DVN is .445121
MEAN is  2.89124E-03 STD DVN is .445121
----------------------------------------
Will you try another case? -- Y/N --? y
Pick a centre value ? 123.99813
and a quantity? 200
MEAN is  123.992     STD DVN is .395285
MEAN is  123.992     STD DVN is .403011
----------------------------------------
Will you try another case? -- Y/N --? n
----------------------------------------
         W A R N I N G    !!!
         --------------------
    Do not use either of these methods with high valued numbers
    or numbers of accuracy of more than about 4 decimal digits.
    For such data rather use a method of FALSE MEANS.  Consult
    one of the references in the appendix or another book.

Ready:
```

Comment

On large sets of numbers errors accumulate faster using method 1 since it is based on squaring the source data. Method 2 produces smaller errors since it is the differences of numbers from the mean which are squared. This is the reason for the variance becoming negative when the centre value is 10000000.

Example A4.6, program MATSTD, in the appendix, demonstrates how statistical calculations can be made much easier when using matrix handling statements. Note, however, that the program does use the non-recommended method for finding the standard deviation when large sets of numbers are involved.

The second warning against rash interpretation of computer results lies in the area of false prediction. As an aid to understanding what is meant by this statement consider the two (absurd) examples below.

1. I've already got two children.
   I'm afraid to have a third because every third child is born Chinese.

2. The government of a country of 50 million people plans to increase average salaries by 100$ a week. It can choose to do this in one of two ways.
   (a) Increase the individual's salary by 100$. The government however reclaims 30$ in tax leaving the wage earner 70$ per week 'real' increase. Total cost to the government is therefore 3500 million dollars.
   (b) Increase the salary of just one individual in the country, say the President, by the equivalent total amount, that is by 5000 million dollars. This too has the effect of raising the 'average' weekly salary by 100$ a week. As super tax rules now apply the President must pay the government 99$ in 100$. The cost to the government in issuing this increase is 50 million dollars. The President's personal gain is 50 million dollars per week, and the 'average' salary rise is 1$ per week.

These ridiculous misapplications of statistics demonstrate the false logic applied to results when not all factors are taken into account. In the second case the 'average' does not reflect the lack of an 'actual' rise in all but one pay packet. Figure 17.1 below illuminates this situation when one extreme outlying point causes a totally wrong impression through falsely raising the average.

Figure 17.1 Illustrating misleading averages

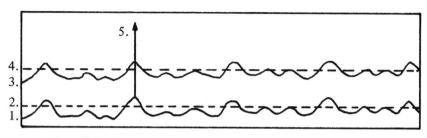

    1.   Old salaries
    2.   Old average
    3.   New salary a)
    4.   New average for cases a) and b)
    5.   New salary for President

Example 17.2 An example with many applications in statistics – the HISTOGRAM

```
100 REM              program  HISTOGRM
110 DIM R(200), V(40)
120 PUT 12 :GRAPH
130 PRINT "Frequency Profile of 200 random numbers"
140 PRINT "One bar represents zone of 3"
150   FOR N = 1 TO 200              :REM generating the numbers
160   R(N) = INT((RND(1)+RND(1))*50)
170   NEXT N
180 PLOT 13, 2, 2 :LINE 13, 59      :REM drawing the axis
190 A = 0
200   FOR Y = 2 TO 59 STEP 6        :REM labelling the Y-axis
210   PLOT 12,Y :PLOT 4,Y,STR$(A) :A=A+1
220   NEXT Y
230 PLOT 13, 2, 2 :LINE 79, 2       :REM drawing the axis
240   FOR X = 13 TO 79 STEP 4       :REM marking the X-axis
250   PLOT X, 1 :NEXT X
260   FOR K = 1 TO 200
270   I = 255
280   P=INT(R(K)/3)
290   IF P/2 = INT(P/2) THEN I = 191  :REM BAR-shade alternator(!)
300   V(P) = V(P) +1
310   DRAW = 15 + P * 2
320   HEIGHT = V(P) * 3
330   IF HEIGHT > 70 THEN 400
340   PLOT DRAW, HEIGHT, I
350     FOR W = 1 TO 20 : NEXT W    :REM WAIT
360   NEXT K
370 A = GET()
380 TEXT
390 GOTO 420
400 REM SUBROUTINE      ERROR MESSAGE
410 PRINT "You've gone off the top !!   So I've stopped !!"
420 END
```

Figure 17.2 Photograph of the RUN of Example 17.2

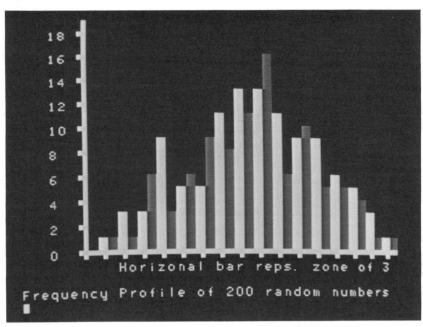

This frequently used and useful visual aid in statistics was produced using low resolution graphics (See Chapter 10).

One other application in statistics is that of RANKING, in chapter 15. See example 15.5, program CRANKY.

This chapter is intentionally brief as those wishing to write statistical programs will, in most cases, have, or have access to, the necessary statistical techniques. With the BASIC language at their fingertips approaching such problems via the computer should be relatively straightforward.

17.2

Q Q Q Q Q Q Q Q Q Q Q Q Q Q Q Q Q Q Q Q Q Q Q Q Q Q Q Q Q Q Q Q Q
Q   PROBLEMS   Q
Q   1. Adapt Example 17.2 in the following ways: Q
Q   (a) DELETE line 160 (for generating the data) and replace it with   Q
Q   relevant READ and DATA statements (or statements to READ   Q
Q   DATA from a file) to suit your own data.   Q
Q   RUN the program.   Q
Q   (b) If necessary increase the quantity of numbers read in (lines 110,   Q
Q   130, 150, 260).   Q
Q   (c) If your data is such that the error message occurs you will need   Q
Q   to introduce a suitable scaling factor.   Q
Q Q Q Q Q Q Q Q Q Q Q Q Q Q Q Q Q Q Q Q Q Q Q Q Q Q Q Q Q Q Q Q Q

CHAPTER 18

Some other applications

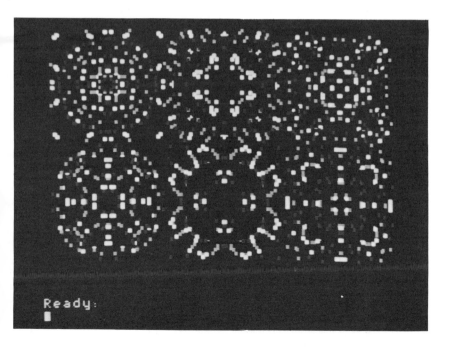

Other applications! These are so many and so varied that choosing a few examples to include in this chapter was no simple task. Just three applications will be considered, namely, compiling an index, (a sorting process), design or pattern generation, and finally, a scientific application in the field of geology.

18.1 THE INDEX PROGRAM

Program BOOKINDX, of example 18.1, is a subset of the one used to produce the INDEX in this book. It is based on FRAMEMOD, example 14.1. In creating an index, the program allows the user first to input a page number and then enter all words on that page required in the index. Words accidentally omitted may be added later and the sets of information merged.

The program can be instructed to write index entries into one of two files. The main file, INDLIST, will normally hold, after the first entries have been made and filed, the already existing index. INDLIST2, a secondary file, is used to collect subsequent entries which may then be appended to the main index.

The best way to understand this program is to RUN it in conjunction with looking at the program listing and instructions. You could type the program in to your computer or better still, if a floppy disk containing the program is available, load it and run it. Try feeding in some 'real data' you want indexed. †

There are many other desirable features required by index-makers not included in this version. If it interests you, follow the suggestions in the problems below, as a start to developing a really useful and versatile program.

Author's note to would be INDEX-makers

Program BOOKINDX requires a large amount of memory space to store the data. It works efficiently in small quantities of data, but on sets larger than, say, 200 items, it is very slow. It runs out of memory space when processing approximately 600 entries.

It is more appropriate when INDEXing large sets of data to enter items via TXED (the TEXT EDITOR) and then submit the file to a different binary tree sort (not in CUB).

---

†   This program is available on floppy 5″ and 8″ floppy disks.
     See References and Further Reading in the appendix.

Example 18.1 Program BOOKINDX

```
1 PUT 12
2 ?"This is ";
4 ?"program  BOOKINDX"                   : REM by Martin Hall
5 ?"Type  I . for instructions"
8 CLEAR 5000
10 QUOTE #10,0:                          : REM Set up for files
20 DIM INDEX$(3000)
30 DEC$ = "*+="                          : REM Mini decision table
100 REM  FRAME body from here to 500 ........................................
110 L$ = "QMXICSL56"                     : REM Command letters  -  use CAPITALS
120 M$ = "ICLS"                          : REM initial (default) macro
130 M8 = 1 : M9 = 0                      : REM M9 pointer to macro-process
160 ?"What next ";                       : REM letter of NEXT instruction
170 ON M8 GOTO 480,320                   : REM M8 = 1 process selected fr. keybd.
175 REM                                       M8 = 2 process selected fr. MACRO
180 FOR N9 = 1 TO LEN(L$)
190 IF LEFT$(K$,1) = MID$(L$,N9,1) THEN GOTO 210 : REM next process identified
200 NEXT N9
210 REM
250 ON N9 GOTO 290,300,310,500           : REM Next process selected
260 ON N9-4 GOTO 1000,2000,3000,4000,5000,6000,7000
270 ON N9-11 GOTO 8000,9000,10000,11000,12000,13000,14000
280 GOTO 160
290 STOP                                 : REM Quit
300 ?"Your MACRO please";:INPUT M$:M9=0  : REM sequence for your processes  ***
310 M8 = 2
320 M9 = M9 + 1                          : REM M9 counts macro commands executed
330 IF M9>LEN(M$) THEN M9=0:M8=1:GOTO170 : REM switch to keyboard as macro ends
340 K$ = MID$(M$,M9,1)
350 ?TAB(10);M$                          : REM M$ the 'newly' defined macro
360 ?TAB(M9+9);"^"                       : REM "^" indicates current command
470 GOTO 180                             : REM
480 INPUT K$                             : REM single instruction
490 GOTO 180
500 ?CHR$(12):?"USE :-"  : REM ....................................................
910 ?"  I  for Instructions"
920 ?"  M  to define a new MACRO"
930 ?"  X  to eXecute current Macro"
940 ?"  Q  to Quit (terminate)
950 ?"  C  to Create an index"
960 ?"  S  to Sort an index"
970 ?"  L  to Look for repeats"
989 REM                          Insert your own 'processes' from here on
990 GOTO 160 : REM------------------------------------------------------------------
```

```
1000 ? "Process C - Creation     Type '**' instead of a page no.to end an index"
1010 ? "                         Type '*' to end a page"
1020 ? "                         Type '+' at the end of an important entry"
1030 ? "                         Type '=' to indicate a sub-heading title"
1040 ? "                         Type '*' to end entries under a sub heading"
1070 INPUT "Page no." ;NUM$                 : REM  Hold page no.
1080 IF NUM$ = "**" THEN 1340               : REM  End of inputting index
1090 IF VAL(NUM$) <= 0 THEN PRINT "Non numeric entry":GOTO 1070
1100 I = I + 1                              : REM  Word counter
1110 INPUT "Word";INDEX$(I)
1120 FOR L = 1 TO LEN(DEC$)                 : REM  Look for control symbol
1130 IF MID$(DEC$,L,1) = RIGHT$(INDEX$(I),1) THEN 1180
1140 NEXT L
1150 IF VAL(INDEX$(I)) <> 0 THEN PRINT "Non alphabetic entry" : GOTO 1110
1160 INDEX$(I) = INDEX$(I) + "-" + NUM$     : REM  Merge word + page no.
1170 GOTO 1100                              : REM  Get new word
1180 ON L GOTO 1190,1210,1240               : REM  Act on control symbol
1190 I = I - 1
1200 GOTO 1070                              : REM  Goto start new page
1210 INDEX$(I) = LEFT$(INDEX$(I),LEN(INDEX$(I))-1) + "-%" + NUM$ + "%"
1220 GOTO 1100                              : REM  1210 marks important page
1240 SCRAT$ = INDEX$(I)                     : REM  Subset title has been inp
1250 INPUT "=>";INDEX$(I)                   : REM  Prompt for sub entries
1260 IF INDEX$(I) = "*" THEN I = I-1 :GOTO 1100: REM  End of subset get new wor
1270 IF RIGHT$(INDEX$,1) = "+" THEN 1320    : REM  Is it an important entry
1280 INDEX$(I)=SCRAT$ + INDEX$(I) + "-" + NUM$
1300 I = I + 1                              : REM  Heading and subset merge
1310 GOTO 1250                              : REM  Get next word of subset
1320 INDEX$(I) = SCRAT$ + LEFT$(INDEX$(I),LEN(INDEX$(I)-1)) + "%-" + NUM$ + %"
1330 GOTO 1250                              : REM  Get next word
1340 I = I + 1                              : REM  Increment word counter
1342 INPUT "Do you wish this file to be the main file(Y/N)";REPLY$
1344 IF ASC(REPLY$) = 89 OR ASC(REPLY$) = 121 THEN REPLY$ = "INDLIST" : GOTO 13
1345 IF ASC(REPLY$) = 78 OR ASC(REPLY$) = 142 THEN REPLY$ = "INDLIST2": GOTO 13
1347 PRINT "Sorry I didn't understand that" : GOTO 1342
1348 GOSUB 15110                            : REM  Write to file
1900 GOTO 160 : REM--------------------------------------------------------
2000 ? "Process S - Sort"
2010 INPUT "Which file do you wish to sort" ; REPLY$
2015 IF REPLY$ = "INDLIST" OR REPLY$ = "INDLIST2" THEN 2030
2020 PRINT "File must be 'INDLIST' or 'INDLIST2'"
2025 GOTO 2010
2030 GOSUB 15000                            : REM  Read from file
```

```
2080 Z = I - 1                                    : REM   Set limit of sort
2090 FOR J = 1 TO Z - 1
2091 A$ = "" : B$ = ""
2092 FOR L=1 TO LEN(INDEX$(J)):A$=A$+CHR$(32 OR ASC(MID$(INDEX$(J),L,1))):NEXT L
2094 FOR L=1 TO LEN(INDEX$(J+1)):B$=B$+CHR$(32 OR ASC(MID$(INDEX$(J+1),L,1))):NEXT L
2100 IF A$ < B$ THEN 2140                         : REM   Swap
2120 SCRAT$ = INDEX$(J) : INDEX$(J) = INDEX$(J+1) : INDEX$(J+1) = SCRAT$
2130 F = 1                                        : REM   Set swap flag
2140 NEXT J
2150 IF F = 0 THEN 2200                           : REM   Test for swap
2160 F = 0 : Z = Z - 1 : GOTO 2090                : REM   Reset and return
2200 GOSUB 15110                                  : REM   Write to file
2900 GOTO 160 : REM--------------------------------------------------------------
3000 ?"Process L - Look for repeats in the main index"
3010 REPLY$ = "INDLIST" : GOSUB 15000             : REM   Read file
3080 FOR J = 1 TO I
3090 SCRAT$ = "" : REPLY$ = ""                    : REM   Clear scratch strings
3095 IF INDEX$(J) = "" THEN 3240
3110 FOR L = 1 TO LEN(INDEX$(J))                  : REM   Get words out
3120 IF MID$(INDEX$(J),L,1) = "-" THEN 3160       : REM   of references
3130 SCRAT$ = SCRAT$ + MID$(INDEX$(J),L,1)        : REM   Put them into
3140 NEXT L                                       : REM   Scratch strings
3160 FOR L = 1 TO LEN(INDEX$(J+1))
3170 IF MID$(INDEX$(J+1),L,1) = "-" THEN 3210
3180 REPLY$ = REPLY$ + MID$(INDEX$(J+1),L,1)
3190 NEXT L
3210 IF REPLY$ <> SCRAT$ THEN 3240                : REM   Compare words
3220 INDEX$(J) = INDEX$(J) + MID$(INDEX$(J+1),LEN(REPLY$) + 1)
3230 INDEX$(J+1) = ""
3240 NEXT J                                       : REM   Combine references
3245 REPLY$ = "INDLIST":GOSUB 15110               : REM   Write to file
3900 GOTO 160 : REM--------------------------------------------------------------
4000 ?"PROCESS 4"
4900 GOTO 160 : REM--------------------------------------------------------------
5000 ?"PROCESS 5"
5900 GOTO 160 : REM--------------------------------------------------------------
6000 ?"PROCESS 6"
6900 GOTO 160 : REM--------------------------------------------------------------
15000 REM   SET COMMON SUBROUTINES HERE.........................................
15020 OPEN #10,REPLY$                             : REM File ready for reading
15030 FOR I = 1 TO 3000
15040 ON EOF GOTO 15070
15050 INPUT #10,INDEX$(I)
15060 NEXT I
15070 CLOSE #10
15080 RETURN : REM..............................................................
15110 ERASE REPLY$
15120 CREATE #10,REPLY$                           : REM File ready for writing
15130 FOR J = 1 TO I
15135 IF INDEX$(J) = "" OR INDEX$(J) = "*" THEN 15150
15140 PRINT #10,INDEX$(J)
15150 NEXT J
15160 CLOSE #10
15170 RETURN : REM..............................................................
20000 END
```

```
RUN
This is program  BOOKINDX
Type  I for instructions
What next ? I

USE :-
  I   for Instructions
  M   to define a new MACRO
  X   to eXecute current Macro
  Q   to Quit (terminate)
  C   to Create an index
  S   to Sort an index
  L   to Look for repeats
What next ? C
Process C - Creation      Type '**' instead of a page no. to end an index
                          Type '*'  to end a page
                          Type '+'  at the end of an important entry
                          Type '='  to indicate a sub-heading title
                          Type '*'  to end entries under a sub heading
Page no.? 2.1
Word? Interactive program
Word? Interactive programming
Word? INPUT
Word? Prompts
Word? *
Page no.? 2.2
Word? Prompts
Word? PRINT
Word? LIST
Word? *
Page no.? 2.4
Word? LIST
Word? PRINTER
Word? INPUT+
Word? *
Page no.? **
Do  you  wish  this file  to be  the main file(Y/N)? Y
What next ? S
Process S - Sort
Which file do you wish to sort? INDLIST
What next ? L
Process L - Look for repeats in the main index
What next ? Q

Interrupted at line 290
Ready:
```

```
INPUT-%2.4%-2.1
Interactive program-2.1
Interactive programming-2.1
LIST-2.2-2.4
PRINT-2.2
PRINTER-2.4
Prompts-2.1-2.2
```

This is a listing of the main index file after a normal run of the program. The main reference to the word 'INPUT' has been marked with '%', this symbol can be used itself as a marker for the main reference or as an indicator for that number to be underlined in the final output.

18.2

Q Q Q Q Q Q Q Q Q Q Q Q Q Q Q Q Q Q Q Q Q Q Q Q Q Q Q Q Q Q Q Q
Q   **PROBLEMS**   Q

1. Write a process to print the contents of either file, INDLIST, or INDLIST2, on request. This process enables the user to check on state of the files at any stage.

2. Develop the program so that INDLIST and INDLIST2 can be merged. The resulting file must be saved in INDLIST. A question to consider before writing this process is: 'Is it better to sort both files before merging them, or to merge the files and then sort?'

3. Index entries are allowed subentries. Write a process to search for such entries and separate the headings from the sub headings indenting these as in the example:

      PROGRAM=design   resulting index: PROGRAM
      PROGRAM=process   design
                                               process

4. Write a process to control the printing out of an INDEX thus developed. Develope this to your own specifications. One suggestion is to start each new letter of the alphabet by first leaving a few blank lines and heading the section with the appropriate letter.

Example: A
                         Algorithm
                         Aardvark
                         Atom

Q Q Q Q Q Q Q Q Q Q Q Q Q Q Q Q Q Q Q Q Q Q Q Q Q Q Q Q Q Q Q Q

18.3 COMPUTER AIDED DESIGN

The second fascinating application is in the area of design. Computer Aided Design is widely used by people such as architects, interior decorators, fabric manufacturers, and others, for generating both plans and patterns. Patterns, for example, can be modified and duplicated until a desirable combination of design and colour is attained. Program DOILYREP, (Example 18.2) is one such pattern generator which could be used by designers. The random start to a pattern for each new RUN of the program gives an almost limitless variety of patterns. Figures 18.1 and 18.2 show one such pattern. In the first figure a single pattern section is shown, whereas the second is the result of duplicating that pattern 5 times.

The program causes 50 random points to be generated. As each point is generated it is reflected and rotated through 360 degrees to give 8 points. The pattern is complete when the fiftieth set of points have been plotted. The pattern is preserved for any one RUN by setting the Random generator to the same start point for each pattern repeat. The simple technique of calling OFFSET makes the task of repeating the pattern really easy. Examine the program for yourself and see if you agree with this statement!

If possible load this program into your computer and watch the fascinating pattern display. Certainly, if you are lacking in ideas for designs for anything from tiles and wall paper to curtains, carpets and doilies(!), you are quite likely to find inspiration here.

18.4

Q Q Q Q Q Q Q Q Q Q Q Q Q Q Q Q Q Q Q Q Q Q Q Q Q Q Q Q Q Q Q Q Q Q Q
Q   Q
Q   PROBLEMS   Q
Q   1. By removing one BASIC statement program DOILYREP will pro-   Q
Q   duce six unique patterns each RUN. Delete the relevant statement Q
Q   and RUN the program.   Q
Q   2. Modify DOILYREP further so that it will RUN 'endlessly'. The ever Q
Q   changing patterns that result will captivate most audiences!! Q
Q   Q
Q Q Q Q Q Q Q Q Q Q Q Q Q Q Q Q Q Q Q Q Q Q Q Q Q Q Q Q Q Q Q Q Q Q Q

Example 18.2 Program DOILYREP

```
100 REM program DOILYREP by Steve Thomas
110 ON BREAK GOTO 420
120 PUT 12
130 CALL "RESOLUTION",0,2
140 RANDOMIZE                        :REM Selects random  start to pattern
150 R=RND(1)
160 N=1
170 FOR O=1 TO 6
180 READ DX,DY
190 CALL "OFFSET",DX,DY
200 JUNK=RND(-R)                      :REM Ensures same pattern each time
210 FOR I=1 TO 50                     :REM X,Y co-ords
220 X=INT(RND(1)*(96-2*N)):Y=INT(RND(1)*(96-2*N))
230 GOSUB 280
240 NEXT I
250 A = GET()                         :REM HALT! after one pattern
260 NEXT O
270 GOTO 420
280 U=95-2*N-X:V=95-2*N-Y
290 REM SUBROUTINE     Reflect/rotate
300 IN=I AND 3
310 A=U+N:B=V+N:GOSUB 400
320 A=V+N:B=U+N:GOSUB 400
330 A=X+N:B=Y+N:GOSUB 400
340 A=Y+N:B=X+N:GOSUB 400
350 A=U+N:B=Y+N:GOSUB 400
360 A=Y+N:B=U+N:GOSUB 400
370 A=V+N:B=X+N:GOSUB 400
380 A=X+N:B=V+N:GOSUB 400
390 RETURN
400 CALL "FILL",A-N,B-N,A+N,B+N,IN
410 RETURN
420 CALL "CLEAR"
430 DATA 0,0,0,-96,-96,0,-96,-96,-192,0,-192,-96
440 END
```

Figure 18.1 First pattern in a RUN of DOILYREP

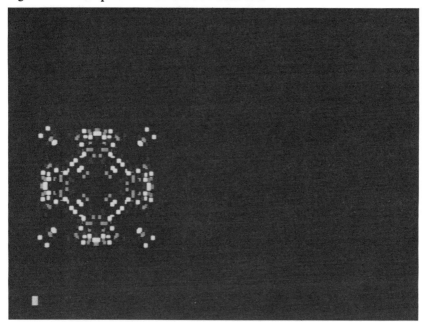

Figure 18.2 Photograph of the completed RUN of DOILYREP

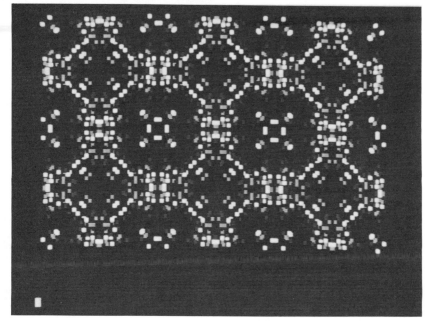

Another example in design is that of the LISSAJOUS figure seen on the cover of this book. It was produced using the program of example 18.3. The pattern is the result of plotting sinusoidal curves at right angles to each other with varying frequencies and phase angles. The 'colourful' effect was produced by plotting squares in XOR mode, (see chapter 10). This enhances the aesthetic appeal at the expense of clarity of the LISSAJOUS figure.

Example 18.3 Program LISS3

```
100 REM   program LISS3  by Steve Thomas
110 CALL "RESOLUTION",1,4
120 N=5
130 M=500
140 P=2*3.14159/M
150 K=3 :J=4
160 RANDOMIZE
170 R=RND(1)
180 FOR O = 1 TO 4
190 READ DX,DY
200 CALL "OFFSET",DX,DY
210 JUNK=RND(-R)
220 FOR A = 1 TO M
230 X=35*COS(K*A*P)+40
240 Y=19*SIN(J*A*P)+24
250 I=32*RND(1)-16
260 GOSUB 300
270 NEXT A
280 NEXT O
290 STOP
300 CALL "FILL",X-N,Y-N,X+N,Y+N,I
310 RETURN
320 DATA 0,0,-80,0,0,-48,-80,-48
330 END
```

18.5 BASIC USED TO CONTROL A MASS SPECTROMETER

The final example of other applications using Interactive BASIC is taken from the Age and Isotope Laboratory in the Department of Geology, our next door neighbour at the University of Oxford. There sophisticated BASIC programs are used to control a mass spectrometer for the isotopic analysis of elements such as strontium (Sr), neodymium (Nd) and lead (Pb), all three of which have important applications in geology for determining the age and the origins of rock samples. Sr, Nd, and Pb isotopic data help geologists to discern whether a rock has crystallized from a melt derived from the earth's upper mantle, or whether it was formed by crystallization of a remelt of old continental crust material.

Figure 18.3 Sketch diagram showing (1) a VG Isomass 54E mass spectrometer with (2) its control console and system monitor, and (3) the Hewlett Packard Microcomputer which controls the instrument.

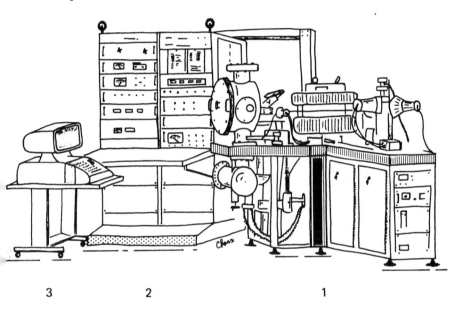

3   2   1

The operation of the mass spectrometer is entirely controlled by a BASIC program. In practice this means that the analysis of up to 16 samples (the maximum capacity of the mass spectrometer) can be made under the complete control of the computer.

The appropriate BASIC program for the analysis of the element concerned is loaded into the computer from a mini-cassette. The programs for Sr, Nd and Pb analysis each occupy approximately 32K of store, but after array declarations most of the 56K available on the computer is required for running the programs.

The computer controls and/or monitors about twenty different functions of the mass spectrometer in addition to collecting, processing and reporting the analytical data. There is a continuous two-way "conversation" between the computer and the mass spectrometer through a multiple interface and system monitor. The computer issues instructions and requests data either for the analysis or in order to take decisions concerning the progress of the run.

Some examples of control instructions would include the order to rotate the turret which contains the 16 samples for analysis to set the selected sample in the analysing position. Each sample is loaded on a filament, and must be heated to approximately 1100 degrees Centigrade for Pb analysis. That is achieved by instruction from the computer to the filament heating current supply unit.

There are, in fact, a host of necessary conditions which must also be controlled and monitored, but this is not a text book on mass spectrometry.

In addition to the controlling function of the computer, there are also monitoring and data-gathering duties. Through the system monitor of the mass spectrometer the computer requests and receives reports on all aspects of the mass spectrometer's operating conditions. Thus such information as the quality of the vacuum in the analysing tube, the stability of the accelerating voltage and the magnetic field strength, the ion beam intensity recorded by the collector system, and the status of the filament in the analysing position (i.e. Has it burnt out?) is frequently sought, assessed and acted upon by the computer.

Decision-making by the computer is a vitally important aspect of automated mass spectrometer analysis, and the development of a program to achieve proper trustworthy computer control necessarily draws on the know-how gained from years of experience in the manual operation of mass spectrometers. One of the main users of the instrument under discussion has said:

"It is difficult to conceive of a more appropriate way of programming than interactive BASIC for this type of application. The need for much testing and trouble-shooting of the programs requires ease of program editing and continuation of execution, because of the difficulties in expressing some very complex decision making processes which a human operator goes through by instinct rather than strict logical deduction. In the particular version of BASIC used on the computer for this application, program execution can be paused, program lines edited, or instructions made to the mass spectrometer from the keyboard prior to the continuing program execution." The computer provides a full printed record of each analysis, including not only the results but the analysing conditions for each set of data, so that any unusual conditions are recorded even when an operator is not present. In addition, the analysis is displayed graphically, so that the stability of a run can be monitored by the operator. Figure 18.4 shows the graphics display for an isotopic analysis of Pb extracted from a cobble in a conglomerate which happens to be the worlds oldest-known sedimentary rock, from Isua, West Greenland.

---

†   See the Glossary in the appendix for unexplained terms.

Figure 18.4 Graphics display of a run of 21 scans over the Mass spectrum of Pb, (lead), measuring the ion beam 6 times in each scan.

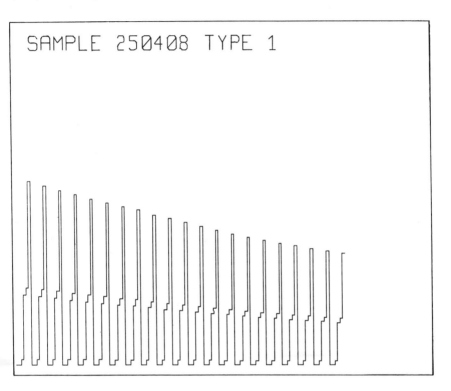

SAMPLE 250408 TYPE 1

The graphics shows a run of 21 scans over the mass spectrum of Pb, measuring the ion beam intensity six times in each scan, twice on the background at atomic mass 203.5, and then 204-Pb, 206-Pb, 207-Pb, 208-Pb. 204-Pb is the least abundant isotope of Pb, and the only one not produced by decay of naturally occurring radio nuclides. 206-Pb in this analysis is less abundant than 207 Pb, though this is an unusual feature characteristic of very old rocks with very low Uranium contents. 208-Pb is, in most natural occurrences, the most abundant isotope of Pb, as seen here.

This analysis represents part of the work to establish the age of the cobbles in the Isua conglomerate at approximately 3770 million years.

18.6 CONCLUSION: THE ADVANCED CAPABILITIES OF BASIC

Obviously an application such as the one above which requires a 32K BASIC program includes many features which cannot be discussed in this brief summary, but even with the sketch outline provided here it should be clear that interactive BASIC has valuable applications in situations involving some very complex interaction between computers and very sophisticated analytical instruments. This is strong evidence to counter that school of thought which denegrates BASIC as a language for beginners only. Certainly the mass spectrometer programs are masterpieces of truly interactive programming.

Variations on a theme

(Some differences in Basics)

Although there is a profusion of dialects in the now well established BASIC language, there is a common core of BASIC words and concepts used by almost all the offshoots of the original language. Words common to most BASICs which have already been defined in this book are, for the most part, not included here. They provide the underlying solid **bass** to the music of the language. Below are some of the words and 'themes' which present the variety.

No attempt has been made to cover all, or even most, of the possible variations. The reader is referred to The BASIC Handbook — An Encyclopedia of the BASIC Language — By David Lien, 1980, (Compusoft Publishing), for a comprehensive list of most words, and variations thereof, in the BASIC language. No references to particular versions of BASIC are given. The manual specific to the BASIC on your computer should be used in conjunction with this book. The reader is especially referred to this when the subject is machine dependent.

Note the meanings of these words in the text below:

none — not included in specification of Minimal BASIC.
same — definition the same as BASICSG.
other BASICs — known variations in other versions of BASIC including some from Tiny BASIC.

RML 380Z BASICSG V 5.0 CUB Chapter References ( )		ANSI Minimal BASIC	Other BASICs

1. Commands, Statements, Functions

DEF	(9)		
DEF FNA(X)		DEF FNA and DEF FNA(X)	DEF FN(X, Y) (two arguments)
single line functions		same	multi line functions
DIM	(4)		
DIM A(10)			
A(0) is first element		A(0) or A(1)	A(1) first element
Total 11 elements			
END	(1, 8)	same	E.
FOR	(4)	same	
the start of a repetition FOR-TO-NEXT loop			under some conditions some computers allow NEXT to be implied
Test for loop termination at end of loop		Test done at beginning	
IF–THEN line no. or statement	(8)	IF . . . THEN line no.	
IF–THEN–ELSE	(8)	none	
INPUT	(2)		I, IN, INP, INKEYS$
INPUT A		same	INPUTL
INPUT "Give ht."; H		none	
INPUT A, A$, B, B$		same	same
LET	(1)		
LET A = B * C		same	LET A=B*C
A = B * C			A=B*C
LVAR	(6, 12)	none	check your manual!
NEW	(1)	SCRATCH	SCRATCH
NEXT	(4)	(see FOR)	(see FOR)
ON X GOTO . . .	(8)	same	GOTO X OF . . .
PRINT	(6)		PRINT USING
PRINT item, item;TAB(n);item		same	(Specifies format) check your manual!
RESTORE	(7)	same	RES
RESTORE n (n-line number)		none	
RETURN	(9)	same	RET
used in conjunction with GOSUB			
RANDOMIZE	(3, 13)	same	RANDOM, RAN, R.
(gives unpredictable start point)			RANDOMISE
RND	(3, 13)	RND	RAND, RANDOM, (see
RND(N)			RANDOMIZE) the effect of the argument differs widely

RML 380Z BASICSG V 5.0 CUB Chapter References	( )	ANSI Minimal BASIC	Other BASICs
RUN RUN 10	(1)	RUN none	RU, R., RUNNH
TAB first column: TAB(0)	(6)	first column: TAB(1)	function missing in some computers

2. *Operators and other Symbols*

: statement separator: allows more than one statement per line	(3)	one statement/line	\ ! ;
↑ raise to power	(3)	**	^ or **
= assignment operator	(8)	same	same
< >	(8)	< >	> < or #
>= or =>	(8)	same	same
<= or =<	(8)	same	same

3. *Language Concepts*

Arrays
  Declaring arrays (see DIM)
  Many dimensions
	(4)	one or two
		dimensions
			check your manual!

Array names
  numeric:
    as for simple variables
  string:
    as for string variables
  For reference to a specific
  element include subscript
  eg. A(7)
	(4)	letter
		
		none
		
		same
			check your manual!
			
			check your manual!
			
			same

File handling	(11)	none	machine dependent
Graphics	(10)	none	a great many variations check your manual!

Line numbers
  range 1–65529
  line length 130 characters
  single or multiple statements/line
	(1)	1–32767
		72
		one statement/line
			check your manual!

Literal string approx. length 120	(5)	65	depends on line length

Names for numbers
  letter, letter & digit,
  a letter followed by sequence
  of letters & digits.
	(1)	letter or letter
		and digit
			check your manual!

RML 380Z BASICSG V 5.0 CUB Chapter References	( )	ANSI Minimal BASIC	Other BASICs
Names for strings as for numbers, followed by a $ sign	(1)	A letter followed by a dollar.	check your manual!
Number precision 6 significant figures	(3)	none	machine dependent
Number range 1E–38 to 1E+38	(3)	none	machine dependent
Strings Needs string space via CLEAR String length 255	(5)	must dimension simple string 127	machine dependent Varies.

4. *System and Peripheral Control*

CTRL Z keys	(1, 2)	none	ESC, ALT MODE, CTRL C etc.
PRINTER	(2)	none	Check your manual!
RETURN key	(1)	same	ACCEPT key ENTER key

APPENDIX 2

Solutions

(by Martin Hall)

The solutions cover the questions set in SECTION I. In each case only one, (and not necessarily the best), of many possible methods of solving the problem is given.

No solutions are provided for section II.

Names given to the programs identify the exercises and problems as follows:

C1E1	Chapter 1	Example 1
C2P1	Chapter 1	Problem 1

List of Solutions Included

C1E1	C4E2	C7P2
C1E3	C4P1(a to d)	C7P3(a to c)
C1P1a	C4P2	
C1P1b	C4P3	C8P1(a and b)
.		C8P2
.	C5P1	.
C1P5	.	.
	.	C8P8
C2P1a	C5P5	
C2P1b		C9P1
C2P2	C6E5	
C2P3	C6P1	C10E10
C2P4	.	C10E11
	.	C10P1
C3E2	C6P6	
C3P1(a to e)		C11P1
C3P2	C7E2	C11P2
C3P3	C7P1	

```
Chapter 1   Example 1     (C1E1)
RUN

C is   1
C is   2
C is   3
C is   4
C is   5
C is   6
```

Chapter 1 Example 3 (C1E3)

1. Lines 60 and 80 cause a blank line to be printed.

2. The PRINT statement will print any text contained in quotes (")

3. Line 130 uses commas to seperate the characters to be printed and prints them in zones 14 characters wide. Line 160 uses semicolons and does not put spaces between the string elements. See page 89.

4. Line 140 using commas to seperate the numbers prints them out in the same format as line 130, but moves them 1 space along. Line 170 using the semicolons prints the individual numbers with one space between each. See chapter 6.

5. When printing numbers BASIC always leaves a space in front of the number for the minus sign. This obviously does not apply to characters and they are not preceded by spaces unless specified.

```
10 REM   Chapter 1 Problem 1a     (C1P1A)
50 IF C > 10 THEN  80

10 REM   Chapter 1   Problem 1b    (C1P1B)
20 LET C = 0
30 PRINT
40 LET C = C + 1
50 IF C > 10 THEN 80
60 PRINT C;
70 IF C <> 5 THEN 74
72 PRINT
74 GOTO 40
80 END

10 REM   Chapter 1   Problem 2   (C1P2)
20 PRINT "Mr John Smith"
30 PRINT "    15 Acacia avenue"
40 PRINT "        Anytown"
50 END

10 REM   Chapter 1   Problem 2   (C1P3)
15 C = 0
20 PRINT "Mr John Smith"
25 C = C + 1
30 PRINT "    15 Acacia avenue"
40 PRINT "        Anytown"
42 PRINT
45 PRINT
50 IF C < 6 THEN 25
60 END
```

```
10 REM    Chapter 1    Problem 4    (C1P4)
20 P = 3.14159
30 R = 5
40 A = P * R * R
50 PRINT "Area is";A
60 C = 2 * P * R
70 PRINT "Circumference is";C
80 END
```

```
10 REM    Chapter 1    Problem 5    (C1P5)
20 P1 = 3.14159
25 PRINT "RADIUS","AREA","CIRCUMFERENCE"
30 R = 0
35 R = R + 1
40 A = P1 * R * R
60 C = 2 * P1 * R
65 PRINT R,A,C
70 IF R = 5 THEN 80
75 GOTO 35
80 END
```

```
5 REM    Chapter 2    Problem 1a    (C2P1A)
10 PRINT "Today's Dollar rate please"
20 INPUT R
30 PRINT "How much sterling"
35 PRINT "To stop me, give me -1"
40 INPUT S
45 IF S < 0 THEN 70
50 PRINT "Dollar value is ";S*R
60 GOTO 10
70 END
```

```
5 REM    Chapter 2 Problem 1b    (C1P1B)
6 REM Alter line 60 to GOTO 30
```

```
100 REM    Chapter 2    Problem 2    (C2P2)
110 PRINT "*** Centigrade to Gas mark converter ***"
130 PRINT "To stop me give me more than a 1000"
140 PRINT "What Temperature ";
150 INPUT F
160 IF F > 275 THEN 190
170 PRINT "Temperature lower than 275"
180 GOTO 140
190 IF F > 1000 THEN 230
200 G = ((F-275)/25)+1
210 PRINT "Gasmark is ";G
220 GOTO 140
230 END
```

```
10 REM   Chapter 2  Problem 3    (C2P3)
20 PRINT "***Currency Converter***"
30 PRINT "To stop me give -1"
40 PRINT "How much sterling ";
50 INPUT S
60 IF S < 0 THEN 140
70 PRINT "DOLLARS    LIRE    FRANCS    MARKS"
80 D = 1.65
90 L = 1450
100 F = 8.38
110 M = 4.02
120 PRINT D*S;"    ";L*S;"";F*S"    ";M*S
130 GOTO 40
140 END
```

```
10 REM   Chapter 2  Problem 4    (C2P4)
20 PRINT "***Spherical Statistics***"
30 PRINT "Input a radius each time a '?' appears"
40 PRINT "To stop, type -1"
50 PRINT "RADIUS", "VOLUME","SURFACE"
60 INPUT R
70 IF R < 0 THEN 120
80 V = (4 * 3.14159 * R^3 )/3
90 A = (4 * 3.14159 * R^2 )/2
100 PRINT R,V,A
110 GOTO 60
120 END
```

```
Chapter 3  Example 2    (C3E2)
100 Implied multiplication is not allowed
200 Multiplication operator missing
300 Adjacent operators are not allowed
400 Implied multiplication is not allowed
500 No error so long as C and D are not 0
600 No error so long as X is not 0
700 No error so long as all the elements are small
```

```
100 REM   Chapter 3  Problem 1a  (C3P1A)
110 PRINT "Input value for X"
120 PRINT "Finish inputting with 999"
130 INPUT X
140 IF X = 999 THEN 190
150 LET Y = ABS(X)
160 PRINT "X","ABS(X)"
170 PRINT X,Y
180 GOTO 130
190 END
```

```
100 REM   Chapter 3  Problem 1b  (C3P1B)
150 LET Y = INT(X)
160 PRINT "X","INT(X)"
130 INPUT X
```

```
100 REM   Chapter 3  Problem 1c  (C3P1C)
150 LET Y = EXP(X)
160 PRINT "X","EXP(X)"
```

```
100 REM   Chapter 3   Problem 1d (C3P1D)
110 LET C = 0
120 PRINT "Random numbers from RND(1)"
130 LET X = 1
140 PRINT RND(X)
150 LET C = C + 1
160 IF C < 10 THEN 140
170 PRINT "Random numbers from RND(0)"
180 LET X = 0
190 LET C = 0
200 PRINT RND(X)
210 LET C = C + 1
220 IF C < 10 THEN 200
230 END
```

```
100 REM   Chapter 3   Problem 1e (C3P1E)
105 RANDOMIZE
120 PRINT "Random numbers from RND(1)"
```

```
100 REM   Chapter 3   Problem 2  (C3P2)
110 C = 1
120 PRINT "Original Rnd","Scaled Rnd"
130 LET X = RND(1)
140 LET Y = INT(X*10)
150 PRINT X,Y
160 C = C + 1
170 IF C < 11 THEN 130
180 END
```

```
100 REM   Chapter 3   Problem 3  (C3P3)
110 LET C = 1
120 LET L = 0
130 PRINT "C O M M O N   L O G A R I T H M S "
140 PRINT "NUMBER","LOGARITHMS"
150 PRINT "-------------------------------------------"
160 LET L = LOG(C) * .4343
170 PRINT C,L
180 LET C = C+ 1
190 IF C / 20 = INT(C/20) THEN 140
200 IF C < 101 THEN 160
210 END
```

```
100 REM   Chapter 4   Example 4.2   (C4E2)
110 REMoved  Lines 100-160 + 320-460
170 DIM A(30)
175 LET T = 0
200 PRINT "Give me some numbers please: to stop me input -1"
205 FOR N = 1 TO 30
210 INPUT A(N)
212 IF A(N) = -1 THEN 245
215 LET T = T + A(N)
240 NEXT N
245 LET L = N - 1
250 PRINT "You have successively entered";L;"numbers into array A"
253 PRINT "The sum is ";T
255 PRINT "The average is ";T/N
257 PRINT "The square of the 7th element is";A(7)^2
258 PRINT "The numbers are :-"
260 FOR N = 1 TO L
270 PRINT A(N);
280 NEXT N
470 END


100 REM   Chapter 4   Problem 1   (C4P1)
105 REM          Chapter 4        Problem 1a
110 DIM Z(10)
120 PRINT "Please input 10 numbers, one on a line"
130 FOR I = 1 TO 10
140 INPUT Z(I)
150 NEXT I
160 REM          Chapter 4        Problem 1b
170 PRINT "Number","N*N","N*N*N"
180 FOR I = 1 TO 10
190 PRINT Z(I),Z(I)↑2,Z(I)↑3
200 NEXT I
210 REM          Chapter 4        Problem 1c
220 PRINT
230 FOR I = 10 TO 1 STEP-1
240 PRINT Z(I);
250 NEXT I
260 REM          Chapter 4        Problem 1d
270 PRINT
280 PRINT
290 FOR I = 1 TO 10 STEP 2
300 PRINT Z(I);
310 NEXT I
320 END


100 REM  Chapter 4  Problem 2    (C4P2)
110 PRINT "Here are the first 100 primes"
120 FOR I = 2 TO 1000
130 FOR J = 2 TO SQR(I)
140 IF I/J = INT(I/J) THEN 210
150 NEXT J
160 LET C = C + 1
170 IF C > 100 THEN 220
180 PRINT I,
190 IF INT(C/5) <> C/5 THEN 210
200 PRINT
210 NEXT I
220 END
```

```
100 REM   Chapter 4   Problem 3    (C4P3)
110 DIM A(5,2),B(2),C(2)
120 FOR I = 1 TO 2
130 FOR J = 1 TO 5
140 LET A(J,I) = INT(RND(1)*100)
150 LET B(I) = B(I) + A(J,I)
160 NEXT J
170 NEXT I
180 PRINT, "Column 1","Column 2"
190 PRINT "Total",B(1),B(2)
200 PRINT "Mean",B(1)/5,B(2)/5
210 LET C(1) = 1000
220 LET C(2) = 1000
230 FOR I = 1 TO 2
240 FOR J = 1 TO 5
250 LET D = ABS(A(J,I)-(B(I)/5))
260 IF D > ABS(C(I) - B(I)/5) THEN 280
270 LET C(I) =A(J,I)
280 NEXT J
290 NEXT I
300 PRINT "Closest",C(1),C(2)
310 PRINT "................................."
320 PRINT "            Whole array"
330 PRINT "Total",B(1)+B(2)
340 PRINT "Mean",B(1)+B(2)/20
350 FOR I = 1 TO 2
360 FOR J = 1 TO 5
370 IF ABS(A(J,I)-B(1)+B(2)/20) > ABS(C(1) - B(1) + B(2)/20) THEN 390
380 LET C(1) = A(J,I)
390 NEXT J
400 NEXT I
410 PRINT"Closest",C(1)
420 END
```

```
10 REM   Chapter 5  Problem 1    (C5P1)
20 LET A$ = "We could go"
30 LET N$ = "ON"
40 LET D$ = "and"
50 PRINT A$;
60 FOR I = 1 TO 6
70 PRINT N$;D$;
80 NEXT I
90 END


100 REM   Chapter 5  Problem 2    (C5P2)
110 DIM L$(40)
120 FOR L = 1 TO 40
130 LET L$(L) = " "
140 NEXT L
150 PRINT "---------------------------------------"
160 LET K = 16
170 LET J = 26
180 FOR N = 1 TO 6
190 LET L$(K) = "5"
200 LET L$(J) = "5"
210 LET L$(12) = "4"
220 LET K = K+1
230 LET J = J-1
240 FOR N1 = 1 TO 40
250 PRINT L$(N1);
260 LET L$(N1) = " "
270 NEXT N1
280 PRINT
290 NEXT N
300 PRINT "---------------------------------------"
310 END
```

C5P3

The line buffer must be cleared before entries are made to it for the next line to be printed.

```
100 REM   Chapter 5  Problem 4   (C5P4)
110 CLEAR 300
120 DIM A(30)
130 LET R$ = "Round the ragged rocks the rugged rascal ran"
140 FOR I = 1 TO LEN(R$)
150 IF MID$(R$,I,1) <> " " THEN 190
160 PRINT W$
170 LET W$ = ""
180 GOTO 200
190 LET W$ = W$ + MID$(R$,I,1)
200 NEXT I
210 PRINT W$
220 PRINT
230 FOR I = 1 TO LEN(R$)
240 IF MID$(R$,I,1) <> "r" THEN 310
250 LET C = C + 1
260 LET A(C) = I
310 NEXT I
320 PRINT R$
330 FOR N = 1 TO C
340 PRINT TAB(A(N)-1);"^";
350 NEXT N
360 PRINT
370 PRINT "There are ";C;" occurrences of 'r' "
380 PRINT
390 LET W$ = RIGHT$(R$,3)
400 LET W$ = W$ + " "
410 LET W$ = W$ + LEFT$(R$,5)
420 PRINT W$
430 END


100 REM    Chapter 5  Problem 5   (C5P5)
110 LET A$="ABCDEFGHIJKLMNOPQRSTUVWXYZ "
120 DIM A(200)
121 PRINT "Type 'C' to Code a message"
122 PRINT "Type 'D' to decode a message"
123 INPUT R$
124 IF R$ = "D" THEN 430
130 PRINT "Input your message "
140 INPUT M$
150 PRINT "The coded message reads"
160 FOR I = 1 TO LEN(M$)
170 FOR J = 1 TO 27
180 IF MID$(M$,I,1) = MID$(A$,J,1) THEN 200
190 NEXT J
200 PRINT J;
210 NEXT I
220 GOTO 530
430 PRINT "Input your coded message, one number"
440 PRINT "on a line, stop with -1"
450 FOR I = 1 TO 200
460 INPUT A(I)
470 IF A(I) < 0 THEN 490
480 NEXT I
490 PRINT "The translated code reads"
500 FOR J = 1 TO I-1
510 PRINT MID$(A$,A(J),1);
520 NEXT J
530 END
```

```
100 REM  Chapter 6  Problem 1   (C6P1)
110 DIM A(10)
115 PRINT "Input 10 numbers when prompted by '?'"
117 PRINT "One number per line "
120 FOR I  = 1 TO 10
130 INPUT A(I)
140 NEXT I
150 FOR I = 1 TO 10
160 PRINT A(I);
170 NEXT I
180 PRINT
190 PRINT
200 FOR I = 1 TO 10
210 PRINT A(I),
220 IF I <> 5 THEN 240
230 PRINT
240 NEXT I
250 PRINT
260 END
```

```
260 REM  Chapter 6  Problem 2   (C6P2)
270 FOR I = 1 TO 10
280 PRINT TAB(I+2);A(I)
290 NEXT I
300 END
```

Chapter 6 Example 5 (C6E5)

The program fails because the variable S reaches −30 which means that the program is trying to TAB(0). A TAB of 0 or less than 0 is obviously not allowed.

```
100 REM  Chapter 6  Problem 3   (C6P3)
110 PRINT "Please give the 5 values for X (one on a line) ";
120 PRINT "when prompted by '?'"
130 PRINT TAB(20);"SIN(X)";TAB(35);"COS(X)"
140 PRINT "................................."
150 FOR I = 1 TO 5
160 INPUT X
170 PRINT TAB(20);SIN(X);TAB(35);COS(X)
180 NEXT I
190 END
180 PRINT
```

```
100 REM  Chapter 6  Problem 4   (C6P4)
110 FOR I = 1 TO 15
120 PRINT "Q ";
130 NEXT I
140 PRINT
150 FOR I = 1 TO 10
160 PRINT "Q";TAB(28);"Q"
170 NEXT I
180 FOR I = 1 TO 15
190 PRINT "Q ";
200 NEXT I
210 END
```

```
100 REM   Chapter 6  Problem 5   (C6P5)
110 PRINT "Give me the numbers please (one on a line), ";
120 PRINT "enter -1 to stop"
130 PRINT
140 PRINT "Number","Square root","Cube root","Fourth root"
150 INPUT X
160 IF X < 0 THEN 190
170 PRINT X,SQR(X),X↑(.3),X↑(.25)
180 GOTO 150
190 END


100 REM   Chapter 6  Problem 6   (C6P6)
110 FOR I = 1 TO 700
120 IF I/7 <> INT(I/7) THEN 240
130 IF C/7 <> INT(C/7) THEN 160
140 LET C = 0
150 PRINT
160 IF I > 10 THEN 190
170 PRINT "   ";I;
180 GOTO 230
190 IF I > 100 THEN 220
200 PRINT " ";I;
210 GOTO 230
220 PRINT I;
230 LET C = C + 1
240 NEXT I
250 END


100 REM   Chapter 7  Problem 1   (C7P1)
110 DATA "This is a valid data item"
120 DATA "Lines 110 to 150 also contain only valid DATA items"
130 DATA 33
140 DATA .5,9, 11, .2, 13, .3, -1, -1
150 DATA "Lark", "Sparrow", "Lammegeiger"
160 DATA And this is an unquoted string,and this the next unquoted string
170 REM >>*   The READ statements below read all the given DATA items   *<<
180 READ D1$,D2$
185 PRINT D1$
187 PRINT D1$
190 READ N
195 PRINT N
200 FOR J = 1 TO 10
210 READ M1,M2
215 PRINT M1,M2
220 IF M1 < 0 THEN 240
230 NEXT J
240 READ B1$,B2$,B3$
242 PRINT B1$
244 PRINT B2$
246 PRINT B3$
250 READ U1$,U2$
254 PRINT U1$
257 PRINT U2$
260 REM >>*           Here endeth the program-segment           *<<
```

```
100 REM   Chapter 7  Problem 2   (C7P2)
110 FOR I = 1 TO 4
120 READ A$,A
130 PRINT A, A$
140 NEXT I
150 DATA "All", 1, "because", 2, "chemistry", 3, "doesn't", 4
160 END
170 REM >>*   The READ statements below read all the given DATA items   *<<
```

```
100 REM   Chapter 7  Problem 3   (C7P3)
110 READ N
120 FOR I = 1 TO N
130 READ N$,A1$,A2$,A3$,B$,S$,W,H
140 IF S$ = "Male" THEN 190
150 LET W1 = W1 + W
160 LET H1 = H1 + H
170 LET F = F + 1
180 GOTO 220
190 LET W2 = W2 + W
200 LET H2 = H2 + H
210 LET M = M + 1
220 PRINT N$;TAB(27);B$
230 PRINT TAB(5);A1$;TAB(27);S$
240 PRINT TAB(10);A2$;TAB(26);W;"Pounds"
250 PRINT TAB(15);A3$;TAB(26);H;"Feet"
260 PRINT
270 PRINT
280 NEXT I
290 PRINT
300 PRINT
310 PRINT "Female average height ";H1/F
320 PRINT "Female average weight ";W1/F
330 PRINT
340 PRINT "Male average height ";H2/M
350 PRINT "Male average weight ";W2/M
360 DATA 3
370 DATA Jane Lipp,120 Dorset st.,Hildown,Dorset,12/03/54,Female,140,5.8
380 DATA Mike Heath,10 Pusey drive,Weston,Bucks,19/11/63,Male,210,6.2
390 DATA Ivor Enjin,23 The Sidings,Lighthill,Gwent,05/10/43,Male,330,6.4
400 NEXT I
100 REM   Chapter 8  Example 8.2   (C8E2)
165 IF X > 0 THEN 170 ELSE PRINT "Negative input"
167 GOTO 150
```

C7E2

Reverse the order of the items in the READ statement: READ A$, A

C8E2

A negative number raised to a fractional power gives a complex result. The BASIC interpreter deals only with REAL numbers and so returns an error.

```
90 REM  Chapter 8  Problem 1   (C8P1)
100 REM Chapter 8     Problem 1a
110 DIM A(100)
120 FOR I = 1 TO 100
130 READ A(I)
140 IF A(I) < 0 THEN 200
150 IF A(I) > 101 AND A(I) < 501 THEN 190
160 PRINT "Error ....Number";A(I);"out of range ";
170 PRINT "101-501"
180 LET A(I) = -1
190 NEXT I
200 REM Chapter 8     Problem 1b
210 FOR J = 1 TO I
220 IF A(J) < 0 THEN 240
230 LET T = T + A(J)
240 NEXT J
250 LET T = T/I
260 PRINT "The average of the numbers in range was"
270 PRINT T
280 PRINT "The above average numbers are "
290 FOR J = 1 TO I
300 IF A(J) < T THEN 340
310 IF A(J) <> T THEN 330
320 LET C = C + 1
330 PRINT A(J);
340 NEXT J
350 PRINT
360 PRINT C;"numbers equalled the average"
370 DATA 456,987,101,348.6,45.8,602,158,149
380 DATA -1
```

```
100 REM   Chapter 8  Problem 2     (C8P2)
110 PRINT "Please input X";
120 INPUT X
130 PRINT "Thank you, now please input the number"
140 PRINT "of the required function"
150 PRINT
160 PRINT "1.Square Root","2.Square"
170 PRINT "3. Cube","4.4th power","5.Factorial"
180 INPUT C
190 ON C GOTO 220,250,280,310,340
200 PRINT "Sorry, I don't understand that number"
210 GOTO 160
220 PRINT "The square root of";
230 LET Z = SQR(X)
240 GOTO 390
250 PRINT "The square of";
260 LET Z  = X*X
270 GOTO 390
280 PRINT "The cube of";
290 LET Z = X↑3
300 GOTO 390
310 PRINT "The fourth power of";
320 LET Z = X↑4
330 GOTO 390
340 PRINT "The factorial of";
350 LET Z = X
360 FOR I = X-1 TO 1 STEP -1
370 LET Z = Z*I
380 NEXT I
390 PRINT X;"is";Z
400 PRINT
410 PRINT "Do you want another go (Y/N)";
420 INPUT A$
430 IF A$ = "N" THEN 470
440 PRINT "Do you want to change your number (Y/N)"
450 INPUT A$
460 IF A$ = "Y" THEN 110:ELSE GOTO 130
470 PRINT "Thank you          Goodbye"
480 END

100 REM   Chapter  8  Problem 3     (C8P3)
110 PRINT "Which number do you wish the factors of"
120 INPUT N
130 PRINT
140 PRINT "Here are the factors of";N
150 FOR I = 1 TO SQR(N)
160 IF N/I <> INT(N/I) THEN 180
170 PRINT I;N/I;
180 NEXT I
190 END
```

```
100 REM   Chapter 8   Problem 4   (C8P4)
110 DIM A(10),B(15)
120 FOR I = 1 TO 10
130 READ A(I)
140 NEXT I
150 FOR I = 1 TO 15
160 READ B(I)
170 NEXT I
180 PRINT "The common numbers are :-"
190 FOR I = 1 TO 10
200 FOR J = 1 TO 15
210 IF A(I) <> B(J) THEN 230
220 PRINT A(I);
230 NEXT J
240 NEXT I
250 PRINT
450 DATA 1,2,3,45,6,7,86,2,98,564
460 DATA 32,4,56,86,54,1,90,73,19,45
470 DATA 23,145,238,50,341
480 END

100 REM   Chapter 8   Problem 5   (C8P5)
110 DIM A(10),B(15)
120 FOR I = 1 TO 10
130 READ A(I)
140 NEXT I
150 FOR I = 1 TO 15
160 READ B(I)
170 NEXT I
180 LET C = 1
190 FOR I = 1 TO 10 STEP 2
200 LET A(C) = A(I)
210 C = C + 1
220 NEXT I
230 C = 1
240 FOR I = 1 TO 15 STEP 3
250 LET B(C) = B(I)
260 NEXT I
270 PRINT
280 PRINT "Subscript","A","B","Total"
290 FOR I = 1 TO 5
300 PRINT I,A(I),B(I),A(I)+B(I)
310 NEXT I
320 DATA 1,2,3,45,6,7,86,2,98,564
330 DATA 32,4,56,86,54,1,90,73,19,45
340 DATA 23,145,238,50,341
350 END
```

```
100 REM   Chapter 8   Problem 6    (C8P6)
110 DIM S(5),W(5)
120 PRINT "Please input identity no.,weight"
130 FOR I = 1 TO 5
140 INPUT S(I),W(I)
150 NEXT I
160 PRINT "Identity";
165 PRINT TAB(2);
170 FOR I = 1 TO 5
180 PRINT S(I);
190 NEXT I
200 PRINT
210 PRINT "Weight";
215 PRINT TAB(2);" ";
220 FOR I = 1 TO 5
230 PRINT W(I);
240 NEXT I
250 PRINT
260 PRINT "Please give the number of the animal"
270 PRINT "you wish to know about"
280 INPUT N
290 FOR I = 1 TO 5
300 IF S(I) = N THEN 320
310 NEXT I
320 PRINT N;"appeared today after 5 weeks absence"
330 PRINT "The weight";W(I);"shows an increase of  .55 grams"
340 END


10 REM   Chapter 8   Problem 7    (C8P7)
20 LET S = 1
30 FOR I = 2 TO 10
40 LET S = S + 1/I
50 NEXT I
60 PRINT "The sum of the series 1 + 1/2 + 1/3.....1/10 is";S
70 END


10 REM   Chapter  8  Problem 8   (C8P8)
20 PRINT "Please give me the number to be factorised"
30 INPUT N
40 LET S= N
50 FOR I = N-1 TO 1 STEP -1
60 LET S = S*I
70 NEXT I
80 PRINT N;"!  = ";S
90 END
```

```
100 REM   Chapter 9  Problem 1    (C9P1)
110 DIM T(20)
120 FOR I = 1 TO 20
130 READ N
140 GOSUB 280
150 NEXT I
160 RESTORE
170 PRINT "Original   List"
180 FOR I= 1 TO 20
190 READ N
200 PRINT N;
210 NEXT I
220 PRINT
230 PRINT "New  List"
240 FOR I = 1 TO 20
250 PRINT T(I);
260 NEXT I
270 STOP
280 REM            Subroutine   Check
290 LET T(I) = N
300 IF N < 32 THEN GOSUB 330
310 IF N > 312 THEN GOSUB 370
320 RETURN
330 REM            Subroutine   Frozen
340 PRINT "Item at";N;"degrees is FROZEN"
350 LET T(I) = 0
360 RETURN
370 REM            Subroutine   Frazzled
380 PRINT "Item at";N;"degrees is FRAZZLED"
390 LET T(I) = 999
400 RETURN
410 DATA 100,25,300,345,500,225,280,21,76,195
420 DATA 44,3,199,55,61,70,12,962,.7,63
```

```
10 REM   Chapter 10 Example 10   (C10E10)
165 CALL "CLEAR"

1 REM Chapter 10 Example 10.11 (C10E11)
10 DEF FNX(A)=40*COS(A)
20 DEF FNY(A)=40*SIN(A)
30 CALL "RESOLUTION",1,1
40 CALL "OFFSET",-80,-48
50 LET PI=3.14159
60 FOR T=0 TO 127
70 LET A=T*PI/64
80 CALL "UPDATE",T AND 1, (T AND 7)/2
90 CALL "PLOT",FNX(A),FNY(A),1
95 CALL "PLOT",30*COS(-A),30*SIN(-A),1
100 NEXT T
110 FOR I=1 TO 100
120 FOR V=0 TO 3
130 FOR P=0 TO 1
135 CALL "COLOUR",1,(I*7 AND 127) + 128
140 CALL "DISPLAY",P,V
150 NEXT P
160 NEXT V
170 NEXT I
180 END



1 REM   Chapter 10  Problem 1   (C10P1)
2 PUT12:CALL"RESOLUTION",0,2:D=160:
S=1.1:FORR=51TO-88STEP-3:FORJ=0TO63:
CALL"PLOT",D+SIN(J/10)*R/S,D-64+COS(J/10)*R*S,3:
NEXT:NEXT
```

```
4 REM   Chapter 11  Problem 1   (C11P1)
5 REM   Fit these segments into FRAMEMOD
8 CLEAR 1000
9 QUOTE #10,34
10 DIM TRANS$(500),DATE$(500),AMOUNT(500)
20 PRINT "Please give the name of your account"
25 PRINT "file, if you are a new user type NEW";
27 INPUT FILE$
30 IF FILE$ = "NEW" THEN 50
40 IF LOOKUP(FILE$) <> 0 THEN 80
45 PRINT "No file ";FILE$:GOTO 20
50 INPUT"Please give me your name";FILE$
60 IF LOOKUP(FILE$) = 0 THEN 70
62 PRINT "I'm sorry that name is not unique, can you modify that":GOTO 50
70 INPUT "PLease give me a password for your file";PWRD$
71 LET TTAL = 0
74 CREATE #10,FILE$:PRINT#10,PWRD$,TTAL:PRINT #10
75 CLOSE #10
76 GOTO 100
80 OPEN #10,FILE$
85 INPUT #10,PWRD$,TTAL
90 INPUT "Password please ";TRY$
91 IF TRY$ <> PWRD$ THEN PRINT "Wrong":GOTO 20000
92 IF TTAL < 0 THEN PRINT "WARNING!!! You are ";TTAL;" overdrawn"
950 ?"  C  to register a Credit"
960 ?"  D  to register a debit"
970 ?"  L  to Look at all transactions"
980 ?"  T  to look at transactions by Type"
982 ?"  P  to look at all transactions by Date"
983 ?"  B  to look at Balance"
990 GOTO160
1000 PRINT "Registering a credit"
1005 GOSUB 15000
1010 PRINT "Please register the credit in the form"
1020 PRINT "100.00,paycheque,29/2/81"
1030 PRINT "To finish type "
1040 PRINT ".999,*,*"
1050 INPUT AMOUNT(I),TRANS$(I),DATE$(I)
1060 IF AMOUNT(I) = .999 THEN 1080
1065 LET TTAL = TTAL + AMOUNT(I)
1070 LET I = I + 1
1075 GOTO 1050
1080 LET I = I-1
1082 GOSUB 15100
1900 GOTO160
2000 PRINT "Please register the debit in the form"
2010 PRINT "100.00,Record Player,02/05/81)
2020 PRINT "To finish type "
2030 PRINT ".999,*,*"
2035 GOSUB 15000
2040 INPUT AMOUNT(I),TRANS$(I),DATE$(I)
2050 IF AMOUNT(I) = .999 THEN 2070
2060 LET TTAL = TTAL-AMOUNT(I)
2062 AMOUNT(I) = -AMOUNT(I)
2065 LET I = I + 1
2067 GOTO 2040
2070 LET I= I-1
2075 GOSUB 15100
2900 GOTO160
3000 PRINT "All Transactions"
```

```
3010 GOSUB 15000
3020 FOR J = 1 TO I
3030 PRINT AMOUNT(J),TRAN$(J),DATE$(J)
3040 NEXT J
3050 PRINT "your balance stands at ";TTAL
3900 GOTO160
4000 PRINT "Listing transactions by type"
4005 GOSUB 15000
4010 INPUT "What transaction do you wish to look at";REPLY$
4020 PRINT " In relation to ";REPLY$; "the following transactions have been ma
4030 FOR J = 1 TO I
4040 IF TRAN$(J) <> REPLY$ THEN 4060
4050 PRINT AMOUNT(J),DATE$(J)
4060 NEXT J
4900 GOTO160
5000 PRINT "Transactions by date"
5005 GOSUB 15000
5010 INPUT "What date are you interested in          ";REPLY$
5020 PRINT
5030 PRINT "On ";REPLY$;" the following transactions were made"
5040 FOR J =1 TO I
5050 IF DATE$(J) <> REPLY$ THEN 5070
5060 PRINT AMOUNT(J),TRAN$(J)
5070 NEXT J
5900 GOTO160
6000 ?"Your balance at the moment stands at              ";TTAL
6900 GOTO160
15000 REM                    Subroutines
15010 REM   Read from file
15012 OPEN #10,FILE$
15017 INPUT #10,PWRD$,TTAL
15020 FOR I = 1 TO 500
15025 ON EOF GOTO 15050
15030 INPUT#10,AMOUNT(I),TRAN$(I),DATE$(I)
15040 NEXT I
15050 CLOSE #10
15060 RETURN
15100 REM   Write to file
15110 ERASE FILE$
15112 CREATE #10,FILE$
15115 PRINT #10,PWRD$,TTAL
15120 FOR J = 1 TO I
15130 PRINT #10,AMOUNT(J),TRAN$(J),DATE$(J)
15140 NEXT J
15145 CLOSE #10
15150 RETURN
20000 END
```

```
1 REM   Chapter 11  Problem 2   (C11P2)
2 REM   These segments fit into FRAMEMOD
8 CLEAR 5000
10 DIM ADD$(500)
950 ?"  E  to Enter a phone number"
960 ?"  F  to Find a phone number"
970 ?"  P  to Print the whole book"
989 REM                          Insert your own 'processes' from here on
990 GOTO160
1000 PRINT "So you want to give me a new address"
1001 IF LOOKUP("BOOK") = -1 THEN GOSUB 15000 ELSE CREATE #10,"BOOK"
1010 PRINT "Please give me the name and address     in the following form"
1020 PRINT "Smith John,35 Sidings st,Oxford,Ox 393933"
1025 PRINT "End by typing a '*'"
1027 INPUT LINE B$
1029 IF B$ = "*" THEN 1330
1209 FOR J = 1 TO I
1210 IF ADD$(J) < B$ THEN 1300
1220 FOR K = I TO J STEP -1
1230 ADD$(K+1) = ADD$(K)
1240 NEXT K
1250 LET ADD$(J) = B$
1260 GOTO 1320
1300 NEXT J
1310 LET ADD$(J) = B$
1320 LET I = I + 1
1325 GOTO 1027
1327 LET I = I +1
1330 GOSUB 15100
1900 GOTO160
2000 PRINT "So you want a phone number eh?"
2005 GOSUB 15000
2010 PRINT "Please give me the name"
2015 LET D = 1
2020 INPUT NAME$
2030 FOR J = 1 TO I
2035 LET A$ = LEFT$(ADD$(J),LEN(NAME$))
2040 IF A$ > NAME$ THEN ON D GOTO 2070,2080
2050 IF A$ <> NAME$ THEN 2060
2055 PRINT ADD$(J)
2057 LET D = 2
2060 NEXT J
2070 PRINT "I'm sorry I don't have that information"
2080 INPUT "Another ";REPLY$
2090 IF REPLY$ = "Y" OR REPLY$ ="y" THEN 2010 ELSE GOTO 2900
2900 GOTO160
3000 PRINT "Printing your whole file"
3005 PRINT "Is this for the printer (Y/N)";
3007 INPUT REPLY$
3010 GOSUB 15000
3020 FOR J = 1 TO I
3029 IF REPLY$ = "N" THEN 3049
3030 LPRINT ADD$(J)
3040 IF J/70 = INT(J/70) THEN PUT #2,12
3042 GOTO 3050
3049 PRINT ADD$(J)
3050 NEXT J
3900 GOTO160
15000 REM  SET COMMON SUBROUTINES HERE
15010 OPEN #10,"BOOK"   :REM  Read from file
```

302 Appendix 2

```
15020 FOR I = 1 TO 500
15025 ON EOF GOTO 15050
15030 INPUTLINE #10,ADD$(I)
15040 NEXT I
15050 CLOSE #10
15060 RETURN
15100 ERASE "BOOK"        :REM  Write to file
15110 CREATE #10,"BOOK"
15120 FOR J = 1TO I
15130 PRINT #10,ADD$(J)
15140 NEXT J
15150 CLOSE #10
15160 RETURN
16000 REM  SET DEFINED FUNCTIONS HERE
17000 REM  DATA STATEMENTS HERE
20000 END
```

APPENDIX 3

ASCII Full character set of the 380Z micro-computer

The ASCII and graphics codes are given in decimal

Reproduced from BASIC + ½
Hertfordshire County Council
Advisory Unit for Computer
Based Education

Code	Char	Code	Char	Code	Char	Code	Char	Code	Code	Code	Code
0	NULL	32	SPACE	64	@	96	—	128	160	192	224
1	▫	33	!	65	A	97	a	129	161	193	225
2	■	34	"	66	B	98	b	130	162	194	226
3	⌐	35	#	67	C	99	c	131	163	195	227
4	⅄	36	S	68	D	100	d	132	164	196	228
5	[:]	37	%	69	E	101	e	133	165	197	229
6	√	38	&	70	F	102	f	134	166	198	230
7	□BELL	39	'	71	G	103	g	135	167	199	231
8	➤	40	(	72	H	104	h	136	168	200	232
9	→TAB	41	)	73	I	105	i	137	169	201	233
10	≡LINE FEED	42	*	74	J	106	j	138	170	202	234
11	Ψ	43	+	75	K	107	k	139	171	203	235
12	▽̈	44	,	76	L	108	l	140	172	204	236
13	⏎CAR RETN	45	-	77	M	109	m	141	173	205	237
14	⊙	46	.	78	N	110	n	142	174	206	238
15	⊖	47	/	79	O	111	o	143	175	207	239
16	⊟	48	0	80	P	112	p	144	176	208	240
17	⊕	49	1	81	Q	113	q	145	177	209	241
18	⊕	50	2	82	R	114	r	146	178	210	242
19	⊖	51	3	83	S	115	s	147	179	211	243
20	⊕	52	4	84	T	116	t	148	180	212	244
21	⤴	53	5	85	U	117	u	149	181	213	245
22	⌂	54	6	86	V	118	v	150	182	214	246
23	⊣	55	7	87	W	119	w	151	183	215	247
24	⅀	56	8	88	X	120	x	152	184	216	248
25	✝	57	9	89	Y	121	y	153	185	217	249
26	⌇	58	:	90	Z	122	z	154	186	218	250
27	⊖ESC	59	;	91	←[	123	{¼	155	187	219	251
28	⊟	60	<	92	⅄\	124	‖	156	188	220	252
29	⊟	61	=	93	→]	125	}¾	157	189	221	253
30	⊡	62	>	94	↑	126	÷	158	190	222	254
31	⊡	63	?	95	#←	127	■DEL	159	191	223	255

APPENDIX 4

Matrices

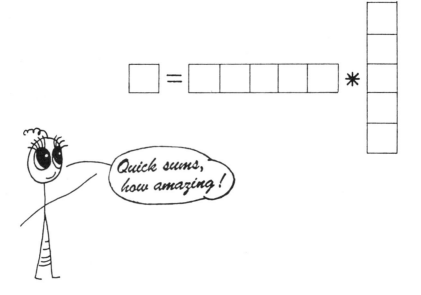

A4.1 PREFACE TO MATRICES

Although Matrices are currently not part of RML 380Z BASICs, they are a very useful and attractive feature of some other BASICs. For example MATREAD and MATPRINT, can reduce human programming effort by a significant factor as illustrated by the first two examples. Work involved in writing statistical examples is again minimised – see Example A4.6.

The programs in this chapter were developed and run on a Computer Technology Limited Modular One (CTL Mod One) Computer.

You have already seen in Chapter 4 a whole list of numbers, or a table, represented by a single letter. For example:

    If Z is a one dimensional array

    Z (20) refers to the 20th element in Z

    If Z is a two dimensional array

    Z (3,5) refers to the 5th element in it's 3rd row

Matrix statements are not strictly necessary. When used wisely they shorten BASIC programs by replacing combinations of statements sometimes by a single statement. This results in faster and more efficient programs. This is partly because there are fewer lines of program but a more significant reason is BASIC MATrix functions are stored in binary. This means these statements do not need to be re-interpreted for each run of the program but are ready for 'immediate' attention by the computer.

A4.2 COMPARE TWO PROGRAMS FOR READING AND PRINTING DATA

Compare the examples A4.1 and A4.2 as an illustration of this point. Both programs read data into a 4 × 6 array and verify the data by printing it out.

Example A4.1 Program USUALRP

```
10 REM           PROGRAM          USUALRP
12 REM
20 REM        READ DATA INTO A
30 DIM A(4,5),B(2,3)
  40 FOR I = 1 TO 4
    50 FOR J = 1 TO 5
    60 READ A(I,J)
    70 NEXT J
  80 NEXT I
85 REM        READ DATA INTO B
  90 FOR K = 1 TO 2
    100 FOR L = 1 TO 3
    110 READ B(K,L)
    120 NEXT L
  130 NEXT K
140 REM        PRINT CONTENTS OF A
  150 FOR I = 1 TO 4
    160 FOR J = 1 TO 5
    170 PRINT A(I,J),
    180 NEXT J
  185 PRINT
  190 NEXT I
195 PRINT
196 PRINT
198 REM        PRINT CONTENTS OF B
  200 FOR K = 1 TO 2
    210 FOR L = 1 TO 3
    220 PRINT B(K,L),
    230 NEXT L
  235 PRINT
  240 NEXT K
250 REM      PHEW ! HOW LONG WINDED CAN YOU GET ?
500 DATA 1,2,3,4,5,2,4,6,8,10
510 DATA 3,6,9,12,15,18,5,10,15,20
520 DATA .1,.1,.1,.3,.3,.3
750 END
```

```
RUN
 1          2          3          4          5

 2          4          6          8         10

 3          6          9         12         15

18          5         10         15         20


.1         .1         .1
.3         .3         .3
DONE
```

Now take a look at example A4.2 and note that lines 40 to 240 inclusive (of example A4.1) have been replaced by 2 matrix statements, MATPRINT and MATREAD.

Example A4.2 Program MATRP

```
10 REM              PROGRAM      MATRP
12 PRINT
15 REM              READ DATA INTO A AND B
30 DIM A(4,5),B(2,3)
35 PRINT
40 MAT READ A, B
45 REM              PRINT CONTENTS OF A AND B
50 MAT PRINT A, B
60 REM              NOW ISN'T THAT SIMPLER ?  !
500 DATA 1, 2, 3, 4, 5, 2, 4, 6, 8, 10
510 DATA 3, 6, 9, 12, 15, 5, 10, 15, 20, 25
520 DATA .1, .1, .1, .3, .3, .3
750 END

RUN
```

1	2	3	4	5
2	4	6	8	10
3	6	9	12	15
5	10	15	20	25

.1	.1	.1
.3	.3	.3

DONE

By now it should be obvious that in BASIC matrix is just another name for array. It may be defined, for example, in a DIMension statement:

```
22 DIM T(3,3), W(3,1), X(1,3), Y(3,2), Z(1,1)
```

The above may be represented as:

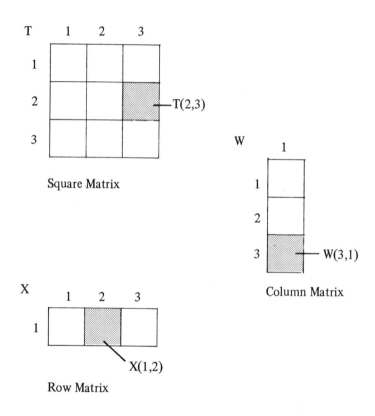

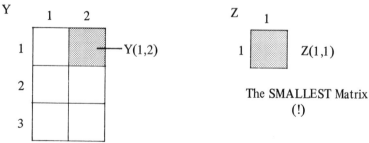

A4.3 MATRIX HANDLING STATEMENTS

MATrix statements follow the conventions of matrix algebra. They are used to manipulate arrays, (matrices).

A matrix may be **defined** implicitly **through usage**

    e.g.   20 LET A(2,5) = 99

               defines A implicitly as size 2 × 5

A matrix may be **defined** explicitly **by declaration**

    e.g.   10 DIM A(2,5), X(20,10)

Note: The maximum size of an implicit matrix is 10 by 10 and of a vector is 10

The ORIGIN is assumed to be 1

e.g. V

	1	2	3	4	5	6	7	8	
1									VECTOR

The first elements are V(1, 1) and M(1, 1)

M

	1	2	3	4	5	
1						MATRIX
2						

A4.4 ROW AND COLUMN DEFINITION

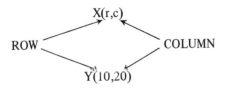

The **row** is always indicated by the **first** subscript, the **column** by the **second**.

A VECTOR matrix is thus a column matrix with only one column. The vector illustrated may be defined as:

    DIM C(5, 1)
or
    DIM C(5)

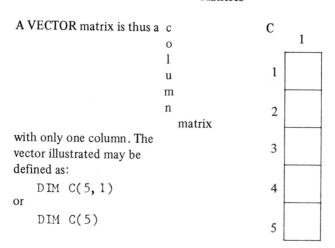

The shapes of vectors (lists) and matrices (tables) must be clearly defined when using MAT instructions.

Sometimes a matrix is used several times within a program. As in example A4.3 it may be a different shape on each occasion. This is permissable as long as the number of locations in the new matrix does not exceed that reserved for the original matrix. These points are illustrated by lines 30, 50, 110, 150.

There are several MATrix statements which allow a new working size to be specified. Without exception these are INPUT statements and include MAT-READ, MATINPUT, ZER and CON. It is **impossible to resize** a matrix **using an output command** such as MATPRINT.

In general the statement MATPRINT will result in widely spaced output. If closer spacing is required line 60 should be changed to read MATPRINT S; as in line 80. The results can be seen in the RUN of Example A4.3.

Example A4.3 Program MATSIZE

```
10 REM              PROGRAM    MATSIZE
20 PRINT
30 DIM S(2,6)
40 PRINT " ORIGINAL SIZE     S(2,6)"
50 MAT READ S
60 MAT PRINT S
70 PRINT " S(2,6)   CLOSELY PRINTED"
80 MAT PRINT S;
90 PRINT " S RE-SIZED TO    S(3,4)"
100 RESTORE
110 MAT READ S(3, 4)
120 MAT PRINT S
130 PRINT " S  RE-SIZED TO    S(1,5)"
140 RESTORE
150 MAT READ S(1, 5)
160 MAT PRINT S
300 DATA 1, 2, 3, 4, 5, 6, 7, 8, 9, 10, 11, 12
500 END

RUN

 ORIGINAL SIZE     S(2,6)

1              2            3         4          5
6
7              8            9         10         11
12
S(2,6)   CLOSELY PRINTED

1  2  3  4  5  6
7  8  9  10  11  12
S RE-SIZED TO    S(3,4)

1              2            3         4
5              6            7         8
9              10           11        12
S  RE-SIZED TO    S(1,5)

1              2            3         4          5
DONE
```

A4.5 MATRIX MULTIPLICATION ILLUSTRATED

If   B is a matrix with 4 rows and 2 columns — B(4, 2)
      C is a matrix with 2 rows and 3 columns — C(2, 3)
      A the product of B and C is   — A(4, 3)
      Multiplication of matrices is only possible when, as in the example above, the number of columns in B is the same as the number of rows in C. The method of multiplication is shown below.

$$\text{MAT } A = B * C$$

The size of the resulting matrix is shown below.

$$B(4, 2) * C(2, 3) \quad \text{gives} \quad A(4, 3)$$

In general $B(i, k) * C(k, j) \quad \text{gives} \quad A(i, j)$

A4.6 THE PRODUCT OF TWO VECTORS

A is a $1 \times m$ matrix: $A = (a_{11}, a_{12}, a_{13}, \ldots a_{1m})$
B is a $m \times 1$ matrix:

$$B = \begin{bmatrix} b_{11} \\ b_{21} \\ b_{31} \\ \vdots \\ b_{ml} \end{bmatrix}$$

The product $A * B$ in that order is:

$$(a_{11}b_{11} + a_{12}b_{21} + a_{13}b_{31} + \ldots a_{1m}b_{ml}) = \sum_{k=1}^{m} a_{1k}b_{kl}$$

Note the operation is **row by column**

Example A4.4 Vector Product

$$\begin{array}{cc} A & B \end{array} \qquad\qquad\qquad C$$

$$(2\ 3\ 4) * \begin{bmatrix} 1 \\ -1 \\ 2 \end{bmatrix} = (2(1) + 3(-1) + 4(2)) = (7)$$

An equivalent matrix statement could be: MAT C = A * B

A4.7. MATRIX STATEMENTS

FUNCTION OR MAT STATEMENT	EXAMPLE	VISUAL AID	DESCRIPTION/COMMENT
MAT + (addition)	MAT E = A + B		E, A, B must be the same size.
MAT − (subtraction)	MAT E = A − B		E, A, B must be the same size.
MAT * (multiplication)	MAT E = A * B		If E is K × N then A must be K × J and B must be J × N.
MAT * (scalar multiplication)	MAT A = (x) * B		A and B must be the same size.
MAT = (assignment)	MAT A = B		A and B must be the same size.
MAT READ	MATREAD A(m, n)		Reads data from DATA statements into A. m, n may set a new size.
MATINPUT	MATINPUT A (m, n)		Data is input from the m, n may set a new size.
MATPRINT	MATPRINT A, B, C		PRINTS matrices A, B, C one after the other. Commas or semi-colons (for output) may be used as separates.

A4.8 MATRIX FUNCTIONS

In CTL Mod One BASIC the maximum matrix size is 16383 elements
maximum size of a subscript (in a 2-dimensional matrix) 255

FUNCTION	EXAMPLE	VISUAL AID	DESCRIPTION/COMMENT
ZER	MAT B = ZER(m, n)	B $\begin{bmatrix} 0 & 0 \\ 0 & 0 \\ 0 & 0 \end{bmatrix}$	All the elements on a matrix are set to ZERO (0). A new working size may be set.
CON	MAT C = CON(m, n)	C $\begin{bmatrix} 1 & 1 & 1 & 1 \\ 1 & 1 & 1 & 1 \end{bmatrix}$	All the elements of C are set to ONE (1). A new working size may be set.
IDN	MAT D = IDN(m, n)	D $\begin{bmatrix} 1 & 0 & 0 \\ 0 & 1 & 0 \\ 0 & 0 & 1 \end{bmatrix}$	An identity matrix is established (all ones down diagonal indicated. D must be square). A new working size may be set.
INV	MAT E = INV(F)	F $\begin{bmatrix} 1 & 2 \\ 3 & 4 \end{bmatrix}$ E* $\begin{bmatrix} -2 & 1 \\ 1.5 & -5 \end{bmatrix}$	Inverts a square matrix into another square matrix of the same size.
TRN	MAT G = TRN(H)	G $\begin{bmatrix} 1 & 0 \\ 2 & 0 \\ 3 & 0 \\ 4 & 0 \\ 5 & 0 \end{bmatrix}$ H* $\begin{bmatrix} 1 & 2 & 3 & 4 & 5 \\ 0 & 0 & 0 & 0 & 0 \end{bmatrix}$	Transposes a m × n matrix into a n × m matrix.
			*These could be any values!

A4.9 SOME EXAMPLES USING MATRICES

1. Quick Summation of Lists of Numbers

(a) **Two Lists** (ref. example A4.4)

50 DIM G(1, 7), M(1, 7), T(1, 7)　defines　G　　M　　T

100 MAT T = G + M　　　　　gives　　T　=　G　+　M

140 MATREAD G(7, 1), M(7, 1)　resizes
　　　　　　　　　　　　　　and fills
　　　　　　　　　　　　　　with data

150 MAT T = ZER(7, 1)　　　resizes
　　　　　　　　　　　　　and fills
　　　　　　　　　　　　　with zeros

Thus:

160 MAT T = G + M　　　　　gives

Note: The MATPRINT statement sometimes results in an unattractive output. For example, there is no way at all in which any further information can be included on the same line as that partly used as a result of a MATPRINT. Of course there are ways round this! Take a look at the output of example A4.5. Line by line 'headings' cannot be included in the first table.

Example A4.5 Program MATMARKS

```
10 REM                              PROGRAM  MATMARKS
30 PRINT "      :::  TEST SCORES:   GEOG & MATHS  -  MAX 50"
50 DIM G(1,7),M(1,7),T(1,7)
70 MAT READ G,M
80 MAT PRINT G; M;
90 PRINT "============================="
100 MAT  T = G + M
110 MAT PRINT T;
120 PRINT "============================="
130 RESTORE
140 MAT READ G(7,1),M(7,1)
150 MAT  T = ZER(7,1)
160 MAT  T = G + M
180 PRINT
200 PRINT TAB(30); "GEOGRAPHY","MATHEMATICS","TOTAL"
220 PRINT TAB(30); "------------------------------------"
  230 FOR N = 1 TO 7
  250 PRINT TAB(30); G(N,1),M(N,1),T(N,1)
  260 NEXT N
270 DATA 11,42,50,35,45,37,25
280 DATA 46,25,33,44,18,42,49
290 END
```

```
LOAD____RUN
    :::  TEST SCORES:    GEOG & MATHS  -  MAX 50

 11  42  50  35  45  37  25

 46  25  33  44  18  42  49
=============================

 57  67  83  79  63  79  74
=============================
```

	GEOGRAPHY	MATHEMATICS	TOTAL

	11	46	57
	42	25	67
	50	33	83
	35	44	79
	45	18	63
	37	42	79
	25	49	74

DONE

(b) A Single List (ref. example A4.6)

```
40 DIM G(1,7), C(7,1), S(1,1)    defines     G   C   S
```
                                                          ‾‾‾‾ □

```
70 MATREAD G
```
causes
G to
fill
with data

```
110 MAT C = CON
```
fills
C with
1's

```
120 MAT S = G * C
```
S holds
sum of   □ =   ‾‾‾‾
numbers
in G.

2.   Summing the Squares of Numbers in a List (ref. example 10.6)

Using the information in (b) above, and that below:

```
50 DIM T(7,1), A(1,1)    defines     T   A
```
                                                          □

```
160 MAT T = TRN(G)
```
fills T   T   G
with   ‾‾‾‾
elements
of G

```
70 MAT A = G * T
```
A holds   A = G *|T
the sum   □   ‾‾‾‾
of squares
of G numbers

Question: Calculate the standard deviation of the numbers: 11, 42, 50, 35, 45, 37, 25

The method used in the program below uses a formula more suited to small numbers:

$$D = \sqrt{\frac{\Sigma X^2}{N} - M^2}$$

Example A4.6 Program MATSTD

```
10 REM                    PROGRAM           MATSTD
20 PRINT
30 PRINT "          CALCULATES STANDARD DEVIATION"
40 DIM G(1,7),C(7,1),S(1,1),T(7,1),A(1,1)
60 PRINT
70 MAT READ G
80 PRINT "NUMBERS    (X'S) :"
90 MAT PRINT G;
100 PRINT
110 MAT  C = CON
120 MAT  S = G * C
130 PRINT "SUMS OF X'S",S(1,1)
140 LET M = S(1,1) / 7
150 PRINT "MEAN OF X'S",M
160 MAT  T = TRN( G )
170 MAT  A = G * T
180 PRINT "SUM OF (X^2)'DS "; A(1,1)
190 LET D = SQR(A(1,1) / 7 - M * M)
200 PRINT "STANDARD DEVIATION    "; D
210 DATA 11,42,50,35,45,37,25
220 END
```

RUN

```
          CALCULATES STANDARD DEVIATION

NUMBERS    (X'S) :

 11   42   50   35   45   37   25

SUMS OF X'S          245
MEAN OF X'S          35
SUM OF (X^2)'DS   9629
STANDARD DEVIATION      12.2708
DONE
```

A4.10 FURTHER USES OF MATRICES ILLUSTRATED

DIM W(4)

DIM X(1, 4)

DIM Y(4, 1)

DIM S(1, 1)

DIM L(4, 4)

Matrix Products			**Equivalent Matrix Statement**	
			MAT S = X * Y	(1
			MAT L = Y * X	(2
			MAT Y = L * Y	(3
			MAT X = X * L	(4
			MAT L = L * L	(5

The above are used in:
* Producing row and column totals   * Finding the sums of squares
* Markov Chain Problems   * Solving Linear equations, etc.

A4.11

Q Q Q Q Q Q Q Q Q Q Q Q Q Q Q Q Q Q Q Q Q Q Q Q Q Q Q Q Q Q Q Q Q

Q   PROBLEMS   Q

1. This question is designed to help you discover some of the merits and limitations in using MATRIX statements and functions.

    Given the following matrices:

    A is 2×5 B is 2×3

    C is 3×4 D is 3×3

    E is 3×1 H is 3×4

    (a) Write suitable DIMension statements for the above.

    (b) Assign the values $1, 2, 3, \ldots 10$ to A

                            $11, 12, \ldots 16$ to B

                            $17, 18, \ldots 28$ to C

    using MATINPUT or MATREAD.

    (c) MATPRINT A, B, C under appropriate headings.

    (d) Attempt the multiplication of $A \times B$

                            and $B \times C$

    What do you conclude? MATPRINT your results.

    (e) Assign zero to every position in D. MATPRINT

    (f) Resize A to a 3×3 matrix with each element equal to 1. MATPRINT A.

    (g) Change each element in A to a 5.

    (h) Is it possible to sum A and D? Explain.

    (i) Assign $3, 6, 9 \ldots$ to D. Sum A and D and PRINT the results.

    (j) Subtract D from A and PRINT the result.

    (k) MATREAD D. Invert D into A, if possible, and MATPRINT A.

    (l) Assign values to E and compute:

    $E \times B$ $B \times E$ $E \times D$ $E \times C$

    Check the results by inspection of the printout of each product. Make sure you understand why not all of these can be done.

2. MATINPUT even numbers into X, a 2×4 matrix. Attempt to print out the contents of X as a 2×4 matrix, and then as a 4×2 matrix. Record your observations.

3. INPUT 25 numbers into T(25). Reorganise T to enable you to MATPRINT T as a 5×5 matrix.

4. I is a 1×5 vector

    J is a 5×1 vector

    K is formed by $I \times J$

    L is formed by $J \times I$

    Write a program that illustrates the above. Your results should include I, J, K, L printed under suitable headings.

5. Write an interactive program to solve up to 5 simultaneous equations using matrices.

6. Write an interactive program to accept up to 50 numbers. Calculate their mean and then the standard deviation of the numbers using the formula:

$$\text{Standard Dev.} = \sqrt{\frac{(X^2) - \dfrac{(\Sigma X)^2}{N}}{N - 1}}$$

Print the set of values followed by their mean and standard deviation. Your program could also be made to print out the following table.

X (numbers)	X − M (diffs)	(X − M)² (diffs²)	X²

Glossary

Aardvark: The antbear. (South African).

Address: Name of a storage location.

Algol: Algorithmic language. General name for a number of distinct programming languages such as Algol 60 and Algol 68.

Algorithm: A sequence of statements or rules defining the solution to a problem in a finite number of steps.

Analogue computer: A computer which uses a process of measurement of continuously variable physical quantities to represent numbers. (cf. **digital computer**.)

ANSI: American National Standards Institution.

Argument: Datum passed to a BASIC statement, e.g. to a function.

ASCII: American Standard Code for Information Interchange, one of a number of standard character codes. (RML 380Z code is almost ASCII.)

BASIC: Beginner's All-purpose Symbolic Instruction Code. Originally developed as a simple language with limited applications, BASIC has evolved into a powerful language with varied complex capabilities. (For further information work through this book!)

Batch processing: A method of processing whereby a user submits a job to a computer and then waits an indefinite length of time before receiving the results; the user has no control over the progress of the job.

Bit: The smallest unit of binary computer memory or logic. A contraction of Binary Digit. (See **byte**.)

Bubble memory: A slow operating magnetic read/write memory device which retains its information after being powered off.

Buffer: An area for temporary storage of information.

Bug: Computer jargon for 'a mistake'.

Byte: A group of **bits** (usually eight).

Character: A digit, letter, or other symbol.

Chip: See **Silicon chip**.

Collector system: The measuring system for assessing the abundance of ions of the different isotopes of strontium or lead in the mass spectrometer. (See Chapter 18).

Compiler: A program for the translation of instructions given in a high level language (examples: FORTRAN, Algol 60), into a low level language, typically machine language. (cf. **interpreter**.)

Computer: A device for taking in, storing, processing, retrieving and giving out information.

Conglomerate: A sedimentary rock made up of pebbles, cobbles, gravel or boulders cemented together in a matrix of sand and/or mud. (See Chapter 18.)

Core: Rapid access memory originally made of many rings (cores) or magnetic material.

CPU: central processing unit. In colloquial speech CPU is sometimes taken to mean the complete computer.

CRT: Cathode-Ray-Tube, a display device for computers and for television.

CUB: Computing using **BASIC** (this book!)

Cursor: An indicator, typically a short line or small rectangle, to the point at which the next display or editing item will appear.

Debugging: Finding and correcting errors in a computer program.

Default value: Values automatically given to a variable in absence of the assignment of specific values.

Diagnostics: Aids to finding the location and nature of errors in a computer program.

Digital computer: A computer which stores and manipulates information by a counting process. (cf. **analogue computer**.)

Disc: a storage device, similar in shape to a gramophone record, coated with a magnetic material. Information is written to it and taken from it while it revolves at high speed.

Execution time: The time taken by the computer in actively processing a job.

Filament: A thin ribbon of metal on which samples for mass spectrometry are loaded. The filament is heated by passage of electric current. (See Chapter 18.)

File: An area for storage of information.

Floating point: A way of representing particularly very large or very small numbers (in a computer).

For example the numbers: 23456789 could be represented as: $2.34567 \text{ E}+07$

.000032 could be represented as: $3.2 \text{ E}-05$

Floppy disc: A small storage disc in which the magnetic coating is on a flexible base material.

FORTRAN: FORmula TRANslation. A programming language designed by IBM in 1957 for scientific use and now widely adapted for other uses.

Graphics: Representation of information pictorially.

Graphics board: A part of the computer **hardware** which supports **graphics**.

Hardware: The physical components and the equipment which go to make up a computer system. (cf. **software**.)

High-level-language: A programming language (e.g. **BASIC, FORTRAN** etc.) designed for ease of use by human beings.

Input device: One which enables information to be fed into the computer. e.g. a keyboard, paper tape, card reader, etc.

Interactive programming: Communicating with a computer in an "alive" way, where the computer responds (talks back) while a program is running.

Interface: The **hardware** or **software** used to enable a computer to communicate with some other device.

Interpreter: A program which translates the text of a program from **source code** into machine language as it encounters it while the program is RUNning (cf. **batch**).

Ion beam: At red heat strontium and lead atoms become electrically charged particles – ions – which are focussed by electric forces into a beam in the mass spectrometer. (See Chapter 18.)

Isotopes: Atoms of a particular chemical element which have the same atomic weight are said to constitute a particular isotope of that element. Many elements have more than one isotope, meaning that not all atoms of the particular element concerned have the same atomic weights. Lead (Pb) has four isotopes: 204–Pb (the lightest) to 208–Pb (the heaviest). (See Chapter 18.)

K: denotes 1000 (Kilo). In describing computer memory K means $2^{10} = 1024$.

Load: Transfer of information from one part of a computer to another.

Loop: Repeated execution of a sequence of instructions.

Low-level language: A programming language designed from the point of view of a machine. It allows efficient translation into machine language.

LSI: Large Scale Integrated circuit.

Machine language: The programming language in which any program must ultimately be expressed, i.e. a set of machine instructions which specify the operations to take place.

Magnetic core: See **core**.

Mainframe computer: A large and expensive computer offering many facilities.

Mass Spectrometer: Instrument for measuring isotopic concentrations etc. (See Chapter 18.)

Memory: A device that saves encoded instructions and information.

Microcomputer: Consists of a processor, plus memory, plus input/output devices built primarily on micro electronic components.

Microprocessor: Control works of a **microcomputer**, usually built on a chip. e.g. the Z80 chip.

MODEM: MOdulator/DEModulator. A device that converts a digital signal to an analog (frequency) signal and vice versa.

Multi-access: A facility apparently enables several users to share a computer facility simultaneously. Although only one user is serviced at a time the high speed of the device gives the appearance of handling many users simultaneously.

Neodymium (Nd): A rare earth element. (See Chapter 18.)

Off-line: Processes or devices not under control of the **CPU** or when used independently of it.

On-line: Devices connected to the **CPU**.

Operating system: A program or collection of programs which supervise the running of the computer. e.g. the execution of other programs.

Output device: One which enables information to be output from a computer. e.g. a printer, disc, etc.

Overflow: A condition in the computer resulting when a number larger than it is capable of handling is input or generated.

Pointer: An indicator of the current position of information in a list, table, or in memory.

Port: A physical connection for an incoming line to the computer.

Processor: See CPU.

Program: A set of instructions for a computer to perform some given task.

Programming language: A language used for writing programs.

PROM: Programmable Read Only Memory.

Radio-nuclide: A radioactive **isotope** of an element. (See Chapter 18.)

RAM: Random Access Memory.

Random access: A means of accessing storage non-sequentially!

ROM: Read Only Memory.

Scrolling: The movement of 'text' up the screen as a scribe of old would read a scroll!

Sedimentary rock: A rock composed of sediment! (See Chapter 18.)

Sequential access: Storage in which the only means of accessing items is sequentially.

Silicon chip: A micro miniaturised electronic circuit built on a tiny 'chip' of silicon.

Simulation: Imitation of a process from real life.

Software: (cf. **hardware**) The programs etc. that make a computer go!

Source code: The original text of a program.

Store: See **memory**.

String: A connected sequence of characters, words, or other symbols.

Strontium (Sr): An element related in its chemistry to the better-known element calcium. (See Chapter 18.)

Subscript: An array index.

Terminal: A device used by a human for communicating with a computer.

Time-sharing: A way of operating a computer so that several users with different purposes appear to use it at the same time.

Turret: A wheel holding the samples loaded on filaments ready for mass spectrometry. (See Chapter 18.)

VDU: Video Display Unit, used as a display device for computers.

VLSI: Very Large Scale Integrated Circuit.

Volatile memory: A system of storage in which all stored information is lost when the power is switched off. e.g. semi-conductor storage.

Word: A unit of storage in the computer which differs in size according to the kind of computer.

Workspace: The area of temporary storage of program and data.

APPENDIX 6

References and further reading

General References

1. EXTENDED BASIC VERSION 5, Reference Manual (for Disc Systems) (1980), Research Machines Limited.
2. THE BASIC HANDBOOK, An Encyclopedia of the BASIC Computer Language.
   Lien, David A. (1980), Compusoft Publishing.
3. BASIC PROGRAMMING
   Kemeny, John G. & Kurtz, Thomas E. (1980), John Wiley & Sons Inc.
4. ILLUSTRATING BASIC
   Alcock, Donald (1978), Cambridge University Press.

Chapter 10

1. HIGH RESOLUTION GRAPHICS, Reference Manual
   (1980), Research Machines Limited.
2. RESEARCH MACHINES 380Z SYSTEMS MANUAL
   (1980), Research Machines Limited.
3. INTERACTIVE COMPUTER GRAPHICS in SCIENCE TEACHING
   edited by McKenzie, J., Elton, L., & Lewis, R. (1978), Ellis Horwood Ltd.

Chapter 12

1. RESEARCH MACHINES 380Z SYSTEMS MANUAL
   (1980), Research Machines Limited.
2. 380Z MINI DISC SYSTEM USER GUIDE (40 character systems) 1981, Research Machines.

Chapter 13

1. MATHEMATICS
   Bergamini, David & the Editors of LIFE. (1965), Time International (Holland).
2. INTRODUCTION TO COMPUTER SCIENCE, Theory and Problems of
   Scheid, Francis (1970), Schaum's Outline Series, McGraw Hill Book Company.
3. PROBABILITY, Theory and Problems of
   Lipschitz & Seymour (1974), Schaum's Outline Series, McGraw Hill Book Company.

4. STATISTICS IN THE COMPUTER AGE
   Craddock, J. M. (1968), Unibooks – English Universities Press.
5. MONTE CARLO METHODS
   Hammersley, J. M. (Oxford Univ. Inst. of Economics & Statistics) &
   Handscomb, D. C. (O.U.C.L.), (1964), Methuen & Co. Ltd.
6. THE RANDOM NUMBER AS A COMPUTING TOOL
   Pettit, Francis R. (1978), (A paper written at Oxford University Computing
   Teaching Centre).

Chapter 14

1. GUIDE TO GOOD PROGRAMMING PRACTICE
   Meek, Brian & Heath, Patricia (1980), Ellis Horwood.
2. MODERN PROGRAMMING TECHNIQUES, (Lecture Notes)
   Pettit, Francis R. (1981), Oxford University Computing Teaching Centre.
3. PROGRAM DESIGN DOCKET USING $FRAME
   Pettit, Francis R. (1979), Oxford University Computing Teaching Centre.

Chapter 15

1. THE ART OF COMPUTER PROGRAMMING, (Volume 3)
   Knuth, Donald E. (1973), Addison-Wesley Publishing Co.
2. INTRODUCTION TO COMPUTER SCIENCE, An Interdisciplinary Approach
   Walker, Terry M. (1972), Allyn and Bacon, Inc. Boston.

Chapter 17

1. A PROGRAMMED TEXT IN STATISTICS
   Hine, J. & Wetherill, G. B. (1975), Chapman & Hall, U.S.A.
2. STATISTICS IN SMALL DOSES, A Livingstone Medical Text
   Castle, W. M. (1972), Churchill Livingstone, Edinburgh and London.
3. STATISTICS, A computer-Oriented Approach (second edition)
   Afifi, A. A. & Azen, S. P. (1979), Academic Press Inc.

Appendix 7 Matrices

1. BASIC (E4)
   Modular One User Handbook (Issue 1), Computer Technology Limited.

Language summary

Note: Some items appear under more than one heading.

A7.1 ELEMENTS OF BASIC

Lines in a BASIC program consist of a line number (in the range 1 to 65529) and normally one statement. As a space-saver more than one statement per line is allowed, in which case statements are separated by colons (:). A line is terminated by a carriage return. Line numbers are omitted from examples in this summary.

Constants are numbers built into the program and are either integer or real, with an optional sign and an optional exponent. Numbers are in the range $-1E+38$ to $+1E+38$.

Variables are named memory locations each of which may hold a variety of numbers in turn during a program RUN.

Arrays may hold a whole collection of data under one name. An array may be a VECTOR or a MATRIX. Individual members of an array are identified by means of subscripts and are called **subscripted variables**. Arrays may be declared using a DIM statement.

Strings A string is a sequence of characters. A **literal string** is a sequence of characters usually enclosed by quotation marks. A **string variable** may consist of up to 256 characters and may have its contents changed during a program RUN. String names end with the dollar sign (**$**). Space for strings may be reserved using a CLEAR statement.

A7.2 OPERATORS

Arithmetic operators	$*$ $/$ $\qquad$ $+$ $-$
Relational operators	$=$ $\quad$ $<>$ $\quad$ $>$ $\quad$ $<$ $\quad$ $>=$ $\quad$ $<=$
Brackets	( )

A7.3 MATHS FUNCTIONS

Note: X represents an expression

SIN(X)	sine of X, angle X in radians.
COS(X)	cosine of X, X in radians.
TAN(X)	tangent of X, X in radians.
ATN(X)	arctangent of X, result in radians (range $-pi/2$ to $pi/2$).
EXP(X)	natural exponent of X.
ABS(X)	absolute value of X.
LOG(X)	logarithm of X to base e.
INT(X)	integer part of X.
SQR(X)	positive square root of X.
RND(X)	random number between 0 and 1.
SGN(X)	gives 1 if $X > 0$
	0 if $X = 0$
	-1 if $X < 0$

A7.4 LOGICAL OPERATORS

An expression is considered FALSE if it is equal to zero, TRUE otherwise. The operators evaluate as follows:

AND	equates to 1 if both operands are non-zero	0 otherwise.
OR	equates to 1 if either operand is non-zero	0 otherwise.
NOT	equates to 1 if the operand is zero	0 otherwise.

A7.5 STRING FUNCTIONS

Function	*Purpose*	*Example*
CLEAR	Clears all variables and arrays. Reserves storage Reserves storage space for up to 2000 characters.	CLEAR CLEAR 2000
FRE	Returns free string storage space or free memory space depending on dummy argument used.	FRE(X$) FRE(X)
ASC("Z")	Gives ASCII code for first character of string argument.	LET B = ASC("Z")
CHR$(N)	Gives ASCII character whose numeric code is the argument. CHR$ is the inverse of ASC.	PRINT CHR$(65)

STRING FUNCTIONS (*ctd.*)

Function	Purpose	Example
HEX$(N)	Converts its numeric argument into a four character string containing a hexadecimal number.	LET G$ = HEX$(12345)
VAL("N")	Gives number represented by string argument.	LET B = VAL("4.5")
STR$(N)	Assigns value of argument to a string. STR$ is the inverse of VAL.	LET B$ = STR$(4.5)
LEN(C$)	Gives the length of string argument.	LET L = LEN("3WORDS")
LEFT$(C$,K)	Returns substring of specified number of left-most characters of string.	LET L$ = LEFT$(A$,2)
RIGHT$(C$,K)	Returns substring of specified number of the right-most characters of string.	LET R$ = RIGHT$(A$,2)
MID$(C$,K,L)	Returns substring, of specified number of characters, starting with character in position specified by second argument and consisting of the number of characters specified by the third argument.	LET M$ = MID$(C$,3,7)

A7.6 GENERAL STATEMENTS AND COMMANDS

Command	Purpose	Example
DIM	Specifies maximum size for numeric or string array.	DIM A(72),B(5,10) DIM A$(10)
DEF FN	Defines a user specified function.	DEF FNA(X)=X*X
REM	A comment in the program.	REM comment
LET	Assignment to a variable.	LET A$="HI" LET A=3.14159

GENERAL STATEMENTS AND COMMANDS (*ctd.*)

Command	Purpose	Example
PRINT	Prints values of items listed. A comma separator determines a zone to be 14 characters wide, a semi-colon separator results in closely packed output.	PRINT A,B$;C(5)
?	Equivalent to PRINT.	? X,Y,"CO-ORD"
TAB	Move to position specified.	PRINT TAB(50);A
FOR	Statements between FOR and NEXT are executed the specified number of times. When STEP is omitted step size defaults to 1.	FOR I=J TO K STEP L
NEXT	Marks lower boundary of a FOR loop.	NEXT I
IF	Conditional test	IF X < 0 THEN 200 IF X < 0 THEN GO TO 200 IF X < 0 GO TO 200 IF A = B THEN PRINT "*" IF P > K THEN 9 ELSE K=J
GOTO	Jump to specified line.	GOTO 500
ON ... GOTO	Jump to line determined by value of the expression.	ON X GOTO 600,900
GOSUB	Program control transferred to specified line.	GOSUB 555
RETURN	Returns control to statement after relevant GOSUB.	RETURN
ON ... GOSUB	Program control transferred to line determined by value of expression.	ON X GOSUB 400,300
RANDOMIZE	Random Number generator is set to a random point in its sequence.	RANDOMIZE
READ	Reads information from a DATA statement.	READ A,B$,D
DATA	Specifies numeric or string data for READ statements.	DATA 10,"YES",99

GENERAL STATEMENTS AND COMMANDS (*ctd.*)

Command	Purpose	Example
RESTORE	Resets data pointer to start for re-reading.	RESTORE
RESTORE 100	Resets data pointer to line 100.	
CLEAR	Clears all variables and arrays, reserves string space.	CLEAR CLEAR 2000
FRE	Returns free string space or free memory space, depending on dummy argument used.	FRE(X$) FRE(X)
INPUT	Allows data to be input from keyboard during a program run. Also described elsewhere.	INPUT A,B$
STOP	Terminates program execution.	STOP
END	Terminates program execution.	END
CONT	Continue program after CTRL Z or STOP.	CONT

A7.7 LINE EDITING

To replace line:	Type original line number with new statement.
To delete line:	Type original line number followed by carriage return.
DELT	Deletes previous character.
CTRL U	Deletes current line.

A7.8 CONTROL CHARACTERS

The control characters marked * act as toggles on the feature they control. Typing them once activates the feature, which persists until they are typed again.

CTRL	A*	Toggle autopaging.
CTRL	C	Return to CP/M.
CTRL	E*	Echo console output to printer.
CTRL	F	To front panel.
CTRL	L	Clears the screen.
CTRL	O*	Suppress console output.

CONTROL CHARACTERS (*ctd.*)

CTRL	P*	Echo console output to printer.
CTRL	Q	Resume execution after **CTRL S**.
CTRL	S	Suspend program execution.
CTRL	U	Deletes current line.
CTRL	Z	Interrupt execution of program.

A7.9 FILES STATEMENTS

Notes:
1. File names may have up to 8 printing characters, drawn from the sets A ... Z, a ... z, 0-9 and $.
2. Only one input and one output file may be selected concurrently. Multiple files are dealt with by selecting them in turn.
3. Data files are sequential files.

A7.9.1 Commands used in conjunction with data files

Note: A channel is specified by a hash (#) character and followed by channel number:
- (0) keyboard (input, output)
- (2) screen (output)
- (10) file (input, output)

Commands in logical sequences for creating a file to receive data:

Command	Purpose	Example
CREATE	A file is created and made ready to receive output from program.	CREATE#10,"elms"
PRINT	PRINTs to file.	PRINT#10,A
CLOSE	CLOSEs output file.	CLOSE#10
OPEN	OPENs file for reading.	OPEN#10, "oaks" OPEN#10,T$
INPUT	Information is INPUT from opened file to current program.	INPUT#10,B
matrix handling:	(not part of BASICSG)	
MATPRINT	Prints specified matrix to file.	MATPRINT #10,A
MATREAD	Reads specified matrices from file.	MATREAD #10,A,B

A7.9.2 Other file handling commands

Command	*Purpose*	*Example*

LOOKUP	Check to see if file exists. LOOKUP returns −1 if file exists and 0 otherwise.	`IF LOOKUP(A$)<>0 THEN 5(`
		`.`
		`.`
		`50 OPEN #10,A$`

INPUT LINE#10	Input entire line from file.	`INPUT LINE#10,A$`

A7.10 INPUT AND OUTPUT COMMANDS

Command	*Purpose*	*Example*
DIR	Get disc directory.	`DIR`
DIR#10	Get disc directory and send to file.	`DIR#10`
LIST#10	List to file.	`LIST#10,50-200`
LVAR	Prints existing variables on console.	`LVAR`
LLVAR	Prints existing variables on printer.	`LLVAR`
TRACE	Sets line number trace.	`TRACE0`
LTRACE	Sets line number trace onto printer.	`LTRACE1`
GET	Single numberic character input.	`LET A = GET(123)`
GET$	Single string character input.	`A$=GET$( )` `A$=GET$(#10)`
PUT#10	Outputs the list of arguments to the selected channel.	`PUT#10,T$` `PUT 12`
WIDTH	Set width of console.	`WIDTH 35`
LWIDTH	Set width of printer.	`LWIDTH 72`
LPRINT	Output to printer.	`LPRINT ZE,B`
PRINT#10	Prints to file.	`PRINT#10,A`
INPUT#10	Information is input from opened file.	`INPUT#10,B`

INPUT AND OUTPUT COMMANDS (*ctd.*)

Command	Purpose	Example
READ	Reads information from a DATA statement.	READ A,A$
DATA	Specifies data, either numeric or string, for READ statements.	DATA 5,"APPLE"
RESTORE	Permits reREADing of DATA by resetting data pointer to start of DATA.	RESTORE

A7.10.1 Commands for controlling input files

Command	Purpose	Example
ON EOF	Trap end of file.	ON EOF GOTO 99
EOF	Generate end of file condition.	EOF

A7.10.2 Commands for controlling format of output

Command	Purpose	Example
NULL	Sets nulls for console.	NULL 3,0
LNULL	Sets nulls for printer.	LNULL 3,0
POS	Returns current console cursor position.	LET A=POS(0)
LPOS	Returns current position of printer head.	LET P=LPOS(0)
QUOTE	Set string quotes on output.	QUOTE#10,0

A7.11 GRAPHIC COMMANDS (Low resolution)

Command	Purpose	Example
GRAPH	Sets scroller to use only bottom	GRAPH
GRAPH 1	four lines and clears the top 20.	GRAPH 1
GRAPH 2	Opens screen for use of PEEK and POKE.	
GRAPH 3	Restores screen to normal state after GRAPH 2.	
GRAPH 0	Screen restored to use full 24 lines.	
TEXT	Use in preference to graph 0.	TEXT

GRAPHICS COMMANDS (Low Resolution *ctd.*)

Command	Purpose	Example
PLOT	Plot string, character, or dot.	`PLOT 10,12,2`
POINT(S)	Test screen location(s).	`LET A=POINT(9,9)`
LINE	Draws a line from last point to this.	`LINE X,Y`

A7.12 GRAPHICS COMMANDS (High and Medium resolution)

Command	Purpose	Example

RESOLUTION	First call to graphics routines, initialises the system. Defines resolution to be used.	`CALL "RESOLUTION",0,B`
		`where B = 1 or 2`
		`CALL "RESOLUTION",1,B`
		`where B = 1,2 or 4`

PLOT	Plots point	`CALL "PLOT",20,30,I`
		`I is 0-15 depending`
		`on number of bits/pixel.`

LINE	Draws line from 'pen' position to specified X, Y position.	`CALL "LINE",30,50,I` `I - as for plot.`
FILL	Fills rectangle specified by points $(X1, Y1)$, $(X2, Y2)$. $X1 <= X2 \quad Y1 <= Y2$.	`CALL"FILL",20,30,30,50,I` `I - as for plot.`

COLOUR	Logical colour takes specified brightness.	`CALL "COLOUR",I,N`
		`I in range 0-15`
		`N in range 0-255`

SETCOL	As for COLOUR but delayed until a call to VIEW is made. Allows a rapid change of colours.	`CALL "SETCOL",I,N,` `as for colour.`
VIEW	Transfers colour changes specified by SETCOL to colour look-up table.	`CALL "VIEW",P` `P - specifies page.`

GRAPHICS COMMANDS (High and Medium Resolution *ctd.***)**

Command	Purpose	Example
UPDATE	Specifies the page and view to be written to.	CALL "DISPLAY",1,2
DISPLAY	Specifies the page and view to be displayed.	CALL "DISPLAY",1,2
CLEAR	Clears current page and view.	CALL "CLEAR"
OFFSET	Co-ordinates of bottom left-hand corner of screen are changed from 0,0 to specified co-ordinates.	CALL "OFFSET",20,20
GLOAD	Loads a picture from BASIC cache memory.	CALL "GLOAD",A
GSAVE	Saves a picture to BASIC cache memory.	CALL "GSAVE",A

A7.13 SYSTEM COMMANDS

Note: System commands are executed immediately. They do not require sequence numbers.

Command	Purpose	Example
CREATE	Opens file for receiving output.	CREATE#10,"RESULTS" CREATE#10,F$
SAVE	A copy of the current program is written to disc.	SAVE "FRED"
FSAVE	Save program in internal format.	FSAVE "POLYGON"
LOAD	Loads a program from specified file, and overwrites old program.	LOAD"OLDFILE"
LOAD?	Verifies that FSAVED file on disc is same as program in memory.	LOAD?"ASH"
LOADGO	Load and execute program.	LOADGO"TOTT" LOADGO"TOTT",200
ERASE	Erases specified file.	ERASE"FRED"
RENAME	Changes name of file.	RENAME NEWNAME,OLDNAME

SYSTEM COMMANDS (*ctd.*)

Note: In the examples below m and n represent sequence line numbers. F and L are positive integers.

Command	Purpose	Example
RENUMBER	RENUMBER program according to instruction. The default gives starting number as 10, and subsequent line numbers in intervals of 10.	RENUMBER RENUMBER 100,10
RUN	Initiates program execution.	RUN
NEW	Clears program area prior to typing in a new program.	NEW
DELETE m	To delete line m.	DELETE 250
DELETE m-n	To delete lines m-n.	DELETE 130-190
DELETE m-	To delete lines m to the end.	DELETE 110-
DELETE -m	To delete lines up to and including m.	DELETE -50
LIST	Lists the whole program.	LIST
LIST m	To list line m.	LIST 20
LIST m-n	To list from line m to n.	LIST 20-80
LIST m-	To list from line m to the end.	LIST 95-
LIST -m	To list up to and including line m.	LIST -130
LLIST	Similar to LIST but listing is to printer if printer option has been selected.	LLIST
BYE	Return to CP/M.	BYE
RANDOMIZE	Sets random number generator to a random point in its sequence.	RANDOMIZE
PRINTER	Use to select printer option. (Check system manual for details).	PRINTER 3

SYSTEM COMMANDS (*ctd.*)

Command	Purpose	Example
RESET	Initialise discs. Use after changing disc.	RESET
ON BREAK	Console interrupt trapped. Program execution redirected to specified line.	ON BREAK GOTO 99
MERGE	Loads specified program and merges it with program in workspace.	MERGE "PATTERNS"
MERGEGO	Merge and execute program.	MERGEGO "COLOUR"
EDIT	Activate line editor to act on specified line.	EDIT 20
FN	Call user defined function.	LET D = FNS(A)

A7.14 MACHINE AND ASSEMBLY LANGUAGE SUPPORT

Command	Purpose	Example
PEEK	Returns contents of memory location.	LET A = PEEK(B)
POKE	Stores value in memory location.	POKE A,0
INP	Returns value from input port.	LET V = INP(P)
OUT	Sends value to output port.	OUT P,V
WAIT	Waits for input status bit.	WAIT P,M,X
VARADR	Returns address of variable.	LET A = VARADR(U)
USR	Calls user supplied function.	LET V = USR(B)
CALL	Calls user supplied subroutine.	CALL "RES",V1,V2

A7.15 ERROR HANDLING COMMANDS

Command	Purpose	Example
ON ERROR	Trap error condition.	ON ERROR GOTO 50
RESUME	Resume execution after error.	RESUME
ERL	Returns number of line on which most recent error occurred.	LET A = ERL
ERR	Returns number of the most recent error.	LET B = ERR
ERROR	Causes error. Default 0 "unknown error" message.	ERROR 12

A7.16 MATRIX STATEMENTS (not part of BASICSG)

Command	Purpose	Example
MAT +	Matrix addition.	MAT C = A + B
MAT −	Matrix subtraction.	MAT A = C − B
MAT *	Matrix multiplication.	MAT C = A * B
MAT *	Multiples each element of a matrix by expression X and assigns the values to another.	MAT A = (X)*B
MAT READ	Reads elements of matrix from DATA statements; a new size may be specified.	MAT READ A(m,n)
MAT INPUT	Input of a matrix from console; a new size may be specified.	MAT INPUT A(m,n)
MAT PRINT	Prints specified matrices on the console. Either semi-colons or commas may be used as separators packed or unpacked output.	MAT PRINT A, B

A7.17 MATRIX FUNCTIONS (Not part of BASICSG)

Notes: 1. There is an absolute maximum matrix size.
2. Neither subscript of a 2-dimensional matrix may exceed 255.

Command	*Purpose*	*Example*
ZER	Sets all elements of a matrix to 0. A new working size may be specified.	MAT B = ZER (m,n)
CON	Sets all elements of a matrix to 1. A new working size may be specified.	MAT C = CON (m,n)
IDN	Establishes an identity matrix (all ones down the diagonal). A new working size may be specified.	MAT D = IDN (n,n)
INV	Inverts a square matrix into another square matrix with the same size.	MAT E = INV (F)
TRN	Transposes a matrix.	MAT G = TRN (H)

Index

V

VAL 322
valid results 207
VARADR **190**
variable 52, 199, 216
   names 207
   exchange of 115
variance 201, 260
Variations on a Theme **277**
VDU 23
VDU screen 160
vector matrix 310
vector product 312, 313
vector sort 233, 235
video display screen 23
VIEW (HRG) **145**
views 165
virtual screen 160
visible screen 160, 162

W

WAIT **190**
warning
   rash interpretation 260
West Greenland 274
wheel 207
WIDTH 93, **173**
windowing 160
wordlists 239
workspace **28**, 77, 181
world's oldest known sedimentary rock 274
XOR mode 272

Z

ZER 310